CONGRESS

By the Same Author

American Constitutional Law (with Katy J. Harriger, 11th ed., 2016)

The Democratic Constitution (with Neal Devins, 2d ed., 2015)

The Law of the Executive Branch: Presidential Power (cloth ed., 2014; paper ed., 2015)

Constitutional Conflicts between Congress and the President (6th ed., 2014)

On the Supreme Court: Without Illusion and Idolatry (2014)

Presidential War Power (3d ed., 2013)

Defending Congress and the Constitution (2011)

Political Dynamics of Constitutional Law (with Neal Devins, 5th ed., 2011)

On Appreciating Congress: The People's Branch (2010)

The Supreme Court and Congress: Rival Interpretations (2009)

The Constitution and 9/11: Recurring Threats to America's Freedoms (2008)

In the Name of National Security: Unchecked Power and the Reynolds *Case* (2006)

Military Tribunals and Presidential Power: American Revolution to the War on Terrorism (2005)

The Politics of Executive Privilege (2004)

Nazi Saboteurs on Trial: A Military Tribunal and American Law (2003)

Religious Liberty in America: Political Safeguards (2002)

Congressional Abdication on War and Spending (2000)

The Politics of Shared Power: Congress and the Executive (4th ed., 1994)

Encyclopedia of the American Presidency (with Leonard W. Levy, 1994)

Constitutional Dialogues: Interpretation as Political Process (1988)

The Constitution between Friends: Congress, the President, and the Law (1978)

Presidential Spending Power (1975)

President and Congress: Power and Policy (1972)

CONGRESS

Protecting Individual Rights

Louis Fisher

UNIVERSITY PRESS OF KANSAS

© 2016 by the University Press of Kansas
All rights reserved

Published by the University Press of Kansas (Lawrence, Kansas 66045), which was organized by the Kansas Board of Regents and is operated and funded by Emporia State University, Fort Hays State University, Kansas State University, Pittsburg State University, the University of Kansas, and Wichita State University

Library of Congress Cataloging-in-Publication Data
Names: Fisher, Louis, author.
Title: Congress : protecting individual rights / Louis Fisher.
Description: Lawrence, Kansas : University Press of Kansas, 2016.
   | Includes index.
Identifiers: LCCN 2015043966 | ISBN 9780700622115 (cloth : alk. paper)
   | ISBN 9780700622122 (ebook)
Subjects: LCSH: United States. Congress—Powers and duties.
   | Civil rights—United States—History. | Separation of powers—United States.
Classification: LCC KF4935 .F575 2016 | DDC 342.7308/5—dc23
LC record available at http://lccn.loc.gov/2015043966

British Library Cataloguing-in-Publication Data is available.

Printed in the United States of America

10 9 8 7 6 5 4 3 2 1

The paper used in this publication is recycled and contains 30 percent postconsumer waste. It is acid free and meets the minimum requirements of the American National Standard for Permanence of Paper for Printed Library Materials Z39.48-1992.

To the Library of Congress

CONTENTS

Preface   xi
Note on Citations   xv

Chapter 1. Judging the Three Branches   1
    Congress   2
    The President   5
    The Judiciary   12
    The Warren Court   17
    Individual Rights at Risk   19
    Seeking a Better Balance   23

Chapter 2. Founding Principles   29
    Breaking with the British Model   30
    Lessons from the Continental Congress   32
    Drafting the Constitution   35
    Proposing a Title for the President   38
    The Bill of Rights   40
    Scope of Public Participation   41

Chapter 3. The Rights of Blacks   47
    Ending Slavery   47
    The Civil War   51
    Congressional Safeguards, Judicial Opposition   53
    Public Accommodations Legislation   55
    From *Plessy* to *Brown v. Board*   58
    The Civil Rights Act of 1964   65
    The Continuing Dialogue   67

Chapter 4. The Rights of Women   69
    Blackstone's Doctrine of Coverture   69
    Myra Bradwell's Effort to Practice Law   70
    Belva Lockwood Goes to Congress   73
    Judicial Rulings from 1875 to 1971   75

Equal Rights Amendment   77
Abortion Rights   80
Equal Pay Legislation   85
The Lilly Ledbetter Case   86
Additional Legislative Activity   90

Chapter 5. The Rights of Children   92
Legislation on Child Labor   92
Invoking the Commerce Power   94
Turning to the Taxing Power   97
Congress Keeps Trying   99
Compulsory Flag Salutes   103
In the Lower Courts   104
The Supreme Court Decides   106
Having Second Thoughts   109

Chapter 6. Protecting Religious Liberty   115
Constitutional Principles   115
Conscientious Objectors   116
Pacifism after World War I   120
Chaplains   124
Legislation on Polygamy   126
Exemptions in Prohibition Statutes   127
The Yarmulke Case   130

Chapter 7. The Rights of Native Americans   137
Propagating the Gospel   137
Indian Removal   139
Stirrings of Reform   142
Protective Legislation   144
Religious Use of Peyote   146
Religious Freedom Restoration Act (RFRA)   149
Edison Chiloquin and Klamath Indians   157

Chapter 8. Strengthening U.S. Democracy   159
Making Time for Legislative Work   160
Protecting Congressional Prerogatives   161
Improving Institutional Resources   164
Eliminating Gerrymandered Districts   166
Limiting Campaign Expenditures   168

About the Author   177
Index of Cases   179
Index of Subjects   184

PREFACE

This book's title may puzzle some readers. They might ask: How could a Congress that functions by majority vote ever reliably protect individual and minority rights? That is certainly a fair question, yet in this book I will provide ample evidence that Congress has performed well at protecting rights for more than two centuries—even in recent decades when Congress is routinely described as dysfunctional and "broken."[1] Does the legislative record include failures? No doubt it does, but the executive and judicial branches have had their share of failures also, often quite major ones. As for Congress voting by majority, that is also true of appellate courts and the Supreme Court. Nevertheless, scholars and the media continue to describe the Supreme Court as "guardian" of individual rights even though its outcomes are also determined by majority vote.

The purpose of this book is to analyze Congress as part of a system of government dedicated to constitutional limits and the protection of individual rights. For some reason, the general public and scholarly studies routinely attribute to the President and the Supreme Court unique and often imaginary institutional qualities that enable them to protect rights. Those studies pay little or no attention to what Congress has accomplished. Moreover, praise for presidential and judicial action is based largely on assumptions and assertions, not on the record. When that history is examined with care, Congress emerges as a remarkably successful institution in meeting the Framers' expectation that government should exist not merely to exercise power but also to protect rights.

Congress, as with other branches during times of perceived dangers to national security, has failed to protect individual rights. This book analyzes those periods in detail. In recent decades, Congress has fallen short in fulfilling its institutional and constitutional duties. The final chapter explores what Congress could do to strengthen itself and restore a capacity to carry out its essential role in self-government. For those discouraged by the recent conduct of Congress, this book can highlight periods when Congress functioned well and provide a constructive model for the future.

1. Thomas E. Mann & Norman J. Ornstein, The Broken Branch: How Congress Is Failing America and How to Get It Back on Track (2008 ed.).

In the chapters that follow, readers will see Congress repeatedly responding in a positive manner to protect the rights of blacks, women, children, religious minorities, and Native Americans. The other branches were involved as well, but on many occasions Congress took the lead in bringing assistance to not only minorities but even minorities within minorities. From 1789 up to World War II, it is difficult to find any federal court decision that upheld and championed individual and minority rights. Blacks, women, and minorities found it necessary to turn to Congress and state legislative bodies for support. There remains (as always) the need for an open political process that can respond to constitutional rights. Congress fills that need. The judicial process is far too closed, limited, and unreliable.

During the court-packing battle of 1937, the Senate Judiciary Committee praised federal courts as guardians of individual and minority rights: "Minority political groups, no less than religious and racial groups, have never failed, when forced to appeal to the Supreme Court of the United States, to find in its opinions the reassurance and protection of their constitutional rights."[2] Given the judicial record at that time, it would be more accurate to replace "never failed" with "rarely succeeded."

In 1937, an article by Henry W. Edgerton, who later became a federal judge, drilled a hole through the assertions offered by the Senate Judiciary Committee. After studying Supreme Court opinions from 1789 to the 1930s, he concluded that judicial rulings "give small support to the theory that Congress had attacked, and judicial supremacy defended, 'the citizen's liberty.'" Far from defending individual and minority rights, the courts "sided uniformly with the interests of government and corporations."[3] In a 1943 study, historian Henry Steele Commager reached a similar position. The Court had "intervened again and again to defeat congressional efforts to free slaves, guarantee civil rights to Negroes, to protect workingmen, outlaw child labor, assist hard-pressed farmers, and to democratize the tax system."[4]

The capacity of Congress to protect individual and minority rights has a long and distinguished history, both in taking the initiative to safeguard rights and in passing remedial legislation to correct errors in the courts. Little in the record over the past two centuries offers convincing evidence that courts are particularly gifted or reliable in coming to the defense of individual rights. That duty necessarily falls on all three branches, the fifty states, and the general public.

My approach to this subject draws from working for Congress for forty

2. S. Rept. No. 711, 75th Cong., 1st Sess. 20 (1937).
3. Henry W. Edgerton, "The Incidence of Judicial Control over Congress," 22 Corn. L. Q. 299 (1937).
4. Henry Steele Commager, Majority Rule and Minority Rights 55 (1943).

years, first as Senior Specialist in Separation of Powers with the Congressional Research Service and later as Specialist in Constitutional Law with the Law Library of Congress. It would be understandable for a reader to wonder how those four decades with Congress might have biased my perspective. I can only say that over that period I never hesitated in my dealings with lawmakers and their staff to push against legislative actions that I regarded as an invasion of executive and judicial powers. I did that on a regular basis, not only in private meetings and reports but in public testimony and books and articles.

The people I dealt with in the executive and judicial branches appreciated that my purpose was not to defend Congress alone but the larger constitutional and political system. That career is explained in a book I published after retiring from Congress in August 2010, *Defending Congress and the Constitution* (2011). Having worked closely with Congress, I fully appreciate both its promise and its pitfalls. In the end, I remain committed to a system of self-government and checks and balances, not to presidential or judicial supremacy.

I very much appreciate meeting with Chuck Myers of the University Press of Kansas to discuss my plans for this project and receive his advice and guidance on individual chapters. Jasmine Farrier and an anonymous reviewer for the University Press of Kansas provided me with detailed comments that proved of great value. Joel Goldstein of Saint Louis University School of Law invited me to send the first two chapters to his students for their comments. For an hour, over Skype, we discussed the major issues. I am indebted to many friends and colleagues who read individual chapters and provided excellent evaluations: Reb Brownell, Henry Cohen, Mike Crespin, Royce Crocker, Jeff Crouch, John Denvir, John Dinan, Chris Edelson, Jenny Elsea, Bruce Fein, Joel Goldstein, Katy Harriger, Henry Hogue, Nancy Kassop, Mike Koempel, Kevin Kosar, Bob Mutch, Walter Oleszek, Ron Peters, Dick Pious, Mort Rosenberg, Mark Rozell, Mark Rush, Mitch Sollenberger, Bob Spitzer, Jerry Waltman, and Don Wolfensberger. Many thanks to Kathleen Kageff for excellent copyediting and thoughtful suggestions.

The book is dedicated to the Library of Congress because it was my home for four decades, allowing me to learn firsthand from the daily process of interacting with experts in all three branches. During my ten years in New York City, I discovered that the speakers I most admired were not those who merely published or litigated. They were those actively involved in their day jobs in applying professional knowledge. They were practitioners, not merely experts. Perhaps I liked that because my undergraduate degree was in chemistry and I did graduate work in physical chemistry. I was used to trying things out in the laboratory. The Library of Congress became my laboratory, where I worked closely with lawmakers, committees, and professional staff. During my five years of retirement I continue to reach out and learn from those contacts.

NOTE ON CITATIONS

All court citations refer to published volumes whenever available: *United States Reports* (U.S.) for Supreme Court decisions, *Federal Reporter* (F.2d or F.3d) for appellate decisions, and *Federal Supplement* (F. Supp. or F. Supp. 2d) for federal district court decisions. There are also citations to *Opinions of the Attorney General* (Op. Att'y Gen.) and *Opinions of the Office of Legal Counsel* (Op. O.L.C.) in the Justice Department. Several standard reference works are abbreviated in the footnotes using the following system:

Elliot   The Debates in the Several State Conventions on the Adoption of the Federal Constitution (5 vols., Jonathan Elliot, ed., Washington, D.C., 1836–1845).

Farrand   The Records of the Federal Convention of 1787 (4 vols., Max Farrand, ed., New Haven, Conn.: Yale University Press, 1937).

The Federalist   The Federalist, Benjamin F. Wright, ed. (New York: Metro Books, 2002).

Landmark Briefs   Landmark Briefs and Arguments of the Supreme Court of the United States: Constitutional Law (Philip B. Kurland & Gerhard Casper, eds., Washington, D.C.: University Publications of America, 1978–).

Richardson   A Compilation of the Messages and Papers of the Presidents (20 vols., James D. Richardson, ed., New York: Bureau of National Literature, 1897–1925).

Stokes   Anson Phelps Stokes, Church and State in the United States, 3 vols. (New York: Harper & Bros., 1950).

Swindler   William F. Swindler, ed., Sources and Documents of United States Constitutions, 10 vols. (Dobbs Ferry, N.Y.: Oceana Publications, 1973–1979).

Thorpe   Francis Newton Thorpe, ed., The Federal and State Constitutions, Colonial Charters, and Other Organic Laws, 7 vols. (Washington, D.C.: Government Printing Office, 1909).

CONGRESS

1

JUDGING THE THREE BRANCHES

The Framers created a constitutional system that depends heavily on checks and balances to avoid the abuse of political power concentrated in one branch. The purpose is to protect individual rights and the aspiration for self-government. That principle largely governed the federal government for the first century and a half. In the years following World War II, the American political and legal culture changed fundamentally to favor a strong President empowered to initiate national security and domestic policy on his own.

Over that same period, the Supreme Court emerged with the reputation of providing the "final word" on the meaning of the Constitution. Both developments would have astonished the Framers. Without a strong and independent Congress, we could not speak of democracy in America. Our political system would operate with two elected officers in the executive branch and none in the judiciary, a form of government best described as elitist.

The pronounced biases that guide contemporary debate on the three branches of the federal government are well displayed in symposia published by the *Boston University Law Review* from 2006 to 2009. The first two titles were neutral in tone: "The Role of the Judge in the Twentieth-First Century" (December 2006) and "The Role of the President in the Twenty-First Century" (April 2008). The third, published in April 2009, carries this weighted theme: "Congress: The Most Disparaged Branch."[1] In one of the articles, David Mayhew put the matter in proper context: "Congress is an unlovely institution, but it has always been unlovely."[2] He recalled what Alexis de Tocqueville said in 1835: "When one enters the House of Representatives at Washington, one is struck by the vulgar demeanor of that assembly."[3] Mayhew included the famous observation by Mark Twain in 1897: "Suppose you were an idiot. And suppose you were a member of Congress. But I repeat myself."[4]

In a democracy, it is appropriate to poke fun at all three branches, but such comments are rarely aimed at the President and the Supreme Court. When Mayhew generalizes about the executive and judicial branches, he is

1. 89 B.U. L. Rev. 331 (2009).
2. David R. Mayhew, "Is Congress 'The Broken Branch'?," id. at 357.
3. Id.
4. Id. at 358.

complimentary. The President offers "speed, coordination, and secrecy," while the judiciary "traffics in coherence, consistency, and justice."[5] The downsides of presidential speed and secrecy are not explored, nor is there any analysis of the incoherence, inconsistency, and injustice that appear in decisions handed down by the Supreme Court. Mayhew observes: "Crisp, clear, decisive, theoretically elegant action is not ordinarily the congressional way."[6] That is true, but when Congress does act crisply, clearly, and decisively, as when it promptly passed the Tonkin Gulf Resolution in August 1964 to authorize war in Vietnam, with only two dissenting votes in the Senate, the resulting national security policy can be a disaster.[7] As a deliberative body, Congress is not supposed to automatically and quickly salute presidential initiatives and assertions. That is not good for Congress or the country. Mayhew ends with a valuable insight: "Congress is not all that defective an institution once its role is properly considered."[8] This book is written to provide that essential consideration.

Congress

In discussing the role of Congress in protecting individual rights, it is important to recognize that entirely different methods are used to evaluate the three branches. Congress is criticized more than the other branches in part because it works largely in the open, particularly in the television age when the public can watch floor debates and committee hearings. Contentious disputes within Congress remain on full display. That is natural, healthy, and inevitable for a legislative body. The open process within Congress makes for better decisions because of public input and scrutiny from private citizens and experts who are called to testify before committee hearings, giving all sides an opportunity to make their case.

There is far less "groupthink" in Congress than in the executive branch, where advisers tend to anticipate what the President wants to hear and to speak accordingly as part of the drive toward consensus. The result of that executive behavior has led to numerous domestic and foreign policy failures ranging from the Korean War and Carter's energy initiative to Clinton's health plan, the war against Iraq in 2003, and military action against Libya in 2011.[9]

5. Id.
6. Id. at 359.
7. Louis Fisher, Presidential War Power 127–44 (3d ed., 2013).
8. Mayhew, "Is Congress 'The Broken Branch'?," at 369.
9. Irving L. Janis, Groupthink (2d ed., 1982). With regard to Korea, Iraq, and Libya, see Fisher, Presidential War Power, at 80–103, 209–32, 238–47 (2013). The Carter-Clinton policies are analyzed by Richard M. Pious, Why Presidents Fail (2008).

Interestingly, Congress pays a cost for its open process. Studies suggest that the general public is "generally dissatisfied with the core tendencies of the democratic legislative process: deliberation, debate, compromise, and disagreement."[10] Yet those qualities are unavoidable for a legislative body composed of 535 lawmakers, two branches, two parties, and a variety of committees and subcommittees. Donald Wolfensberger, after working for Congress from 1969 to 1997 in high-level staff positions, published a perceptive book in 2000 regarding the capacity of Congress to deliberate on matters of public policy. In examining the last two centuries, he concluded Congress "has adapted and drawn closer to the people while expanding individual rights, liberties, and opportunities. . . . Deliberative democracy has been on continuous trial from the beginning. And, over the long haul, members of Congress have acquitted themselves honorably."[11]

Deliberation, debate, compromise, and disagreement occur in the executive and judicial branches, but they are not as visible and on public display to the same extent as in Congress. White House, executive branch, and judicial branch activities are far more closed. We don't watch the President discuss public policy with Cabinet officials, debate national security issues in the Situation Room at the White House, or participate in meetings with lawmakers and lobbyists. As noted in one study: "Nasty, visible disputes within the executive branch are fairly rare, and interest-group activity there is seldom reported."[12] The President has a White House Press Secretary who attempts to present coherent reasons to justify executive actions. No such person speaks for Congress.

The Supreme Court listens to oral argument in public, but few people gain access to watch the proceedings. Proposals to televise oral arguments at the Supreme Court have thus far failed. A transcript and oral recording of the argument are made public, but no cameras are permitted in the courtroom. When Justices discuss pending cases in conference, that process remains closed. Perhaps decades later, in the papers of retired Justices, we may have the opportunity to read and interpret notes taken in conference.

Because of these marked differences in observing the three branches, operations by the President and the Supreme Court generally look more coherent, reasonable, and impressive than for Congress. In that sense, we use

10. Jessica C. Gerrity, "Understanding Congressional Approval: Public Opinion from 1974 to 2014," in The Evolving Congress, Senate Committee on Rules and Administration, S. Prt. 113-30, 113th Cong., 2d Sess. 195 (2014).

11. Donald R. Wolfensberger, Congress and the People: Deliberative Democracy on Trial 283 (2000).

12. John R. Hibbing & Elizabeth Theiss-Morse, Congress as Public Enemy: Public Attitudes toward American Political Institutions 61 (1995).

two entirely different methods to evaluate the three branches: realistic for Congress, idealistic for Presidents and the Supreme Court. That bias and illusion grew more pronounced in the years following World War II, in large part because of the manner in which scholars began to describe the President and the judiciary. The result: severe misconceptions about the way the three branches govern and protect individual rights.

Evaluations of Congress are typically down-to-earth. See it for what it is. No need to invent imaginary properties that are complimentary and admiring. Praise and flattery are extremely rare. More likely are comments from humorists like Will Rogers: "This country has come to feel the same when Congress is in session as when the baby gets hold of a hammer." Generalizations about the President and the Supreme Court lie on an entirely different plane. Remarks are elevated, if not celestial, expressing broad acclaim.

Members of Congress take time from their official duties to regularly deride their own institution. Consider these titles of books written by lawmakers: *Congress: The Sapless Branch*, by Senator Joseph S. Clark (1964), *House Out of Order*, by Representative Richard Bolling (1965), and *The Futile System: How to Unchain Congress and Make the System Work Again*, by Representative John J. Rhodes (1976). On occasion, Presidents and federal judges will concede misjudgments in their branches, but not in a book that wholly attacks their institution.

Professors who teach courses on Congress typically concentrate on legislative procedures, parliamentary precedents, congressional leaders and parties, committees and subcommittees, campaigns and elections, lobbyists and interest groups, the President and the judiciary, and legislative oversight of executive agencies. Given the complexity and detail of those subjects, it would be highly unusual for a professor to devote any time to the contributions of Congress in protecting individual and minority rights. The focus is on process, not outcomes, and thus overlooks the substantial contributions of Congress in protecting individual rights. Students are likely to leave college without any appreciation for that legislative record.[13]

Richard Fenno has published insightful studies of Congress, relying heavily on interviews with lawmakers and their staff. Often he traveled with House members to their districts to observe their contacts with constituents. His research method "was largely one of soaking and poking—or just hanging around."[14] Through these visits he could appreciate that the Supreme Court "does not even claim to be representative," and that when a President claims

13. For an excellent analysis by someone who teaches Congress and highlights the capacity of state legislatures to protect individual rights, see John J. Dinan, Keeping the People's Liberties: Legislators, Citizens, and Judges as Guardians of Rights (1998).
14. Richard F. Fenno, Jr., Home Style: House Members in Their Districts (1978).

to be "president of all the people," it is "just that—a claim, not a fact." Congress, not the President, "best represents the diversity of the country; and members of Congress, not the president, are in closest touch with the people who live in the country."[15]

Unless they are rich and powerful, citizens have little access to the executive and judicial branches. They do with members of Congress and their staff, not only in offices on Capitol Hill but in field offices within states and congressional districts, with personal visits, phone calls, and e-mails. Members return home to meet with constituents personally and in town hall meetings. Self-government means more than voting in elections. Citizens need to be connected to Congress throughout the year to receive assistance on personal matters and give their thoughts on economic, social, and political issues.

The President

In the years prior to World War II, social scientists and the public made little effort to lionize the American President and manufacture heroic properties. The President was not placed on a pedestal and clothed with wondrous qualities, acting instinctively for the "national interest" and surrounded by advisers with unrivaled experience and unerring political judgment. On occasion, a glowing spotlight might be placed on a particular President, especially George Washington and Abraham Lincoln. Although revered now, the praise of Lincoln came after his assassination. Washington may have been the only President with an aura during his time in office.

Beginning with World War II and continuing into the Cold War and the current war against terrorism, many social scientists have increasingly singled out the President as best equipped to protect the nation, not only from foreign threats but in confronting and settling domestic disputes. On a regular basis these expectations and hopes are dashed by Presidents who fall short of what they promised and what voters hoped for. This cycle of high expectations followed by public dismay continues on a regular course from one administration to the next.

In the 1950s, such scholars as Clinton Rossiter, Richard Neustadt, James McGregor Burns, and Arthur Schlesinger championed inflated and wholly unrealistic models of presidential power. In previous periods and the years that followed, the executive branch established a clear pattern of operating with faulty facts, relying on mistaken judgments, and making misleading statements to Congress and the public. The result: costly wars and botched

15. Id. at 244.

domestic initiatives, demonstrating on numerous occasions a lack of executive branch capacity to formulate and implement effective policies.[16]

Rossiter's *The American Presidency*, published in 1956 and followed by a paperback edition in 1960, promoted an idealized image of executive power. Insisting he was not creating something new, he borrowed this 1861 praise from an Englishman, John Bright, about the U.S. President: "I think the whole world offers no finer spectacle than this; it offers no higher dignity; and there is no greater object of ambition on the political stage on which men are permitted to move." In Bright's estimate, after referring to various hereditary rulers, "there is nothing more worthy of reverence and obedience, and nothing more sacred, than the authority of the freely chosen magistrate of a great and free people; and if there be on earth and amongst men any right divine to govern, surely it rests with a ruler so chosen and so appointed."[17] It is interesting to see such words as reverence, sacred, and divine. No such language would be used to describe a legislative body.

Rossiter defined the purpose of his book: "to confirm Bright's splendid judgment by presenting the American Presidency as what I honestly believe it to be: one of the few truly successful institutions created by men in their endless quest for the blessings of free government."[18] Conceding that the office of the presidency had "its fair share of warts," he wanted "to make clear at the outset my own feeling of veneration, if not exactly reverence, for the authority and dignity of the President."[19] Veneration and reverence? Those words typically express respect, awe, and devotion, describing an office as holy and sacrosanct. Nothing in the American presidency from 1789 to 1960 merited that level of flattery and idolatry. Those who write on Congress would not express themselves in that manner. What is it about the President that provokes such praise? Has the office retained some of the divine rule earlier attributed to monarchs, who could not only do no wrong but not even think wrong?[20]

Other presidential scholars trumpeted the need for bold and unchecked presidential leadership. Arthur M. Schlesinger, Jr., ironically credited with exposing "the imperial presidency" (a phrase he also used as the title of his 1973 book), earlier played a major role in manufacturing a larger-than-life U.S. President. His book *The Age of Jackson* (1945) looked to Andrew Jackson as a model for preserving democracy under the 1940s threat of world fascism. He praised Theodore Roosevelt for "usher[ing] in a period of energetic

16. Louis Fisher, "Teaching the Presidency: Idealizing a Constitutional Office," 45 PS: Political Science & Politics 17 (2012); http://www.loufisher.org/docs/ci/teach.pdf.
17. Clinton Rossiter, The American Presidency 15 (1960).
18. Id.
19. Id. at 15–16.
20. See the first section in chapter 2.

government" and paid tribute to Woodrow Wilson for understanding "the need for executive vigor and government action."[21] His three-volume work *The Age of Roosevelt* celebrated activism and leadership by Franklin D. Roosevelt.[22] Certainly presidential actions pursued merely to showcase "energy" and "vigor" can damage U.S. interests.

Writing in *The Crisis of Confidence* (1969), Schlesinger explained that the President did not have in internal affairs "the same constitutional authority he has in foreign policy," and here he cited the Supreme Court's decision in the 1936 *Curtiss-Wright* case and its reference to the President "as the sole organ of the federal government in the field of international relations."[23] As a professional historian, Schlesinger should have read John Marshall's sole-organ speech in 1800 to see if it promoted plenary and exclusive power for the President in the field of external affairs. Clearly it did not. In an amicus brief I filed with the Supreme Court on July 17, 2014, I pointed out what other scholars have said over the years: John Marshall merely argued that President John Adams, in turning over to Great Britain a British citizen charged with murder, was simply exercising extradition authority granted to him by the Jay Treaty.[24] On June 8, 2015, in *Zivotofsky v. Kerry*, the Supreme Court finally—after seventy-nine years—discarded the sole-organ doctrine. In adding extraneous dicta to *Curtiss-Wright*, Justice George Sutherland implied that Marshall recognized for the President plenary and exclusive powers in foreign affairs. That is plainly false, as even a cursory examination of Articles I and II of the Constitution would reveal.

Richard Neustadt's *Presidential Power*, first published in 1960 and reissued as a paperback four years later, has had a profound impact among scholars, students, and the public. The book attracted broad support because it focused on stories, case studies, and the examination of presidential power in practical terms. The downside of Neustadt's approach, as explained by Ronald Moe, was to jettison institutional, legal, and constitutional values, divorcing presidential studies from the framework of public law previously established by Edward S. Corwin.[25]

21. Arthur M. Schlesinger, Jr., The Age of Jackson (paper ed., 1949; originally published in 1945).

22. Arthur M. Schlesinger, Jr., The Crisis of the Old Order, 1919–1933 (1957); The Coming of the New Deal (1958); The Politics of Upheaval (1960).

23. Arthur M. Schlesinger, Jr., The Crisis of Confidence 220 (1969).

24. Louis Fisher, Brief *Amicus Curiae* of Louis Fisher in Support of Petitioner, Zivotofsky v. Kerry, No. 13-626, In the Supreme Court of the United States, July 17, 2014; http://www.loufisher.org/docs/pip/Zivotofsky.pdf.

25. Ronald C. Moe, "At Risk: The President's Role as Chief Manager," in James P. Pfiffner, ed., The Managerial Presidency (1999); Ronald C. Moe, "Governance Principles: The Neglected Basis of Federal Management," in Thomas H. Stanton & Benjamin Ginsberg, eds., Making Government Manageable (2004).

It is easy to misread Neustadt. He begins with a modest and attractive theme by defining presidential power as "the power to persuade."[26] Persuasive power "amounts to more than charm or reasoned argument. . . . For the men he would induce to do what he wants done on their own responsibility will need or fear some acts by him on his responsibility." The formal powers of Congress and the President "are so intertwined that neither will accomplish very much, for very long, without the acquiescence of the other." In a phrase that seems consistent with the constitutional system of checks and balances, Neustadt refers to political power as "a give-and-take."[27] In probably the most celebrated statement in the book, Neustadt wrote that the Framers did not create a government of separated powers. Instead, they "created a government of separated institutions *sharing* powers."[28]

Such remarks offer a reassuring and soft glow of mutual accommodations among the branches, fully consistent with the American system of checks and balances designed to safeguard individual rights. However, those comforting and familiar themes appear early in the book. As the reader proceeds deeper into the study, Neustadt urges Presidents to take power, not give it or share it. Power is to be acquired and concentrated in the presidency and used for *personal* reasons. Neustadt's favorite President was Franklin D. Roosevelt, and he criticized Dwight D. Eisenhower for failing to seek political power for personal use. "The politics of self-aggrandizement as Roosevelt practiced it affronted Eisenhower's sense of personal propriety."[29]

Of the many case studies in the book, one focuses on the Korean War. Neustadt faults Truman for giving too much latitude to General Douglas MacArthur and discusses the Supreme Court's *Youngstown* decision in 1952, striking down Truman's effort to seize steel mills to prosecute the war. At no time, however, did Neustadt inquire whether Truman possessed constitutional or legal authority to go to war against North Korea without coming to Congress to seek its approval. Other than meeting with a few congressional leaders, Truman made no effort to "persuade" Congress to grant him authority to take the country to war against another nation, as all Presidents before Truman felt compelled to do. Truman acted unilaterally. For Neustadt, there was no need for "give-and-take" or "shared power." It was Truman's job "to make decisions and to take initiatives." Among Truman's private values, "decisiveness was high upon his list." Truman's image of the President was "man-in-charge," and Neustadt wrote for "a man who seeks to maximize his

---

26. Richard E. Neustadt, Presidential Power 23 (1964; originally published in 1960).
27. Id. at 43, 45, 47.
28. Id. at 42, emphasis in original.
29. Id. at 157.

power."[30] Taken logically, that form of government would justify the decisions and actions of any autocrat.

To exercise authority, Neustadt argued that a President needed confidence "that his image of himself in office justify an unremitting search for personal power."[31] He measured presidential success by action, vigor, decisiveness, initiative, energy, and personal power. Absent from his analysis were constitutional checks, separation of powers, federalism, sources of authority, and the ends to which power is put. As political scientist John Hart has observed, Neustadt evaluates a President "on the basis of his influence on the outcome, but not on the outcome itself."[32]

When Neustadt reissued his book in 1990 under a different title, he seemed to alter his model of the President after the abuse of executive power during Lyndon Johnson's Vietnam War and the scandals of Nixon's Watergate and Reagan's Iran-Contra. He now wrote in a manner entirely different from the tone of his 1960 and 1964 editions: "To share is to limit; that is the heart of the matter, and everything this book explores stems from it."[33] Nothing in his earlier editions advanced those basic constitutional values that protect individual rights.

Thomas Cronin has helped puncture imaginary and misleading qualities that other scholars bestowed on the American President. In a paper delivered at the 1970 American Political Science Association Annual Meeting, he objected to romantic and idealized models of the presidency. Entitled "The Textbook Presidency and Political Science," Cronin faulted scholars for promoting "inflated and unrealistic interpretations of presidential competence and beneficence." Infatuation with the presidency, Cronin said, necessarily diminished the role of Congress, the Constitution, checks and balances, separation of power, and democratic processes.[34]

In his book *On the Presidency* (2010), Cronin reviewed the record of fourteen Presidents from 1920 to 2009. He concluded: "Maybe about three were successful. At least half a dozen failed in one way or another."[35] He deleted from the list of successful Presidents those who were forced from office, impeached, rejected when they sought reelection, or decided to step aside rather than face voter rebuke. Three Presidents survived this winnowing process: Franklin D. Roosevelt, Dwight D. Eisenhower, and Ronald Reagan. Despite

30. Id. at 166, 171.
31. Id. at 172.
32. John Hart, "Presidential Power Revised," 25 Political Studies 48, 56 (1977).
33. Richard E. Neustadt, Presidential Power and the Modern Presidents: The Politics of Leadership from Roosevelt to Reagan x (1990).
34. Thomas E. Cronin. "The Textbook Presidency and Political Science," 116 Cong. Rec. 34914–28 (1970).
35. Thomas Cronin, On the Presidency: Teacher, Soldier, Shaman, Pol 2 (2010).

this bleak record, some contemporary scholars continue to attribute to the presidency romantic qualities of integrity, honesty, and competence rarely seen in those who actually sit in the Oval Office. It should be evident that the political skills required to survive primaries and general elections do not automatically translate into sound judgments needed to effectively exercise presidential power.

John Burke and Fred Greenstein compared how Presidents Dwight D. Eisenhower and Lyndon Johnson decided whether to intervene militarily in Vietnam. Eisenhower chose to stay out; Johnson entered and escalated the war. Contrary to those who might view Johnson as the stronger leader, Eisenhower comes across as better equipped through personal judgment and advisers to reach more thoughtful judgments about prospective costs and benefits.[36] In a subsequent study, Greenstein examined presidential styles from Franklin D. Roosevelt to Barack Obama. Rather than attempt to generalize about "Presidents," he found a wide variety of skills in terms of public communication, organizational competence, and programmatic knowledge, as well as a range of self-destructive qualities.[37]

In 2008, Richard Pious incisively analyzed presidential actions from Eisenhower through George W. Bush to highlight the reasons behind a pattern that led to repeated failings in office. His examples covered national security (Eisenhower and the U-2 flights, Kennedy and the Bay of Pigs, Johnson and Vietnam, Ford and the *Mayaguez*, Reagan and Iran-Contra, Bush II and Iraq) and domestic policy (Carter's energy policy, Bush I and the budget summit, and Clinton's health care proposal).[38] James Pfiffner focused on the extent to which Presidents resorted to telling lies about public policy and engaging in systematic deception.[39] Studies by Harold Bruff, Gene Healy, and Peter Shane explored the capacity of Presidents and their legal advisers to manipulate the law for political objectives, resulting not only in damage to the constitutional order but catastrophic policy outcomes.[40] Notwithstanding the quality of these works, outsized and unrealistic notions of presidential authority retain a firm foothold in the media and the White House, and among some scholars.

36. John P. Burke & Fred I. Greenstein, How Presidents Test Reality: Decisions on Vietnam, 1954 and 1965 (1989).

37. Fred I. Greenstein, The Presidential Difference: Leadership Style from FDR to Barack Obama (3d ed., 2009).

38. Richard M. Pious, Why Presidents Fail (2008).

39. James P. Pfiffner, The Character Factor: How We Judge American Presidents (2004). See also his Power Play: The Bush Presidency and the Constitution (2008).

40. Harold H. Bruff, Bad Advice: Bush's Lawyers in the War on Terror (2009), Gene Healy, The Cult of the Presidency: America's Dangerous Devotion to Executive Power (2008), and Peter M. Shane, Madison's Nightmare: How Executive Power Threatens American Democracy (2009).

A serious shortcoming in academic work on the presidency is the extent to which the discipline of political science has largely cut ties with public law and constitutional analysis. Similar weaknesses apply to studies on Congress. When political science developed in the United States in the 1880s, the study of politics necessarily incorporated public law. Politics and law were "interdependent." Investigating one required investigating the other. A research project on government and public policy could not be pursued by excluding law. Beginning in the 1950s, behavioral studies gained traction in political science, and scholars began to divorce the Constitution from their studies.[41] By 1963, behavioralism topped the list of fields in which significant work was being done. Located at the bottom: public law. Fortunately, a number of political scientists continue to orient their research to public law and monitor legal boundaries to presidential power.[42]

Not only has the discipline of political science placed less weight on public law analysis, but so have some law professors. They remain attracted to a system of government that concentrates power in the President without any legal or constitutional checks, either from Congress or the courts. In *Terror in the Balance* (2007), Eric Posner and Adriane Vermeule describe the executive branch as the only institution of government with the resources, power, and flexibility to respond to national security threats. Individual civil liberties, they argue, are appropriately subordinated and marginalized because they "interfere with the effective response to the threat."[43] They urge lawyers to "restrain other lawyers and their philosophical allies from shackling the government's response to emergencies with intrusive judicial review and amorphous worries about the second-order effects of sensible first-order policies."[44]

What if the policies are senseless and abusive? What happens to individual rights when there are no external restraints on executive actions? It is curious that the work of Posner and Vermeule would appear several years after the George W. Bush administration went to war against Iraq on the basis of six claims that Iraq possessed weapons of mass destruction. Those assertions, of highly dubious quality, proved to be entirely false.[45] Moreover, the U.S. military intervention lacked competent preparation for what would happen to the

41. Mitchel A. Sollenberger, "Presidential Studies, Behavioralism, and Public Law," 44 Pres. Stud. Q. 758 (2014).

42. Louis Fisher, "Connecting Presidential Power to Public Law," 44 Pres. Stud. Q. 157 (2014). For a list of political scientists grounded in public law, see the individuals discussed in Louis Fisher, "Political Scientist as Practitioner," 46 PS: Political Science & Politics 519, 520–23 (2013).

43. Eric Posner & Adriane Vermeule, Terror in the Balance: Security, Liberty, and the Courts 7 (2007).

44. Id. at 167.

45. Fisher, Presidential War Power, at 216–31.

country after toppling Saddam Hussein. Especially harmful was the decision to disband the Iraqi Army and exclude members of the Baath Party from the new Iraq government. The two decisions alienated hundreds of thousands of Iraqi troops and undermined the technical capacity needed for social and economic activity.[46]

Posner and Vermeule developed the same theme, and even a more radical one, in *The Executive Unbound* (2010). Their advice is to trust not in law or the Constitution to constrain the President. Instead, they rely solely on public opinion and political elections, "substituting the rule of politics for the rule of law."[47] To reach that position they follow two contradictory methods of analysis. For Congress and the judiciary, they review various deficiencies and weaknesses before dismissing both branches in the fight against terrorism. When they turn to the President and the executive branch, they create an imaginary and idealistic world, attributing to Presidents and executive officials an unmatched and unverified capacity to respond effectively to emerging threats. They express confidence that the President "knows the range of options available, their likely effects, their costs and benefits—thanks to the resources and expertise of the executive branch—and so, if he is well-motivated, he will choose the best measures available."[48] The primary issue is not motivation. It is competence and the historical record, and yet Posner and Vermeule do not test their model against a string of presidential errors ranging from Korea to the Bay of Pigs, Vietnam, Iran-Contra, and finally the Iraq War in 2003.

The Judiciary

We are generally advised that courts, not the elected branches, are far better structured to protect individual rights. Constitutional scholar Laurence Tribe has written that the Supreme Court "often stands alone as the guardian of minority groups. The democratic political process, by its very nature, leaves political minorities vulnerable to the will of the majority." His fundamental premise: majorities cannot protect minorities. Tribe conceded that the Court's record "in championing the cause of oppressed minorities is hardly unstained."[49] Other legal scholars conclude that it is necessary to place political power in an unelected Court to protect minorities "from democratic

46. James P. Pfiffner, "US Blunders in Iraq: De-Baathification and Disbanding the Army," Intelligence and National Security," Vol. 25, No. 1, Feb. 2010, at 76–85.

47. Eric Posner & Adriane Vermeule, The Executive Unbound: After the Madisonian Republic 14 (2010).

48. Id. at 130.

49. Laurence H. Tribe, God Save This Honorable Court 20 (1985).

excess."[50] Yet from 1789 through World War II, it is difficult to find federal court decisions that upheld and championed individual rights.

In a recent study, Noah Feldman correctly notes that not until the Supreme Court decided *Brown v. Board of Education* in 1954 could it be seen "as rightly devoted to the protection of minorities."[51] He further observes that the unanimous decision, widely praised, "was a compromise and, in that sense, incoherent as a statement of constitutional law." The "mess" that resulted in the following years "reflected this incoherence."[52] The next section focuses on the record of the Warren Court in protecting individual rights. Chapter 3 examines *Brown* in greater detail.

In looking for early examples of judicial protection to minorities, one could cite the 1943 decision that struck down a school policy that compelled students who were Jehovah's Witnesses to salute the American flag or be expelled. However, three years earlier the Court had upheld the policy by a resounding 8-to-1 majority, provoking severe criticism throughout the country. Those decisions are analyzed in chapter 5.

A famous footnote written by Justice Stone in a 1938 decision suggested that the Supreme Court might have a special responsibility to protect "discrete and insular minorities," especially when "those political processes ordinarily to be relied upon to protect minorities" have been curtailed.[53] His statement recognized that individual and minority rights were often protected by the elected branches. Indeed, blacks, women, children, and other minorities regularly found it necessary to turn to Congress and state legislatures for support.

In *Law's Empire* (1986), Ronald Dworkin created a model that entrusts to the Supreme Court the protection of individual rights: "The United States is a more just society than it would have been had its constitutional rights been left to the conscience of majoritarian institutions."[54] In a footnote, he acknowledged that he offered "no argument for this flat claim" and he would have to take into account that the Court's record "has been spotty."[55] The material in this book finds little support for his generalization. As demonstrated in chapters 3 through 7, many judicial decisions regarding blacks, women, children, religious minorities, and Native Americans led to a less just society. Repeatedly, the corrective force came from legislative bodies and public participation.

50. William Mishler & Reginald S. Sheehan, "The Supreme Court as a Countermajoritarian Institution? The Impact of Public Opinion on Supreme Court Decisions," 87 Am. Pol. Sci. Rev. 87, 87 (1993).

51. Noah Feldman, Scorpions: The Battles and Triumphs of FDR's Great Supreme Court Justices 406 (2010).

52. Id. at 407.

53. United States v. Carolene Products Co., 304 U.S. 144, 153, n.4 (1938).

54. Ronald Dworkin, Law's Empire 356 (1986).

55. Id. at 449, n.2.

Following World War II, the Supreme Court and scholars frequently announced that when the Court decides a case it speaks with finality. Justice Robert Jackson offered this assessment in 1953: "We are not final because we are infallible, but we are infallible only because we are final."[56] A clever sentence, but it is misleading for two reasons. First, Jackson could only have been referring to decisions about constitutional, not statutory, questions. It is widely accepted that when the Court decides that a statute means A not B, Congress is at liberty to say: "No, it means B (or C), not A," and pass another statute. That happens on a regular basis, as discussed in the Lilly Ledbetter equal pay issue in chapter 4.

Second, even confining Jackson's statement to constitutional matters, he is clearly incorrect. Nothing in the Court's record points to any evidence of judicial infallibility or finality. Jackson was too good a student of constitutional history to believe what he said. As explained in chapter 5, the Supreme Court's decision in 1940 to uphold a compulsory flag salute for public school children produced intense criticism from the press, religious organizations, and the general public. In the face of this opposition, three Justices who had joined the majority changed their minds and publicly stated two years later that the 1940 case had been "wrongly decided." Two other Justices from the majority retired, and their replacements helped form a 6–3 majority in 1943 to strike down the compulsory flag salute.[57] The author of the 1943 decision: Robert Jackson.

More broadly, the Supreme Court lacks finality on constitutional issues for the simple reason that it makes mistakes and has done so throughout its history. This book covers many examples. Chief Justice William Rehnquist put the matter crisply in 1993: "It is an unalterable fact that our judicial system, like the human beings who administer it, is fallible."[58] Despite that plain talk, the Court and scholars continue to defend the "last word" doctrine. In a religious liberties case in 1997 discussed in chapter 6, the Court announced: "When the Court has interpreted the Constitution, it has acted within the province of the Judiciary Branch, which embraces the duty to say what the law is. Marbury v. Madison, 1 Cranch, at 177." The Court concluded that when a conflict occurs between a Court precedent and a congressional statute, the Court's ruling "must control."[59]

Over two centuries of constitutional history demonstrate that the Court's position in 1997 is false. Many examples in this book will underscore that point. What of the famous case of *Marbury v. Madison* (1803)? It states: "It

56. Brown v. Allen, 344 U.S. 443, 540 (1953).
57. West Virginia State Board of Education v. Barnette, 319 U.S. 624 (1943).
58. Herrera v. Collins, 506 U.S. 390, 415 (1993).
59. City of Boerne v. Flores, 521 U.S. 507, 535–36 (1997).

is emphatically the province and duty of the judicial department to say what the law is. Those who apply the rule to particular cases, must of necessity expound and interpret that rule. If two laws conflict with each other, the courts must decide on the operation of each."[60] Three points need be said about this frequently misunderstood passage from *Marbury*.

First, read the first sentence as often as you like, and it says nothing about judicial finality. One could easily rewrite it to produce another claim: "It is emphatically the province and duty of the legislative department to say what the law is." No one could disagree with that, but it wouldn't establish congressional finality or supremacy either. Second, if two laws conflict they can be resolved by the Court but also by subsequent legislation passed by Congress, which happens frequently. Examples will be given. Third, invoking this sentence from *Marbury* ignores what Chief Justice Rehnquist said in 1993: the Supreme Court makes errors, often major ones. Abundant details in this book reinforce that obvious point.[61]

Politically and legally, Marshall was too sophisticated a student of the Constitution and politics to believe that the Supreme Court was superior to the other two branches. Having declared a statutory provision unconstitutional in *Marbury*, he thereafter used judicial review only in a positive sense by consistently *upholding* congressional authority. His respect for the elected branches appears in a note he sent to Justice Samuel Chase on January 23, 1805, while the Senate considered whether to remove Chase from the Court after being impeached by the House. Marshall did not promote judicial supremacy. Instead, he recommended that it would be better to replace the impeachment process with "an appellate jurisdiction in the legislature. A reversal of those legal opinions deemed unsound by the legislature would certainly better comport with the mildness of our character than [would] a removal of the Judge who has rendered them unknowing of his fault."[62] This is not the language of a Chief Justice who believes the Court delivers the final word on legal and constitutional matters.

Nevertheless, scholars and reporters continue to promote judicial supremacy, claiming that a Supreme Court ruling can be reversed only through constitutional amendment or if the Justices change their minds. Writing in 2012, Jeffrey Toobin said that a Supreme Court decision "interpreting the

60. 5 U.S. (1 Cr.) 137, 177 (1803).
61. For closer analysis of the many misconceptions that flow from *Marbury v. Madison*: Louis Fisher, On the Supreme Court: Without Illusion and Idolatry 1–33, 221–28 (2014); Louis Fisher, Defending Congress and the Constitution 22–47 (2011).
62. 3 Albert J. Beveridge, The Life of John Marshall 177 (1919). Marshall dated the letter January 23, 1804, but modern scholarship fixes the date a year later; 6 The Papers of John Marshall 348, n.1 (Charles F. Hobson, ed., 1990). Like the rest of us, Marshall forgot to switch to the new year.

Constitution can be overturned only by a new decision or by a constitutional amendment."[63] Tom Goldstein, who frequently argues cases before the Supreme Court, stated on June 20, 2013, that when the Court "interprets the Constitution, that is the final word. The President and Congress can't overturn its decision. The only option is to amend the Constitution which is basically impossible."[64] Reporters for major newspapers continue to promote judicial finality. Adam Liptak, writing for the *New York Times* on August 21, 2012, noted that "only a constitutional amendment can change things after the justices have acted in a constitutional case."[65] Reporting for the *Washington Post* on October 25, 2014, Robert Barnes wrote that *Marbury v. Madison* "established the court as the final word on the Constitution."[66]

A contemporary example will establish that when the Supreme Court decides a constitutional issue, Congress has an opportunity to respond with legislation that gives individual rights greater protection. In the early 1980s, Captain Simcha Goldman objected that an Air Force regulation violated his religious liberty by prohibiting him from wearing his yarmulke indoors while on duty. A 5–4 Court held for the Air Force.[67] Within one year, Congress passed legislation directing the military to permit soldiers to wear religious apparel unless it interfered with military duties. How could Congress countermand the Court's interpretation on this constitutional issue? The answer comes from language in Article I, Section 8, granting to Congress the power to make "Rules for the Government and Regulation of the land and naval forces." That constitutional determination is left to Congress, not the judiciary. Details on this case appear in chapter 6.

In *Obergefell v. Hodges* (2015), the Supreme Court upheld the constitutionality of same-sex marriages. Although divided 5–4 with many bitter dissents, including one by Chief Justice Roberts, who said the majority's opinion had nothing to do with the Constitution, the decision extended new rights to millions of people. Certainly other Supreme Court decisions have protected individual rights, particularly over the past six decades, but this book covers many instances of the elected branches advancing individual rights far better than the judiciary. Examples include Congress providing equal accommodations for blacks in 1875, only to be struck down by the Supreme Court in 1883; the Court in *Bradwell v. State* (1873) denying women the right to

63. Jeffrey Toobin, The Oath: The Obama White House and the Supreme Court 194 (2012).

64. http//www.scotus.blog.com/2013/06/power.

65. Adam Liptak, "In Congress's Paralysis, a Mightier Supreme Court," N.Y. Times, Aug. 21, 2012, at A10.

66. Robert Barnes, "Addressing the Supreme Court with Fun," Wash. Post, Oct. 25, 2014, at A1.

67. Goldman v. Weinberger, 475 U.S. 503 (1986).

practice law; the Court's decision in *Plessy v Ferguson* (1896) upholding racial discrimination; the child-labor decisions of 1918 and 1922; the decisions in 1943 and 1944 that upheld a curfew for and detention of Japanese Americans, two-thirds of them U.S. citizens; and more recent cases such as the *Goldman* yarmulke decision, just covered, and the equal pay decision involving Lilly Ledbetter in 2007.

The Warren Court

Those who associate the Supreme Court with protecting individual rights often have in mind the decisions handed down under Chief Justice Earl Warren. The school desegregation case in *Brown v. Board of Education* (1954) is frequently cited as a leading example of the Court safeguarding the rights of individuals. The previous section included the views of Noah Feldman about *Brown* and the implementing decision a year later in *Brown II*, but those decisions will be analyzed in detail in chapter 3.

The Warren Court gained a reputation for extending new rights to individuals charged with crimes, such as its decision in *Gideon v. Wainwright* (1963), which granted indigent defendants the right to counsel provided by the government. Such procedural safeguards are important, but the Court was not breaking new ground. A century earlier, several states had already begun to recognize that right. In 1854, the Supreme Court of Indiana stated that a "civilized community" could not prosecute a poor person and withhold counsel. Five years later, the Wisconsin Supreme Court called it a "mockery" to promise a pauper a fair trial and tell him he must employ his own counsel.[68] In 1892, Congress passed legislation to provide counsel to represent poor persons and extended that provision in 1910.[69]

The Warren Court defended many other individual rights. *Griswold v. Connecticut* (1965) struck down a state law that made it a crime for any person, including married couples, to use any drug or article to prevent conception. There was little support for a statute that reached back to 1879, but the opinion by Justice Douglas was widely criticized for relying on "penumbras, formed by emanations" in the Bill of Rights. In *Baker v. Carr* (1962) and *Gray v. Sanders* (1963), the Court established the one person, one vote standard for reapportionment, and it helped the poor by abolishing poll taxes in *Harper v. Virginia Board of Elections* (1966). Other branches were involved with the issue of poll taxes. In 1962, Congress had passed a constitutional amendment

68. Gideon v. Wainwright, 372 U.S. 335 (1963); Webb v. Baird, 6 Ind. 13 (1854); Carpenter v. Dane, 9 Wis. 248 (1859).
69. 27 Stat. 252 (1892); 36 Stat. 866 (1910).

to eliminate the poll tax for federal elections, and it was ratified two years later. The Voting Rights Act of 1965 declared that the poll tax placed an unreasonable hardship on voter rights and gave federal courts jurisdiction to decide cases involving state and local elections. That statute led to the decision in *Harper*. Other noteworthy Warren Court decisions include a unanimous decision in *Torcaso v. Watkins* (1961), holding unconstitutional a Maryland provision that required all public officials to affirm a belief in God.

The Court's controversial decision in *Engel v. Vitale* (1962) struck down New York's "Regents' Prayer," which required public school children to acknowledge their dependence on God. Writing for the Court, Justice Black said, "it is no part of the business of government to compose official prayers for any group of the American people to recite as a part of a religious program carried on by government."[70] He explained that his decision did not indicate hostility toward religion or prayer. Instead, the Constitution left religious practices and beliefs to the individual, not to government.

In a concurrence, Justice Douglas offered unfortunate and unnecessary references to the fact that the Supreme Court convenes with the words "God save the United States and this Honorable Court," each House of Congress opens the day's business with guest chaplains who say a prayer, the Pledge of Allegiance includes the words "under God," and congressional legislation in 1865 authorized the placement of "In God We Trust" on coins. In his dissent, Justice Stewart observed that Presidents from George Washington to John F. Kennedy in their Inaugural Addresses ask the protection and help of God.

A number of newspapers incorrectly reported that the Court had prohibited prayer, when in fact it had banned *official* prayer. One newspaper headline announced: "Court outlaws God."[71] Representative George Andrews of Alabama added: "They put Negroes in the school and now they've driven God out."[72] Strong pressure developed to pass a constitutional amendment to nullify the Court's decision, but the movement lost steam after congressional hearings revealed broad support for the ruling by Protestant, Catholic, and Jewish organizations.[73] In 1963, the Court in *Abingdon School Dist. v. Schempp* decided that states may not require that students in public schools read verses from the Bible or cite the Lord's Prayer at the beginning of each day. Public criticism of this decision was not near as intense as with *Engel*.[74]

70. Engel v. Vitale, 370 U.S. 421, 425 (1962).

71. Lucas A. Powe, Jr., The Warren Court and American Politics 187 (2000).

72. Id. at 188.

73. Louis Fisher and & Katy J. Harriger, American Constitutional Law 623–24 (10th ed., 2013).

74. Powe, The Warren Court and American Politics, at 361–63,

Building on cases involving coerced confessions, self-incrimination, and right to counsel, the Warren Court in 1966 handed down *Miranda v. Arizona*, announcing various rights for defendants held in police custody. To prevent compulsion by law enforcement officials, the person in custody must be informed before interrogation of the following: the right to remain silent, anything said may be used in court, the right to consult with an attorney and to have a lawyer present during interrogation, and the right to have a lawyer appointed if the accused is indigent. *Miranda* was bitterly attacked for interfering with the efforts of law enforcement officials, but the Court correctly noted that its holding was not "an innovation in our jurisprudence."[75] *Miranda*-type warnings had been given routinely by federal agents in the past and had been given by state officials.[76]

Individual Rights at Risk

In times of perceived emergencies and fears of disloyalty at home, all three branches have failed to protect individual rights. That has been the pattern from 1789 to the years following the terrorist acts of September 11, 2001. On a repeated basis, government turns against various groups and violates basic constitutional rights, at times apologizing decades later. At fault here is not merely Congress but also the President and the Supreme Court.

Congress passed the Alien and Sedition Acts in 1798, and they were signed by President John Adams. It is remarkable that the two elected branches could support such repressive legislation seven years after ratification of the Bill of Rights. When pressure mounted for going to war against France in 1798, individuals within the country fell into two discrete categories: loyal and disloyal. The nation's leading periodical for the Federalist Party, Philadelphia's *Gazette of the United States*, warned: "He that is not for us, is against us."[77] Those who faced repression in 1798 were the foreign born: "enemy aliens" and "alien friends."

Some of the incentive in passing these statutes lay in partisan calculations. The Federalists believed that immigrants were more likely to vote for the Republican-Jeffersonian Party. The legislation extended the waiting period for citizenship from five years to fourteen years. The Alien Friends Act authorized the President to deport any alien "he shall judge dangerous to the peace

75. 384 U.S. 436, 442 (1966).

76. McNabb v. United States, 318 U.S. 332, 336 (1943); Haley v. Ohio, 332 U.S. 596, 598, 604 (1948).

77. James Morton Smith, Freedom's Fetters: The Alien and Sedition Laws and American Civil Liberties 15 (1956).

and safety of the United States": a standard broad enough to put all aliens at risk. Deportation was allowed if the President had "reasonable grounds" to believe that an alien was involved in "any treasonable or secret machinations" against the federal government. Individuals targeted by this legislation had no right to a public trial to be heard by a jury, to confront witnesses, or access to other basic procedural safeguards. A separate statute covered "alien enemies," subjecting all noncitizen males fourteen years or older to removal from the country. Mere identification with an enemy nation was sufficient to merit removal.[78]

Under the Sedition Act of 1798, which applied to both aliens and citizens, individuals could be fined and imprisoned if they wrote or said anything about Congress or the President deemed by the government to be "false, scandalous and malicious," intended to "defame" those political institutions or bring them into "contempt or disrepute," "excite" any hatred against them, or "stir up" sedition or act in combination to oppose or resist federal laws or any presidential effort to implement those laws. Mere criticism of the government could result in prosecution.

The Adams administration prosecuted not only individuals but also newspapers deemed too critical of the Federalist Party and its policies. Most newspapers in the country were Federalist, not Republican-Jeffersonian. When Thomas Jefferson was elected President in 1800, he used his pardon power to relieve those punished by the Sedition Act.[79] In 1840, a congressional statute provided funds to reimburse those fined under the statute. A committee report accompanying the legislation denounced the statute as "unconstitutional, null, and void."[80] Although the two elected branches subsequently pushed back against the Sedition Act, no such resistance came from the judiciary. The courts during the John Adams administration were safely Federalist, with no political interest or independence to check prosecutions by the executive branch. In *New York Times Co. v. Sullivan* (1964), the Supreme Court acknowledged that the Sedition Act was not struck down by a court of law but by the "court of history."[81]

America has several times passed sedition laws to intimidate and punish citizens who thought and spoke in ways the government found unacceptable. In 1917, after the United States became involved in World War I, several states passed sedition legislation. Under a Minnesota law, one individual was prosecuted for remarking in public: "We were stampeded into this war by

78. Geoffrey R. Stone, Perilous Times: Free Speech in Wartime 16–70 (2004).
79. 11 Writings of Thomas Jefferson 43 (Albert Bergh, ed., 1904), letter to Mrs. John Adams, July 22, 1804).
80. H. Rept. No. 86, 26th Cong., 1st Sess. 2 (1840); 6 Stat. 802, ch. 45 (1840).
81. 376 U.S. 254, 276 (1964).

newspaper rot to pull England's chestnuts out of the fire."[82] Congress relied on a Montana statute as model legislation. With the change of only three words it became the federal sedition act of 1918. Those convicted faced a fine of $10,000 and twenty years in prison, or both. In the 1940 Smith Act, Congress passed legislation to punish seditious utterances. The statute did not use the word sedition, but the government nonetheless proceeded to hold sedition trials.[83]

Another period of repression is the "Red Scare" of 1919–1920. Following the Russian Revolution of 1917 and the growth of the American radical movement, congressional committees investigated what it considered to be suspect organizations. Attorney General A. Mitchell Palmer took the lead in infiltrating these organizations and gathering names to be deported. State and local governments turned against groups suspected of being unpatriotic. As government abuses mounted and became public, the Red Scare ran its course.[84]

In 1927, Justice Louis Brandeis warned about what fear can bring in a time of perceived threats, particularly unreasoned fear: "Fear of serious injury cannot alone justify suppression of free speech and assembly. Men feared witches and burnt women. It is the function of speech to free men from the bondage of irrational fears."[85] The Framers, he said, "did not exalt order at the cost of liberty."[86] To protect self-government, members of Congress must demonstrate a capacity to think independently and explain their views clearly. If they merely take direction from the President or the Supreme Court, they cease being representatives, forsake their oath of office, and undermine the system of checks and balances that safeguards constitutional government.

In 1938, the House created the Un-American Activities Committee (HUAC), chaired by Martin Dies of Texas. Increasingly the committee turned its attention to Communism. Published hearings identified 640 organizations, 483 newspapers, and 280 labor organizations as "Communistic." The list included the Boy Scouts, the American Civil Liberties Union, the Catholic Association for International Peace, and the Camp Fire Girls.[87] During House debate on February 1, 1943, lawmakers took turns singling out writers, publishers, political activists, and executive officials thought to be linked to the Communist Party.[88]

---

82. Stone, Perilous Times, at 211.
83. Louis Fisher, The Constitution and 9/11, at 131–38 (2008).
84. Stone, Perious Times, at 220–26.
85. Whitney v. California, 274 U.S. 357, 376 (1927) (Brandeis, J., concurring).
86. Id. at 377.
87. Stone, Perilous Times, at 246.
88. 89 Cong. Rec. 475–78 (1943).

The House created a special subcommittee to evaluate claims against federal employees considered to be disloyal or subversive. The subcommittee offered draft language to deny the use of federal appropriations to pay the salaries of three executive officials: William E. Dodd, Jr., Robert Morss Lovett, and Goodwin B. Watson. Although the Senate objected to discharging government employees based on secret testimony developed by the House subcommittee, eventually a bill denying salaries for the three men was sent to President Roosevelt. Because the bill contained emergency funding for World War II, he signed it but condemned the provision as an unconstitutional bill of attainder (legislative punishment without trial).[89] In 1946, the Supreme Court reached the same judgment.[90]

World War II led to additional violations of individual rights, brought about by all three branches. On the basis of an executive order issued by President Franklin D. Roosevelt in 1942, followed by supportive legislation from Congress, the federal government acted against more than one hundred thousand Japanese Americans on the West Coast. Initially they were subject to a curfew order and later taken from their homes and placed in detention camps inland.[91] In the *Hirabayashi* and *Korematsu* cases of 1943 and 1944, the Supreme Court upheld these actions, steps so damaging to individual rights that the nation later issued an apology to those injured. How could the Supreme Court sustain these policies?

In a 1962 article, Chief Justice Earl Warren reviewed the capacity of the judiciary to defend individual rights when endangered by the elected branches. To Warren, the two decisions underscored "the limitations under which the Court must sometimes operate" in an area in which the elected branches "must bear the primary responsibility for determining whether specific actions they are taking are consonant with our Constitution." The fact that the Court rules in a case like *Hirabayashi* "that a given program is constitutional, does not necessarily answer the question whether, in a broader sense, it actually is." In other words, Warren advised his readers not to seek constitutional answers always from the courts. In a democratic society, the legislative and executive branches still have "the primary responsibility for fashioning and executing policy consistent with the Constitution." He even warned against excessive reliance on the political branches: The "day-to-day job of upholding the Constitution really lies elsewhere. It rests, realistically, on the shoulders of every citizen."[92]

89. The Public Papers and Addresses of Franklin D. Roosevelt, 1943 Volume, at 385–86 (1950).
90. United States v. Lovett, 328 U.S. 303 (1946). For further details: Fisher, The Constitution and 9/11, at 138–43.
91. Fisher, The Constitution and 9/11, at 144–51.
92. Earl Warren, "The Bill of Rights and the Military," 37 N.Y.U. L. Rev. 181, 202 (1962).

Following World War II, individual rights were jeopardized by elected branch actions. On March 25, 1947, President Harry Truman issued procedures to determine the loyalty of federal employees. Procedures were so carelessly drafted that employees, although entitled to a hearing, were often unable to learn the names of confidential informants. Truman's executive order, by blocking access to confidential files, permitted irresponsible trials that wrecked federal careers.[93] Initiatives by Senator Joseph McCarthy to seek out Communists and disloyal Americans produced additional violations of individual rights. On December 2, 1954, the Senate voted 67 to 22 to "condemn" him for bringing the Senate into "dishonor and disrepute" and acting to "impair its dignity."[94]

Seeking a Better Balance

There is no evidence that the Framers ever intended the judiciary to be the "last word" on the meaning of the Constitution. No language in the Constitution supports that doctrine, either expressly or by implication. Some reasons have already been offered to reject the theory of judicial supremacy. Other evidence in this book will underscore that the Constitution has always been shaped by all three branches and the states, with no branch occupying a dominant position. To accept the Supreme Court as the ultimate arbiter of constitutional questions would do grave damage to the Framers' aspiration for self-government and individual rights.

President Abraham Lincoln framed the issue well in his first inaugural address. He did not question that some constitutional questions are decided by the Supreme Court, and that "such decisions must be binding in any case upon the parties to a suit as to the object of that suit." With *Dred Scott v. Sandford* (1857) in mind, a case in which the Court justified slavery on the ground that blacks were by nature permanently inferior to whites, he said: "The candid citizen must confess that if the policy of the Government upon vital questions affecting the whole people is to be irrevocably fixed by decisions of the Supreme Court, the instant they are made in ordinary litigation between parties in ordinary actions the people will have ceased to be their own rulers, having to that extent practically resigned their Government into the hands of that eminent tribunal."[95]

93. Fisher, The Constitution and 9/11, at 151–58.
94. 100 Cong. Rec. 16392 (1954).
95. Arthur M. Schlesinger, Jr., & Fred L. Israel, eds., My Fellow Citizens: The Inaugural Addresses of the Presidents of the United States, 1789–2009, at 146 (2010).

An early constitutional conflict, involving all three branches of government, came from the decision of Congress to create a U.S. Bank. Although nothing in the Constitution provided express authority to establish such an institution, the Court in 1819 upheld it as within the broad power of the Necessary and Proper Clause. As author of *McCulloch v. Maryland*, Chief Justice Marshall seemed to adopt the principle of judicial supremacy. He said that if a constitutional dispute must be decided, "by this tribunal alone can the decision be made. On the supreme court of the United States has the constitution of our country devolved this important duty."[96]

McCulloch has been described as one of the "fixed stars in our constitutional constellation."[97] No doubt it is, but the decision had nothing to do with judicial finality. At stake in the U.S. Bank debate was whether the two elected branches possessed constitutional authority to create such an institution. It was left to them to create it or not. The Court had no role in that decision. Even if the Court were to bless their efforts, as it did in *McCulloch*, a future Congress or President could change their position on the constitutionality or the necessity of a U.S. Bank. If Congress were to decide not to reauthorize it, that political decision would be closed and final. The Court could have no part in that judgment. If Congress reauthorized the bank and the President vetoed it on policy or constitutional grounds and Congress failed to override the veto, the Court would again be excluded in such considerations.

Precisely that happened in 1832 when President Andrew Jackson decided to veto a bill reauthorizing the Bank. He was advised that he had to sign the bill because the Bank had been endorsed by previous Congresses, previous Presidents, and the Supreme Court. He disagreed, holding that "mere precedent" was a "dangerous source of authority." He reviewed the checkered history of the Bank. The elected branches favored a national bank in 1791, decided against it in 1811 and 1815, and offered support in 1816. As to *McCulloch*, Jackson said it "ought not to control the coordinate authorities of this Government." All three branches "must each for itself be guided by its own opinion of the Constitution." His analysis of the bill convinced him that the Bank was neither necessary nor proper under Article I of the Constitution.[98] Congress did not override his veto. Last word on the U.S. Bank? The elected branches, not the Court.

Consider what happened in 1852 when the Supreme Court decided that the Wheeling Bridge over the Ohio River, constructed under Virginia state law, represented a nuisance because the structure was so low it obstructed

---

96. McCulloch v. Maryland, 17 U.S. (4 Wheat.) 316, 401 (1819).
97. Jamal Greene, "The Anticanon," 125 Harv. L. Rev. 379, 385 (2011).
98. 3 Richardson 1144–45.

navigation.[99] Congress responded by debating a bill to make the Wheeling Bridge "a lawful structure."[100] Lawmakers discovered what the Court had missed: vessels had deliberately elevated their smoke chimneys so they would not clear the bridge.[101] The bill provided that rather than altering the bridge to accommodate vessels, ships must adjust to the bridge.[102]

The dispute now returned to the Supreme Court. Writing for the majority, Justice Samuel Nelson explained that in 1852 the Court regarded the bridge as inconsistent with the authority of Congress to regulate interstate commerce. But the new statute removed that objection.[103] Three dissenting Justices could not believe that the Court's earlier decision that the bridge marked an unconstitutional obstruction of commerce could be reversed by congressional action. One Justice, Robert Grier, protested that allowing Congress to annul or vacate a Supreme Court decree "is without precedent, and, as a precedent for the future, it is of dangerous example."[104] He ignored *McCulloch*. The fact that the Court decided the Bank was constitutional did not prevent Congress or the President from deciding it was not.

A similar dispute occurred in the 1890s, but by now the Court had learned that constitutional issues could go back and forth between the judiciary and the elected branches and in some cases the elected branches could prevail. In 1890, the Court ruled that Iowa's prohibition of intoxicating liquors from outside its borders could not be applied to original packages or kegs coming from a firm in Illinois. Only after the original package entered Iowa and was broken into smaller packages could the state regulate the product. However, the Court added a caveat: the power of Congress over interstate commerce necessarily trumped the power of a state "unless placed there by congressional act."[105] States could not exclude incoming articles "without congressional permission."[106]

The Court's opinion was issued on April 28, 1890. By May 14, the Senate reported a bill granting Iowa authority to regulate incoming intoxicating liquors.[107] The remedial legislation was enacted on August 6. The statute made intoxicating liquors, upon their arrival in a state or territory, subject to the police powers of a state "to the same extent and in the same manner as

99. Pennsylvania v. Wheeling and Belmont Bridge Co., 54 U.S. (13 How.) 518 (1852).

100. Cong. Globe, 32d Cong., 1st Sess. 2195 (1852).

101. Id. at 2440 (Senator James Murray Mason).

102. 10 Stat. 112 (1852).

103. Pennsylvania v. Wheeling and Belmont Bridge Co., 18 How. 421, 430 (1856).

104. Id. at 449. For further details on the Wheeling Bridge cases, see Fisher, On the Supreme Court: Without Illusion or Idolatry, at 78–83.

105. Leisy v. Hardin, 155 U.S. 100, 108 (1890).

106. Id. at 125.

107. 21 Cong. Rec. 4642 (1890).

though such liquids or liquors had been produced in such State or Territory, and shall not be exempt therefrom by reason of being introduced therein in original packages or otherwise."[108] Unanimously, the Supreme Court upheld this statute.[109]

Subsequent chapters in this book reinforce the constitutional dialogue that occurs between the Supreme Court and the elected branches, including the effort for nearly a century to enact public accommodations legislation for blacks (chapter 3), to enable women to practice law (chapter 4), to pass child labor legislation after the Court twice struck down earlier congressional efforts (chapter 5), to secure religious liberty for minorities (chapter 6), and to protect the rights of Native Americans (chapter 7).

The constitutional system is strengthened when members of Congress, Presidents, courts, academics, reporters, the media, and the public at large treat all three branches of government as legitimate parts of a political system that debates and decides the meaning of the Constitution. Members of Congress take an oath to support the Constitution, not to defer to the Court or the President. It is appropriate for them to respect the Court and the President, just as the Court and the President should respect Congress. Members of Congress defer far too often to presidential claims and assertions. Similarly, at times they find it difficult to criticize judicial rulings, as though it is improper to do so. They announce support for a decision after first denouncing its reasoning and persuasive quality. Here are recent statements by three senior lawmakers who all chaired the House and Senate Judiciary Committees.

In a floor statement in 2001, Senator Patrick Leahy said he had become "increasingly concerned about some of the recent actions of the U.S. Supreme Court. As a member of the bar of the Court, as a U.S. Senator, as an American, I, of course, respect the decisions of the Supreme Court as being the ultimate decisions of law for our country." Referring to himself again as "an American," he accepted "any of its decisions as the ultimate interpretation of our Constitution, whether I agree or disagree."[110]

Members of Congress should not automatically accept a Supreme Court decision. They should feel at liberty to state their disagreement with a decision, explaining in plain words why it is unsound. Frank and informed criticism can help the Court rethink its reasoning. Total deference will not. Members of Congress know that the Court is capable of making errors and has a long record of doing so, at substantial cost to the rights and liberties of individuals and minorities. There is no reason to imply it is unpatriotic

108. 20 Stat. 313 (1890).
109. In re Rahrer, 140 U.S. 545 (1891). For further details on this case and congressional debate, see Fisher, On the Supreme Court, at 84–86.
110. 147 Cong. Rec. 2457 (2001).

or un-American to find fault with decisions of the Supreme Court. Blunt criticism is not only acceptable but reflects support for the system of self-government. Leahy noted that judicial activism "can work both ways. It can work to expand protections for all our rights or it can be used to limit our rights."[111] If the latter, it is important to say so.

Leahy objected that a recent decision by the Court was "just the latest in a long and ever growing line of 5–4 decisions that second-guess congressional policy judgment[s] to strike down Federal statutes and generally treat Congress as a least favored administrative agency rather than a coequal branch of the Federal Government."[112] A key point, and all the more reason to insist on coequality and not subordinate Congress to the Court as the ultimate interpreter. Leahy concluded with this thought: "Again, as I have said, I have stood on the floor of the Senate defending the Supreme Court as much or more than anybody I know in my 26 years here. I have defended the Supreme Court on decisions even when I disagreed with the Court."[113]

Why defend what you disagree with? Robert Katzmann, now a federal judge on the Second Circuit, wrote in 1997 about the need for candid public comments on court rulings: "Reasoned criticism of judicial decisions and of the administration of justice are useful and valuable; but excesses in rhetoric and political attacks can heighten insecurity about legislative intention." Courts need to understand that "not every disagreement is a threat to independence."[114] Because courts are part of making public policy, they should be subject to frank public evaluation.

Senator Orrin Hatch has had a long career in following and commenting on Supreme Court decisions. He knows how much the quality of court rulings can vary. When the Court decided *Boumediene v. Bush* in 2008, holding that Guantánamo detainees have a right of habeas corpus to federal district courts, Hatch announced his disagreement: "This decision, written by Justice Kennedy, gives terrorists one of the most important rights enjoyed by the people of the United States." Actually, at issue were not the rights of terrorists but of detainees *suspected* of terrorism. The questions were difficult, Hatch admitted, but "I do not believe that the Supreme Court has provided the correct answer." He understood that it is natural to be concerned about people's rights, "even those of terrorists, but sometimes we have to be practical and pragmatic and do the things that have to be done to protect the American people, and our citizens overseas."[115]

111. Id.
112. Id. at 2458.
113. Id.
114. Robert A. Katzmann, Courts and Congress 112 (1997).
115. 154 Cong. Rec. 12426 (2008).

Hatch might have left it at that. However, like Leahy, he gave full support to a decision he disagreed with: "There are many who will believe that the Supreme Court made the right decision and others, such as myself, who believe that the Court made a lousy decision. However, I will uphold the Supreme Court, even though it was a 5-to-4 decision. Nevertheless, it is a decision by one-third of the separated powers of this country, and must be recognized as such."[116] Why give one-third of the government the final say? Like the other two branches, the judiciary is fully capable of making errors and should be held publicly accountable for its decisions.

The third illustration of legislative deference to the Supreme Court comes from Representative John Conyers, who chaired the Judiciary Committee for several years and has a close understanding of legislative-judicial relations. In 2009, he participated in floor debate on the Supreme Court's decision in *Ledbetter v. Goodyear Tire & Rubber Co.* (2007), which rejected Lilly Ledbetter's effort to receive back pay to compensate for years of gender discrimination. Although Conyers called the decision "wrongheaded," he said he believed that "our courts are our last line of defense when it comes to protecting the fundamental rights enshrined in our Constitution and in our civil rights laws."[117] Judicial action was not the last line of defense for Lilly Ledbetter. That defense came from Congress when it passed legislation in 2009 to give greater protection to women that encounter pay discrimination. That dispute is covered in chapter 4.

Before turning to individual chapters on the rights of blacks, women, children, religious minorities, and Native Americans (chapters 3 through 7), the next chapter covers the constitutional principles that apply to all three branches, how the Framers were guided by some English precedents but broke with others, the steps from colonial status to national independence, the role of public participation in democratic government, and the risk to individual rights in times of perceived danger.

116. Id.
117. 155 Cong. Rec. 441–42 (2009).

2

FOUNDING PRINCIPLES

Deciding the appropriate role for Congress and its institutional ability to protect individual rights requires an appreciation of historical precedents and constitutional principles. The Framers were heavily influenced by the Enlightenment and its belief that individuals have the capacity to develop and participate in self-government. In America they would be citizens, not "subjects" ruled by a monarch. Long before the Declaration of Independence, Americans learned how to run their lives, hold meetings to discuss public issues, and find ways to forge a consensus on what should be done. England could exercise control only in a highly theoretical sense from London. Popular sovereignty gradually took root in America. Under the press of daily demands, representative assemblies emerged in colonial America to safeguard the people.

A purpose of the U.S. Constitution is to protect the dignity and worth of individuals, enabling them to promote their skills and talents. James Madison believed that an individual "has property in his opinions and in the free communication of them." He did not associate property solely with material things. It included religious opinions, personal safety and liberty, and the "free use of his faculties and free choice of the objects on which to employ them." Flowing from those fundamental values were the rights of free speech, free press, religious liberty, and protection against arbitrary arrest and seizure of property. Conscience, he said, "is the most sacred of all property." Invading someone's conscience was a greater violation than invading a person's home.[1] In Federalist No. 10, Madison spoke of the "diversity in the faculties of men, from which the rights of property originate." The protection of those faculties, he said, "is the first object of government."[2]

Protection of constitutional rights requires individual participation in government through representative assemblies, in both Congress and local and state legislative bodies, not by entrusting rights and liberties to the President and the Supreme Court. In Federalist No. 49, Madison noted that "the people are the only legitimate fountain of power."[3] It is frequently said

1. Madison's essay on property appeared in the National Gazette on March 29, 1792, and is reprinted in 6 The Writings of James Madison 101–3, Gaillard Hunt, ed.
2. The Federalist 130–31.
3. Id. at 348.

that if Congress does not protect its constitutional powers and abdicates—or acquiesces—to the President and the Supreme Court, it is at fault and deserves no sympathy or support. Partly true, but the problem lies deeper. A decline in congressional power is a decline in the power of the people the legislature represents.

A republic is a form of government in which the supreme power rests with the people, exercised through their representatives. The value of a republic appears in the Pledge of Allegiance: "I pledge allegiance to the flag of the United States of America and to the Republic for which it stands." Contrary to views often heard today, the overriding value in the pledge is not the flag. It is the republic. Lose the republic and the flag stands for nothing.

In a concurrence in 1927, Justice Louis Brandeis explained important values in America. The Framers who won independence from England believed that "the final end of the State was to make men free to develop their faculties; and that in its government the deliberative forces should prevail over the arbitrary."[4] The purpose of government was not to crush independent thought but to encourage it. The Framers valued liberty "both as an end and as a means. They believed liberty to be the secret of happiness and courage to be the secret of liberty. They believed that freedom to think as you will and to speak as you think are indispensable to the discovery and spread of political truth; that without free speech and assembly, discussion would be futile; that with them, discussion affords ordinarily adequate protection against the dissemination of noxious doctrine; that the greatest menace to freedom is an inert people; that public discussion is a political duty; and that this should be a fundamental principle of the American government."[5]

Breaking with the British Model

For most of recorded history, individuals accepted that political decisions over their lives would be made by a select few: by princes, monarchs, and a hereditary aristocracy. The general public was considered too ignorant to participate in public affairs. Like children, they were expected to follow the direction of those who knew best and were trained to make and enforce government policy. To shore up the legitimacy of these governing bodies, kings would claim to rule by divine right.[6] Policies and decisions somehow descended from Heaven, even if the impact on the country was calamitous. Under this

4. Whitney v. California, 274 U.S. 357, 375 (1927) (Brandeis, J., concurring).
5. Id.
6. John Neville Figgis, The Divine Right of Kings (1994 ed.). His work was first published in 1896 with a second edition in 1914.

system, legislative bodies were in no position to take independent action to protect individual rights.

Royal government in England faced repeated challenges. With the Magna Carta of 1215, King John at Runnymede promised not to capture or imprison a freeman "except by the lawful judgment of his peers or by the law of the land." Magna Carta, representing a partial concession to barons, was reissued several times by subsequent kings, serving as an initial check on arbitrary and unjust rule. Within a few months, John appealed to Pope Innocent III for release from any limitations to his royal authority, and by mid-August both sides mobilized for war.[7] John died in October 1216. Parts of Magna Carta were carried to America by English settlers and adopted by some colonies.[8]

Another curb on royal power took the form of the Petition of Right in 1628. Language drafted by members of the House of Commons placed limits on arbitrary arrest, imprisonment without cause, forced loans by the king, and martial law. After studying the draft language, Charles I agreed to grant certain benefits not by some concept of individual right but by royal grace. Parliament rejected his proposal.[9] After Parliament passed the Petition of Right, Charles I chose to rule the country without Parliament and did so from 1629 to 1640. Conflicts between the royalists and Parliament led to years of civil war and ultimately the beheading of Charles I in 1649.

The "Glorious Revolution" of 1688 marked the overthrow of King James II by English parliamentarians and the ascension to the English throne of William III and his wife, Mary II. Various initiatives by James led to repeated conflicts with Parliament and the courts. After he agreed to leave England, Parliament enacted the Bill of Rights in 1689, stating that his actions subverted "the laws and liberties of this kingdom." Some of the rights announced in 1689 would later be incorporated in the U.S. Constitution: freedom of speech and debate in Parliament, not allowing excessive bail and fines, and prohibiting cruel and unusual punishments.[10]

During this period, England made efforts to break with absolute monarchy and divine right, but those concepts did not disappear entirely. Writing in 1765, William Blackstone explained that the king "is not only incapable of *doing* wrong, but even of *thinking* wrong: he can never mean to do an

7. Ralph V. Turner, "The Making of Magna Carta: The Historical Background," in Daniel Barstow Magraw, Andrea Martinez, & Roy E. Brownell II, eds., Magna Carta and the Rule of Law 41 (2014).

8. A. E. Dick Howard, The Road from Runnymede: Magna Carta and Constitutionalism in America (1968).

9. Stephen D. White, Sir Edward Cook and "the Grievances of the Commonwealth," 1621–1628, at 222–53 (1979).

10. E. N. Williams, ed., The Eighteenth Century Constitution: Documents and Commentary 26–33 (1965).

improper thing: in him is no folly or weakness."[11] He also recognized in the king certain powers and capacities that he "enjoys alone," and in the exertion of "lawful prerogative, the king is and ought to be absolute; that is, so far absolute, that there is no legal authority that can either delay or resist him."[12] Among the king's absolute powers were making treaties, appointing ambassadors, and declaring war.[13] The powers that Blackstone placed with the king are vested either entirely in Congress or shared between the Senate and the President (making treaties and appointing ambassadors).

The appeal of popular government in America prompted the Continental Congress to meet in 1774. With the Declaration of Independence two years later, Americans were prepared to reject monarchy and embrace broad public participation. Thomas Jefferson is often credited as author of the Declaration of Independence, but some of the main features (and actual language) had already been stated by George Mason in the Virginia Declaration of Rights in 1776. For example, Mason began with these words: "That all men are created equally free and independent, and have certain inherent natural rights, of which they cannot, by any compact, deprive or divest their posterity; among which are the enjoyment of life and liberty, with the means of acquiring and possessing property, and pursuing and obtaining happiness and safety. That all power is by God and Nature vested in, and consequently derived from, the people; that the magistrates are their trustees and servants, and at all times amenable to them."[14]

Lessons from the Continental Congress

Unlike England, with its history of monarchy over which Parliament gradually gained control, America as a national government began with a legislative branch and no other. After America declared its independence from England, all national powers (including executive and judicial) were vested in a Continental Congress.[15] The ninth article of the first national constitution, the Articles of Confederation, provided: "The United States in Congress assembled, shall have the sole and exclusive right and power of determining on peace and war." The single exception to that principle, which rejected Blackstone's model of royal prerogative, lay with the sixth article, which allowed

11. 1 William Blackstone, Commentaries on the Laws of England 239 (1765) (emphases in original).

12. Id. at 232, 243.

13. Id. at 244–50.

14. See Helen Hill Miller, George Mason of Gunston Hall (1958).

15. Edmund Cody Burnett, The Continental Congress 118–21 (1964 ed.).

states to engage in war if invaded by enemies or when threatened by Indian tribes. That understanding carried forward in Article I, Section 10, of the U.S. Constitution: "No State shall . . . engage in War, unless actually invaded, or in such imminent Danger as will not admit of delay."

The powers of the new national government were severely limited by the need to receive approval from nine of the thirteen states when it wanted to engage in war, enter into treaties, borrow money, appropriate money, and make other commitments. The Articles of Confederation did not provide for a national executive or judiciary. There was a President of the Continental Congress, but he was merely a presiding officer who lacked independent executive power. Studies look to this period as a forerunner for the U.S. President.[16] Members of Congress had to handle not only legislative duties but executive and judicial as well. After finishing legislative business they served on special committees to deal with administrative and adjudicative matters.[17]

Dissatisfaction with this system led to the creation of boards composed of men from outside Congress. For example, in November 1776 Congress authorized the appointment of three commissioners to execute the business of the navy. Known as the Navy Board, it was subject to the direction of the Marine Committee. Other boards were established. This experiment helped relieve lawmakers of some committee work, but often the work of boards proceeded at too slow a pace and without a single person held responsible. By 1781, Congress decided to take the next step and appoint single officers to handle administrative matters. In a practical sense, some members of legislative committees were already functioning as single executives.[18] This experience helped inform members of Congress in 1789 when they created the first executive departments.

On January 10, 1781, Congress heard the committee on the Department of Foreign Affairs recommend the establishment of a permanent office "as a remedy against the fluctuation, the delay and indecision to which the present mode of managing our foreign affairs must be exposed." Responsibility for the overall direction of the Department would fall to a Secretary for Foreign Affairs. On February 7, Congress created three new executive officers: the Superintendent of Finance, the Secretary at War, and the Secretary of Marine. The office of Attorney General was created on February 16 to prosecute all suits on behalf of the United States and to advise Congress on all legal

16. William B. Michaelsen, Creating the American Presidency, 1775–1789; Jennings B. Sanders, The Presidency of the Continental Congress, 1774–89: A Study in American Constitutional History (1971); Charles C. Thach, Jr., The Creation of the Presidency, 1775–1789 (1969; originally published in 1923).

17. Louis Fisher, President and Congress: Power and Policy 6–8 (1972).

18. Id. at 9–11.

matters submitted to him. This separation of power—the result of a painfully slow evolution of executive departments—stands as a victory not for abstract doctrine but of *force majeure*. In a striking phrase, Francis Wharton said the Constitution "did not make this distribution of power. It would be more proper to say that this distribution of power made the Constitution of the United States."[19]

Although Congress used the titles "Department" and "Secretary," these executive officers functioned solely as agents of the legislative branch. A separate executive branch would not be created until delegates met at Philadelphia to draft a new Constitution. Their work was strongly informed by evident weaknesses in the Articles of Confederation, placing all three powers of national government in the Continental Congress. It was widely understood that the new national government would be composed of three separate branches to handle executive, legislative, and judicial duties. In 1789, when the First Congress created the executive departments of State, War, and the Treasury, they were to be headed by a single executive, not a board.

Just as a separate executive branch was seen as necessary from the experience of the Articles of Confederation, the same lesson applied to the need for an independent judiciary. The Continental Congress created Courts of Admiralty to decide all controversies over captures and distribution of prizes. Provisions were made in January 1777 for appeal to a standing committee, which handled fifty-six cases over a three-year period. In January 1780, a separate and permanent court was established to try all appeals: the Court of Appeals in Cases of Capture. Pending cases were transferred from Congress to this new court. Following the conclusion of the war with England and the signing of the peace treaty, the business of the Court declined, and in February 1786 Congress resolved that the salaries of all judges be terminated. Financed on a per diem basis, the Court continued to function until its last session on May 16, 1787, at the State House in Philadelphia, across the hall from the room in which delegates were assembling to write a new constitution.[20]

19. 1 Francis Wharton, The Revolutionary Diplomatic Correspondence of the United States 663 (1889). For further details on the experience with single executives in the Continental Congress, see Fisher, President and Congress, at 11–16.

20. Henry J. Bourguignon, The First Federal Court: The Federal Appellate Prize Court of the American Revolution, 1775–1787 (1977); Sidney Teiser, "The Genesis of the Supreme Court," 25 Va. L. Rev. 398 (1939); F. Regis Noel, "Vestiges of a Supreme Court among the Colonies and under the Articles of Confederation," 37–38 Records Colum. Hist. Soc. 123 (1937).

Drafting the Constitution

By the time the delegates met in Philadelphia, it was widely understood that the new national government would consist of three separate branches, with each branch empowered to check encroachments by the others. Separating the powers created a political system designed to protect individual rights from government abuse. Instead of being ruled by a king who possessed a wide range of prerogative powers, an independently elected Congress possessed sufficient authority and legitimacy to conduct effective controls over the President and executive officers.

On June 1, 1787, delegates at the constitutional convention debated a resolution to create a separate President. The language reflects the influence of the Articles of Confederation and its search for an effective administrative officer: "Resolved, that a national executive be instituted; to be chosen by the national legislature; for the term of   years . . . and that besides a general authority to execute the national laws, it ought to enjoy the executive rights vested in Congress by the confederation." The delegates initially chose to fill up the blank with the word "seven" and postponed action on a proposal to have Congress select the President.[21] Later they agreed to have the President chosen by an Electoral College and serve a four-year term.

Debate on June 1 revealed the determination of delegates to reject the British model that relied on monarchical powers. Charles Pinckney said he was "for a vigorous Executive but was afraid the Executive powers of [the existing] Congress might extend to peace & war &c which would render the Executive a Monarchy, of the worst kind, towit an elective one." James Wilson moved that the Executive consist "of a single person," seconded by Pinckney. John Rutledge, most likely recalling the problems with boards during the Continental Congress, agreed that the executive power should be placed in a single person. A single individual would feel the greatest responsibility and administer the public affairs best, "tho' he was not for giving him the power of war and peace."[22]

Roger Sherman promoted a limited view of the President, considering the office "as nothing more than an institution for carrying the will of the Legislature into effect."[23] He would later describe presidential power in more generous terms. Wilson said he preferred "a single magistrate, as giving most energy dispatch and responsibility to the office," but did not consider "the Prerogatives of the British Monarch as a proper guide in defining the Executive powers." Some of those prerogatives, he said, "were of a Legislative

21. 1 Farrand 62–64.
22. Id. at 64–65.
23. Id. at 65.

nature," including "war & peace &c."[24] He added that the British model was inapplicable to the United States because of its greater size and "manners so republican."[25]

On June 18, Alexander Hamilton delivered a lengthy speech on constitutional principles, stating that his personal view "almost led him to despair that a Republican Govt. could be established over so great an extent." In his opinion, "he had no scruple in declaring, supported as he was by the opinions of so many of the wise & good, that the British Govt. was the best in the world: and that he doubted much whether any thing short of it would do in America."[26] There could be no "good Govt. without a good Executive. The English model was the only good one of this subject." Because of his admiration for the British king, he suggested it might be best for the U.S. President to serve for life.[27]

As he continued to speak, Hamilton began to break free of the British model and royal prerogatives. The U.S. President, he said, would "have the direction of war when authorized or begun."[28] He proposed to give the Senate "the sole power of declaring war."[29] Hamilton agreed that the President could make treaties only with the "advice and approbation of the Senate."[30] He concluded that the power to appoint ambassadors should not be given solely to the President. It would require Senate approval.[31] In urging ratification of the Constitution in 1788, Hamilton in Federalist No. 69 detailed the vast difference between the powers vested in the British king and the "inferior" powers granted to the President.[32]

On August 17, the delegates turned to the power to initiate war. The draft constitution stated that Congress would have the power "To make war." Pinckney objected that legislative proceedings "were too slow" and it would meet "but once a year." Moreover, the House of Representatives "would be too numerous for such deliberations." The Senate, he said, would be "the best depository, being more acquainted with foreign affairs, and most capable of proper resolutions." Pierce Butler saw no need for a legislative role. He was for "vesting the power in the President, who will have all the requisite qualities, and will not make war but when the Nation will support it."[33]

24. Id. at 65–66.
25. Id. at 66.
26. Id. at 288.
27. Id. at 289.
28. Id. at 292.
29. Id.
30. Id.
31. Id.
32. The Federalist, at 446.
33. 2 Farrand 318.

At that point, James Madison and Elbridge Gerry moved to insert "declare" for "make," leaving to the President "the power to repel sudden attacks." Roger Sherman approved, believing that the President should be able "to repel and not to commence war." Gerry, disturbed by Butler's recommendation, "never expected to hear in a republic a motion to empower the Executive alone to declare war."[34] George Mason spoke against giving the power of war to the President "because not [safely] to be trusted with it; or to the Senate, because not so constructed as to be entitled to it. He was for clogging rather than facilitating war; but for facilitating peace." On the motion to insert "declare" for "make," it was agreed to.[35]

At the state ratifying conventions, it was understood that the decision to take the country from a state of peace to a state of war would reside in Congress, not the President. In Pennsylvania, James Wilson expressed the prevailing opinion that the American system of checks and balances "will not hurry us into war; it is calculated to guard against it. It will not be in the power of a single man, or a single body of men, to involve us in such distress; for the important power of declaring war is vested in the legislature at large."[36] In North Carolina, James Iredell compared the limited powers of the President with those of the British monarch. The king of Great Britain was not only the Commander in Chief "but has the power, in time of war, to raise fleets and armies. He has also authority to declare war." By contrast, the President "has not the power of declaring war by his own authority, nor that of raising fleets of armies. These powers are vested in other hands."[37] In South Carolina, Charles Pinckney assured his colleagues that the President's powers "did not permit him to declare war."[38]

Remarks by Pierce Butler at the South Carolina ratifying convention are quite instructive, if not amusing. In Philadelphia he expressed total trust in the President's judgment to involve the country in war. Not a single delegate supported him. He now fully distanced himself from his initial position. In recalling the debate in Philadelphia, he said, "some gentlemen were inclined to give the power to the President; but it was objected to, as throwing into his hands the influence of a monarch, having an opportunity of involving his country in a war whenever he wished to promote her destruction." Of course the unnamed "gentleman" was Butler.

The preamble to the Constitution, particularly the first three words, would have been unimaginable in other countries: "We the People of the United

34. Id.
35. Id. at 319.
36. 2 Elliot 528.
37. 4 Elliot 107.
38. Id. at 287.

States, in Order to form a more perfect Union, establish Justice, insure domestic Tranquility, provide for the common defence, promote the general Welfare, and secure the Blessings of Liberty to ourselves and our Posterity, do ordain and establish this Constitution for the United States of America." Nothing in those words or in the seven Articles that followed contemplated a Congress subordinate to unchecked presidential and judicial power.

The Committee of Detail had proposed: "We the people of the States of New Hampshire, Massachusetts," followed by the other states and ending with Georgia. Gouverneur Morris fashioned that into "We the People." Instead of underscoring the power of states and their possible exercise of independent status, he created a phrase "that would ring throughout American history, defining every American as part of a single whole."[39]

Proposing a Title for the President

On August 6, 1787, at the Philadelphia Convention, the Committee of Detail reported a "stile" for the President: "The President of the United States of America" and a title: "His Excellency."[40] On September 10, with a week remaining in the proceedings, the Committee of Style made those same recommendations.[41] Yet the final draft of the Constitution merely provided in Article II this language: "The executive power shall be vested in a president of the United States."[42] There was no effort to propose a separate style or title.

When the First Congress met in 1789, lawmakers debated the need to give the President a style or title. Would the terms be consistent with republican government or borrow from British or European precedents? On April 23, the Senate proposed a committee of three members to consider and report "what style or titles it will be proper to annex to the offices of President and Vice President of the United States." A resolution to that effect passed the following day.[43] On April 24, the House appointed five members to consider those same issues.[44] They reported on May 5 that "it is not proper to annex any style or title to the respective styles or titles of office expressed in the Constitution." The House agreed to that report.[45]

---

39. Richard Brookhiser, Gentleman Revolutionary: Gouverneur Morris—The Rake Who Wrote the Constitution 90–92 (2003).
40. 2 Farrand 185.
41. Id. at 572.
42. Id. at 597.
43. 1 Annals of Cong. 24 (1789).
44. Id. at 192.
45. Id. at 247.

The two chambers disagreed fundamentally on the issue, the Senate preferring the types of titles adopted in Europe for high public officials, and the House regarding such titles as incompatible with republican government. On May 8, the House voted down a Senate proposal to address the President as "His Excellency."[46] Three days later the House again debated the issue. Thomas Tucker of South Carolina objected that conferring a "high title" would lead to "an embroidered robe, a princely equipage, and finally, a Crown and hereditary succession."[47] If lawmakers expected a title would please President George Washington they would be "greatly disappointed" because the President had "a real dignity of character, and is above such little vanities."[48] Tucker continued: "This spirit of imitation, sir, this spirit of mimicry and apery will be the ruin of our country. Instead of giving us dignity in the eye of foreigners, it will expose us to be laughed at as apes."[49]

James Madison of Virginia recommended that, out of respect, the House agree to meet with the Senate. Still, he said his strongest objection to titles "is founded on principle; instead of increasing, they diminish the true dignity and importance of a Republic, and would in particular, on this occasion, diminish the true dignity of the first magistrate himself."[50] Echoing some of the points made by Tucker, Madison said that if Congress gave titles "we must either borrow or invent them." If lawmakers borrowed, "the servile imitation will be odious, not to say ridiculous also."[51] The House appointed a committee of five, including Madison, to meet once again with the Senate committee.[52]

The Senate committee had proposed this title: "His Highness, the President of the United States of America, and Protector of their Liberties."[53] Some lawmakers objected not merely to that title but the claim that the President had a unique role or special competence in protecting individual liberties. Senator Robert Morris of Pennsylvania said he believed the protection of rights "lay with the Whole Congress."[54] To preserve harmony with the House, the Senate resolved that the address should be "The President of the United States," without the addition of any other title. That resolution passed.[55]

46. Id. at 33.
47. Id. at 319.
48. Id.
49. Id. at 320.
50. Id. at 321.
51. Id.
52. Id. at 324.
53. Id at 35.
54. Kathleen Bartoloni-Tuazon, For Fear of an Elective King: George Washington and the Presidential Title Controversy of 1789, at 106 (2014).
55. 1 Annals of Cong. 36.

The Bill of Rights

In Federalist No. 84, Hamilton acknowledged that critics of the draft Constitution objected it "contains no bill of rights."[56] He considered a bill of rights "not only unnecessary in the proposed Constitution, but would even be dangerous."[57] As checks on governmental abuse, Madison argued in Federalist No. 49 that "the people are the only legitimate fountain of power, and it is from them that the constitutional charter, under which the several branches of government hold their power, is derived. . . ."[58] Still, he expressed concern that "the tendency of republican governments is to an aggrandizement of the legislative at the expense of the other departments."[59] After warning about legislative encroachments, he concluded in Federalist No. 51 that in "republican government, the legislative authority necessarily predominates."[60]

The draft Constitution provided checks on legislative authority. Article I, Section 9, provided that the privilege of the writ of habeas corpus "shall not be suspended, unless when in Cases of Rebellion or Invasion the public Safety may require it." That same section provides that no bill of attainder (legislative punishment without judicial trial) or ex post facto law shall be passed. Article I, Section 9, prohibits states from passing a bill of attainder, ex post facto law, or law impairing the obligation of contracts. Article III, Section 3, states that treason against the United States shall consist "only in levying War against them, or in adhering to their Enemies, giving them Aid and Comfort," and no person shall be convicted of treason unless on the testimony of two witnesses "to the same overt Act, or on Confession in open Court." Under Article IV, Section 2, the citizens of each state shall be entitled "to all Privileges and Immunities of Citizens of the several States." Article VI provides that "no religious Test shall ever be required as a Qualification to any Office or public Trust under the United States."

Even with those safeguards, it was understood that one of the first orders of business by the First Congress would be passage of a bill of rights and submitting it to the states for ratification. On May 4, 1789, Madison gave notice that "he intended to bring on the subject of amendments to the Constitution."[61] For guidance, he could consult state constitutions, including the Virginia Bill of Rights of June 12, 1776, drafted by George Mason. It included the right in a criminal trial to be confronted with accusers and witnesses, to have a speedy

56. The Federalist 532.
57. Id. at 535.
58. Id. at 348.
59. Id. at 350.
60. Id. at 356.
61. 1 Annals of Cong. 247 (1789).

trial by an impartial jury without being compelled to give evidence against oneself, limits on excessive bail and fines, prohibitions on cruel and unusual punishments, prohibitions on general warrants, freedom of the press, and the free exercise of religion.[62]

In discussing his proposed bill of rights, Madison said it was "less necessary to guard against the abuse in the Executive Department than any other; because it is not the stronger of the system, but the weaker. It therefore must be leveled against the Legislative, for it is the most powerful, and most likely to be abused, because it is under the least control."[63] He added: "independent tribunals of justice will consider themselves in a peculiar manner the guardians of those rights; they will be an impenetrable bulwark against every assumption of power in the Legislative or Executive."[64] His judgment was put to the test with enactment of the repressive Alien and Sedition Acts, passed by Congress in 1798 and signed by President John Adams (discussed in chapter 1). No federal court came to the defense of individuals prosecuted under those statutes. On the contrary, some judges were conspicuous advocates. Federal courts, consisting entirely of Federalists, "joined the campaign against republicanism with such fervor as to taint its capacity to conduct impartial trials."[65] Many judges "fanned political passions, applied the Sedition Act to further partisan interests, and actively cooperated in ferreting out potential violators."[66]

Scope of Public Participation

In 1792, Congress debated a bill to establish a uniformed militia drawn from the various states. Some lawmakers expressed concern that a militia could not only fulfill its statutory purpose (suppressing insurrections and repelling invasions) but turn against the public. During House debate, William Vans Murray warned: "Of all the offices of politics, the most irksome and delicate is that by which a Legislature directs the military forces of the community to its own conservation, as it presupposes situations in which resistance to the Government itself is contemplated. Hence, we see a jealousy even in England of the use of the sword, when drawn against any part of the community."[67]

62. Henry Steele Commager, ed., Documents of American History 103–4 (7th ed., 1963).
63. 1 Annals of Cong. 437 (1789).
64. Id. at 439.
65. Geoffrey R. Stone, Perilous Times: Free Speech in Wartime from the Sedition Act of 1798 to the War on Terrorism 68 (2004).
66. Id.
67. Annals of Cong., 2d Cong., 1st–2d Sess. 554 (1792).

To curb unwarranted and unjustified use of the militia, an amendment provided that information of any insurrection would have to be communicated to the President by either a Supreme Court Justice or a federal district judge. A judicial check would thus operate on executive power.[68] Moreover, in case of an insurrection in any state against the government, the President needed to be so informed by the state legislature or the governor.[69] The statute specified that these emergency powers to use the militia to suppress rebellion would be available to the President only "if the legislature of the United States be not in session."[70]

President Washington learned a lesson during this period on the capacity of the general public to check his initiatives. He issued what has come to be known as the Neutrality Proclamation of 1793, warning Americans to avoid any involvement in the war between France and England. He instructed law officers to prosecute all persons who violated his proclamation. Jurors balked at a presidential initiative to punish individuals. Insisting that criminal law required congressional action through the regular legislative process, jurors made it clear they would acquit any individual charged with acting contrary to the proclamation. In England, perhaps the king could issue legally binding proclamations, but America was committed to republican government. Jurors asserted their independent right to safeguard constitutional principles.[71] Unable to cite statutory support to justify actions in court, the government dropped other prosecutions.[72] Washington turned to Congress for statutory authority. He presented the matter to lawmakers, stating that it rested with "the wisdom of Congress to correct, improve, or enforce" the policy set forth in his proclamation.[73] Congress passed the Neutrality Act of 1794, providing the administration the legal authority it needed to prosecute and punish individuals who violated national policy.

On March 3, 1791, Congress enacted a federal excise tax on spirits distilled within the United States. Excise taxes had a long history of inflaming the public and provoking protests.[74] To American farmers, converting grain into alcohol "was considered to be as clear a national right as to convert grain

68. Id. at 577 (amendment by Abraham Baldwin).

69. 1 Stat. 264, sec. 1 (1792).

70. Id., sec. 2.

71. Francis Wharton, State Trials of the United States during the Administrations of Washington and Adams 84–85 (1849); Henfield's Case, 11 F. Cas. 1099 (C.C. Pa. 1793) (No. 6, 360).

72. 2 John Marshall, The Life of George Washington 273 (1832).

73. Annals of Cong., 3d Cong., 1st–2d Sess. 11 (1793).

74. Townsend Ward, "The Insurrection of the Year 1794, in the Western Counties of Pennsylvania," 6 Pa. Hist. Soc. Memoirs 119, 119–27 (1858).

into flour."[75] Beginning in September 1791, excise agents who attempted to collect revenue were seized, tarred and feathered, and stripped of horse and money.[76] President Washington understood the checkered history of excise taxes. An excise law was "of odious character with the people; partial in its operation; unproductive unless enforced by arbitrary and vexatious means; and committing the authority of the Government in parts where resistance is most probable, and coercion least practicable."[77]

By September 1792, Washington learned that citizens in western Pennsylvania had used violence against federal officers attempting to collect duties on distilled spirits.[78] Concerned that the rebellion might spread to other states, he issued a proclamation on September 15, 1792, warning those who resisted the law that it was his duty "to take care that the laws be faithfully executed." He directed all courts, magistrates, and officers to see that the laws were obeyed and the public peace preserved.[79]

On August 7, 1794, Washington issued another proclamation, itemizing a long list of abuses against federal agents and stating he had put into effect the procedures of the Militia Act.[80] He provided Justice James Wilson evidence needed to verify the rebellion and received from Wilson a certification that ordinary legal means were insufficient to execute national law.[81] Washington called on the militias of four states to put down the rebellion.[82] District Judge Richard Peters joined Treasury Secretary Alexander Hamilton and District Attorney William Rawle to accompany the troops. Hamilton and Rawle conducted hearings before Judge Peters to identify the instigators, who were later tried in Philadelphia.[83]

The story now turns from citizens who used violence against federal agents to citizens who merely wanted to discuss public policy in their homes and other places. In his response to the Whiskey Rebellion, Washington publicly objected to citizens holding "certain irregular meetings" to express their disagreement with government policies. Political clubs had indeed emerged, supported by opposition newspapers that helped sharpen rhetoric and crystallize grievances.[84] In a letter of September 15, 1794, Washington concluded that

75. Id. at 126.
76. Id. at 130–31.
77. 32 The Writings of George Washington 96, John C. Fitzpatrick, ed. (1939). Letter to Secretary of the Treasury Alexander Hamilton.
78. Thomas P. Slaughter, The Whiskey Rebellion 179–81 (1986).
79. 1 Richardson 116–17.
80. Id. at 150.
81. Id. at 152.
82. Id. at 153.
83. Homer Cummings & Carl McFarland, Federal Justice 43–45 (1937).
84. Slaughter, The Whiskey Rebellion, at 163–65, 194–95.

the Whiskey Rebellion "may be considered as the first *ripe fruit* of the Democratic Societies."[85] Who were these societies? How dangerous were they to public peace? Washington, directing his ire at those who joined these groups and participated in their discussions, expressed no support for citizens who wanted to discuss public affairs. He asked: "can any thing be more absurd, more arrogant, or more pernicious to the peace of Society, than for self created bodies, forming themselves into *permanent* Censors, and under the shade of Night in a conclave?"[86] He said these individuals had no right to offer personal judgments that statutes passed by Congress were mischievous or unconstitutional. In his mind, citizens had no right to disagree with national policy.

Washington distinguished the activities of Democratic Societies from the constitutional right of the people "to meet occasionally, to petition for, or to remonstrate against, any Act of the Legislature &c."[87] To him, Democratic Societies endeavored "to destroy all confidence in the Administration, by arraigning all its acts, without knowing on what ground, or with what information it proceeds and this without regard to decency or truth."[88] In short, any individual or group that chose to criticize governmental policy would have to be dealt with harshly. As noted in one study, he sought to "delegitimize them as participants in the political process."[89]

On October 8, 1794, Washington again voiced his contempt for citizens who met in private organizations to discuss government policy. The "daring and factious spirit which has arisen (to overturn the laws, and to subvert the Constitution) ought to be subdued. If this is not done, there is, an end of and we may bid adieu to all government in this Country, except Mob and Club govt. from whence nothing but anarchy and confusion can ensue."[90] He worried that Edmond Genet, the French diplomat he called a "diabolical leader," intended "to sow sedition, to poison the minds of the people of this Country."[91]

A week later, Washington predicted that others would soon understand the ill designs of those who led these self-created societies. He said he "should be extremely sorry therefore if Mr. [Madison] *from any cause whatsoever* should get entangled with them, or their politics."[92] In his judgment, these political

85. 33 The Writings of George Washington 506 (letter to Burges Hall, emphasis in original).
86. Id. (emphasis in original).
87. Id.
88. Id. at 507.
89. Robert M. Chesney, "Democratic-Republican Societies, Subversion, and the Limits of Legitimate Dissent in the Early Republic," 82 N.C. L. Rev. 1525, 1528 (2004).
90. 33 The Writings of George Washington 523 (letter to Maj. Gen. Daniel Morgan).
91. Id. at 524.
92. 34 The Writings of George Washington 3 (letter to Secretary of State Edmund Randolph, emphasis in original).

clubs "will destroy the government of this Country."[93] He received support from some members of his Cabinet. Secretary of State Edmund Randolph told Washington that he "never did see an opportunity of destroying these self-constituted bodies, until the fruit of their operations was discharged in the insurrection." Randolph counseled: "They may now, I believe, be crushed. The prospect ought not to be lost."[94]

Washington's Sixth Annual Address to Congress, delivered on November 18, 1794, reviewed his efforts to suppress the whiskey rebellion in four western counties of Pennsylvania. He said that based on a belief that the government's excise tax operation "might be defeated, certain self-created societies assumed the tone of condemnation."[95] Toward the end of his address he took another slap at Democratic Societies, urging Congress to unite "to turn the machinations of the wicked to the confirming of our constitution: to enable us at all times to root out internal sedition, and put invasion to flight."[96]

Washington's sharp rebuke of Democratic Societies provoked lengthy debate in Congress. The Senate generally supported Washington's objection to private clubs that met to discuss political issues. In its formal response to Washington's annual address, the Senate said that resistance to laws in the western counties of Pennsylvania "has been increased by the proceedings of certain self-created societies relative to the laws and administration of the Government; proceedings, in our apprehension, founded in political error, calculated, if not intended, to disorganize our Government, and which, by inspiring delusive hopes of support, have been influential in misleading our fellow-citizens in the scene of insurrection."[97]

House debate was more mixed. William Smith warned that if the House failed to endorse Washington's views about Democratic Societies, the silence of lawmakers "would be an avowed desertion of the Executive."[98] Quite an extraordinary position. Any attempt by a member of Congress to think independently about a presidential policy would amount to desertion. Other members, however, insisted they had a constitutional right and a personal need to speak their minds. Was it expected, asked John Nicholas, "that I am to abandon my independence for the sake of the PRESIDENT?"[99] Josiah Parker suggested that Washington, "for whose character and services he felt as much

93. Id.

94. Letter of Edmund Randolph to George Washington, Oct. 11, 1794, George Washington Papers, Series 5, Reel 106, Library of Congress, Manuscript Division.

95. 34 The Writings of George Washington 29.

96. Id. at 37.

97. 1 Richardson 160. For a fine analysis of the political clubs forming in the 1790s, see Eugene Perry Link, Democratic-Republican Societies, 1790–1800 (1942).

98. Annals of Cong., 3d Cong., 1st–2d Sess. 901 (1794).

99. Id. at 910.

respect and gratitude as any man in America, had been misinformed on this point." Notwithstanding his admiration for the President, "he was not to give up his opinions for the sake of any man."[100] Parker believed that his constituents in Virginia would be repelled by any form of censorship or repression: "They love your Government much, but they love their independence more."[101]

William Giles, after noting his respect for Washington, asked what purpose was served by rebuking such abstractions as "self-created societies." There was not an individual in the country, he said, "who might not come under the charge of being a member of some one or the other self-created society. Associations of this kind, religious, political, and philosophical, were to be found in every quarter of the Continent."[102] Giles suggested that the Baptists, the Methodists, and the Friends might be called self-created societies. He insisted that members of the House were elected "not for the purpose of passing indiscriminate votes of censure, but to legislate only." Giles repudiated "all aiming at a restraint on the opinions of private persons."[103] The public "have a right to censure us," he said, but "we have *not* a right to censure them."[104]

James Madison reinforced those points by insisting that Congress had an essential role in protecting individual rights. To him opinions "are not the objects of legislation." Any indiscriminate censure that falls on classes or on individuals "will be a severe punishment." Such conduct was incompatible with constitutional principles: "If we advert to the nature of Republican Government, we shall find that the censorial power is in the people over the Government, and not in the Government over the people."[105] Should government, asked Abraham Bedford Venable, "show their imbecility by censuring what we cannot punish? The people have a right to think and a right to speak."[106] Thus ended a misguided effort by President Washington, some of his Cabinet officials, and certain lawmakers to single out political societies for censure and upbraid them for expressing opinions about public policy.

How the three branches apply constitutional principles to protect individual rights is explored in chapters 3 through 7, starting first with the treatment of blacks from slavery through the Civil War and to contemporary times. Subsequent chapters cover the rights of women, children, religious minorities, and Native Americans.

100. Id. at 913.
101. Id. at 914.
102. Id. at 899–900.
103. Id. at 901.
104. Id. at 917 (emphasis in original).
105. Id. at 934.
106. Id. at 910.

3

THE RIGHTS OF BLACKS

At the time the Framers met at the Philadelphia Convention, slavery was an established institution in southern states and some in the North. In dealing with that reality, fundamental constitutional principles of human rights were violated. The Constitution, as Justice Thurgood Marshall aptly remarked in 1987, "was defective from the start, requiring several amendments and a civil war."[1] Progress toward extending constitutional rights to blacks did not come primarily from the elected branches or the Supreme Court. Credit for abolishing slavery belongs to citizens and private organizations willing to fight against it.

Ending Slavery

The Framers could not reconcile slavery with the values announced in the Declaration of Independence, which held certain truths "to be self-evident, that all men are created equal, that they are endowed by their Creator with certain unalienable Rights, that among these are Life, Liberty and the pursuit of Happiness." In the original draft, Thomas Jefferson sharply condemned slavery. He charged that King George III "has waged cruel war against human nature itself, violating its most sacred rights of life and liberty in the persons of a distant people," capturing and carrying them "into slavery in another hemisphere." The result: "miserable death in their transportation thither," creating a market where men were bought and sold in "this execrable commerce."[2] That passage was deleted.

The Northwest Ordinance of 1787, governing territory northwest of the Ohio River, contained this provision: "There shall be neither slavery nor involuntary servitude in the said territory, otherwise than in the punishment of crimes whereof the party shall have been duly convicted." Nevertheless, if any person escaped into the Northwest territory, "from whom labor or service is lawfully claimed in any of the original States," fugitives "may be lawfully

1. Remarks of Justice Thurgood Marshall, Annual Seminar of the San Francisco Patent and Trademark Law Association, in Maui, Hawaii, May 6, 1987.
2. Carl L. Becker, The Declaration of Independence: A Study in the History of Political Ideas 212 (1958 ed.).

reclaimed and conveyed to the person claiming his or her labor or service as aforesaid."[3]

Although the word "slavery" does not appear in the Constitution, its existence is implied in several places. Article V provides that no amendment to the Constitution prior to 1808 "shall in any Manner affect the first and fourth Clauses in the Ninth Section of the First Article." The first clause in Section 9 states that the "Migration or Importation of such Persons as any of the States now existing shall think proper to admit" shall not be prohibited by Congress before 1808. This grace period for the slave trade prompted Madison to remark: "Twenty years will produce all the mischief that can be apprehended from the liberty to import slaves. So long a term will be more dishonorable to the National character than to say nothing about it in the Constitution."[4]

The first clause in Section 9 permitted a tax or duty on imported slaves "not exceeding ten dollars for each Person." Some delegates found it offensive to tax slaves as though they were incoming goods or articles of merchandise. Others thought a tax might discourage the importation of slaves. The level of the tax suggests the purpose was revenue more than prohibition.[5] Madison objected it was "wrong to admit in the Constitution the idea that there could be property in men."[6]

Slavery became a factor in deciding how to apportion taxes and Representatives among the states. The fourth clause in Section 9 of Article I prohibited capitation or other direct taxes unless in proportion to population. How was population to be measured? Should slaves be counted like whites, giving the southern states additional representation because of their "peculiar institution"? Or should representation be based solely on free inhabitants? William Paterson of New Jersey, objecting to giving any credit to the South for slaves, did not want to give "an indirect encouragemt. of the slave trade."[7]

As with other matters, the Framers adopted a compromise. Under Article I, Section 2, Representatives and direct taxes were to be apportioned among the states "according to their respective Numbers, which shall be determined by adding to the whole Number of free Persons, including those bound to Service for a Term of Years, and excluding Indians not taxed, three fifths of all other Persons." This language is often misinterpreted as evidence that the Framers regarded blacks as three-fifths of a person, or subhuman. However, the fraction was a partial penalty for practicing slavery. Maximum human

---

3. Henry Steele Commager, Documents of American History 132 (7th ed., 1963).
4. 2 Farrand 415.
5. Id. at 416–17.
6. Id. at 417.
7. 1 Farrand 561.

dignity would have counted each slave not as one but as zero, to give southern states no political or constitutional credit for this institution.

Under Article IV, Section 2, persons "held to Service or Labour" in one state shall be delivered back to that state in case they escaped to another. At the Virginia ratifying convention, Madison explained that this clause was inserted to "enable owners of slaves to reclaim them."[8] The language resulted in a number of fugitive slave laws passed by Congress and interpreted by the Supreme Court.

From 1794 to 1803, Congress passed legislation to regulate and restrict the slave traffic.[9] A statute in 1807 required the traffic to stop altogether, effective January 1, 1808, but slaves continued to be brought into the country illegally, requiring additional legislation.[10] In response to the constitutional provision on runaway slaves, the Fugitive Slave Act of 1793 authorized the return of slaves to their owners.[11] In 1842, the Supreme Court decided that congressional legislation on fugitive slaves preempted state laws on that subject.[12] In this case, Pennsylvania had passed legislation in 1826 establishing procedures to govern fugitive slaves from other states. In an effort to reach a compromise, Congress amended the Fugitive Slave Act in 1850, and it was upheld by a unanimous Supreme Court.[13] These legislative and judicial actions did not halt the move toward secession and civil war.

During this period, Congress attempted to strike a balance between free states and slave states. Land acquired by the Louisiana Purchase threatened to upset that balance. In response, the Missouri Compromise Act of 1820 admitted Missouri as a slave state but prohibited slavery in future states north of the 36°30' line. That remedy was undermined when the United States acquired a vast tract of new territory in the West because of the Mexican War. Congress passed the Compromise of 1850 followed by the Kansas-Nebraska Act of 1854. As a result, the decision over slavery shifted to the new territories (and future states) by adopting a policy called "popular sovereignty." Whether a new territory would be slave or not would now be left to voters in those areas. Slavery could expand.

Opposition to slavery during this period came from the public, not from Congress, the President, or the Supreme Court. Individual Americans, untu-

8. 3 Farrand 325.
9. 1 Stat. 347 (1794); 2 Stat. 70 (1800); 2 Stat. 205 (1803).
10. 2 Stat. 426 (1807); 3 Stat. 450 (1818); 3 Stat. 532 (1819); 3 Stat. 600, §§ 4, 5 (1820).
11. 1 Stat. 302 (1793).
12. Prigg v. Pennsylvania, 16 Pet. 539 (1842).
13. 9 Stat. 462 (1850); Abelman v. Booth, 21 How. 506 (1859). For details on the Fugitive Slave Act of 1850, see Harold M. Hyman & William M. Wiecek, Equal Justice under Law: Constitutional Development, 1835–1875 (1982), at 146–59.

tored in the fine points of law, viewed slavery as repugnant to fundamental
political and constitutional principles, including those embedded in the Declaration of Independence. The essential antislavery documents were private
writings and speeches, not court decisions, legislative statutes, or presidential
initiatives.[14] Citizens felt a strong duty to express their opinions on constitutional rights. They deferred neither to courts nor the elected branches. Americans of the mid-nineteenth century "were not inclined to leave to private
lawyers any more than to public men the conception, execution, and interpretation of public law. . . . Like politics, with which it was inextricably joined,
the Constitution was everyone's business."[15]

As far back as 1688, a number of churches led the fight against slavery.[16]
Quakers expelled slave-owning Friends in 1776.[17] The Pennsylvania Abolition Society was founded in 1794, and in 1800 the Methodist Conference
advocated the gradual emancipation of slaves.[18] In 1818, the General Assembly of the undivided Presbyterian Church unanimously adopted a manifesto
declaring slavery to be "utterly inconsistent with the law of God," although
counseling against "hasty emancipation."[19] Other members of the clergy defended slavery as "clearly established in the Holy Scriptures, both by precept
and example."[20] England abolished slavery in 1833.[21] The American Anti-
Slavery Society was created that year to keep slavery out of the territories.

The First Amendment authorizes individuals "to petition the Government
for a redress of grievances." Beginning in the 1830s, opponents of slavery
established abolitionist newspapers, held public meetings, and presented
abolitionist petitions to Congress. When the volume of these petitions hit a
certain level, Congress in 1836 ordered that all such petitions be simply laid
on the table without debate. Representative John Quincy Adams fought this
so-called gag rule until it was finally lifted in 1844.[22]

14. William M. Wiecek, The Sources of Antislavery Constitutionalism in America, 1760–
1848 (1977).

15. Harold M. Hyman, A More Perfect Union 6 (1975).

16. Louis Fisher, Defending Congress and the Constitution 106–7 (2011).

17. Robert Booth Fowler & Allen D. Hertzke, Religion and Politics in America: Faith,
Culture, and Strategic Choices 18 (1995).

18. Luke Eugene Ebersole, Church Lobbying in the Nation's Capital 3 (1951).

19. Sydney E. Ahlstrom, A Religious History of the American People 648 (1972).

20. Michael Corbett & Julia Mitchell Corbett, Politics and Religion in the United States
95 (1999).

21. Abolition Act, 1833, 3 and 4 Will. 4, ch. 73.

22. Stanley M. Elkins, Slavery: A Problem in American Institutional and Intellectual Life
187 (2d ed., 1968); William M. Wiecek, The Sources of Antislavery Constitutionalism in
America, 1760–1848, at 182–89, 214 (1977).

The Civil War

With neither members of Congress nor Presidents willing to resolve the issue of slavery, they waited for the Supreme Court to issue its decision in the case of *Dred Scott v. Sandford*. Newly elected James Buchanan wanted to mention slavery in his inaugural address on March 4, 1857. First he endorsed the Kansas-Nebraska Act: "What a happy conception, then, was it for Congress to apply this simple rule, that the will of the majority shall govern, to the settlement of the question of domestic slavery in the Territories."[23] As to admitting the Territory of Kansas as a state with or without slavery, it was, he said, "happily, a matter of but little practical importance." To Buchanan, "is is a judicial question, which legitimately belongs to the Supreme Court of the United States, before whom it is now pending, and will, it is understood, be speedily and finally settled." To that decision, "in common with all good citizens, I shall cheerfully submit, whatever this may be."[24]

Buchanan accurately predicted the speed of the Court's decision. It was released two days after the inaugural address. He was incorrect that it would finally settle the issue of slavery. Writing for the Court, Chief Justice Roger Taney held that Dred Scott, as a black man, was not a citizen of Missouri within the meaning of the Constitution, was not entitled to sue in federal court, and Congress possessed no authority to prohibit slavery in the territories. He considered blacks to be "a subordinate and inferior class of beings, who had been subjugated by the dominant race, and, whether emancipated or not, yet remained subject their authority, and had no rights or privileges but such as those who held the power and the Government might choose to grant them."[25] To Taney, the Constitution recognized "the right of property of the master in a slave" and made "no distinction between that description of property and other property owned by a citizen."[26]

The Court's decision helped precipitate a civil war that left, out of a population of thirty million, more than six hundred thousand dead and four hundred thousand wounded. In a book published in 1936, Chief Justice Charles Evans Hughes remarked that "in three notable instances the Court has suffered severely from self-inflicted wounds." His first choice: *Dred Scott*.[27] All nine Justices issued opinions that offered a wide variety of views, depriving

---

23. Arthur M. Schlesinger, Jr., & Fred I. Israel, eds., My Fellow Citizens: The Inaugural Addresses of the Presidents of the United States, 1789–2009, at 131 (2010).
24. Id. at 132.
25. Dred Scott v. Sandford, 60 U.S. 393, 404–5 (1857).
26. Id. at 451.
27. Charles Evans Hughes, The Supreme Court of the United States 50 (1936).

the ruling of credibility and an authoritative voice. The decision "certainly pushed the nation closer to disunion."[28]

A few years after *Dred Scott*, the elected branches dismissed its two principal positions. As to the issue of slavery, in his inaugural message on March 4, 1861, Abraham Lincoln denied that "vital questions affecting the whole people" could be "irrevocably fixed by decisions of the Supreme Court."[29] In 1862, an opinion by Attorney General Edward Bates concluded that men of color, if born in America, were citizens of the United States. To those who claim that "persons of color," though born in the United States, were incapable of being U.S. citizens, he called it a "naked assumption" because the Constitution "contains not one word upon the subject." To the "new-found idea" that citizenship depends on color, other nations would react "with incredulity, if not disgust."[30] Bates repudiated Taney's remarks about citizenship as pure dicta and "of no authority as a legal decision."[31] Also in 1862, Congress passed legislation prohibiting slavery in the territories.[32] During debate on the bill, not a single lawmaker referred to the Court's decision. Members of Congress never doubted their independent constitutional authority to prohibit slavery in the territories, with or without the Court.

In ending slavery, prominent credit is generally given to President Lincoln for issuing the Emancipation Proclamation on January 1, 1863. Little attention is given to previous initiatives by Congress. In addition to abolishing slavery in the territories in 1862, it passed two confiscation acts of August 6, 1861, and July 17, 1862. They established national policy to seize all property, including slaves, of southern states that had taken up arms against the Union.[33] On March 13, 1862, Congress prohibited military and naval officers from returning fugitive slaves to their masters.[34] A month later, on April 10, it declared that the United States should cooperate with states willing to gradually abolish slavery by offering financial aid to compensate them.[35] In that same month, it abolished slavery in the District of Columbia.[36]

While preparing various drafts of the Emancipation Proclamation, Lincoln expressed concern that Congress moved too rapidly and even considered

28. Lackland H. Bloom, Jr., Do Great Cases Make Bad Law? 90 (2014).

29. Schlesinger, Jr., & Israel, My Fellow Citizens, at 146 (2010).

30. 10 Op. Att'y Gen. 382, 397 (1862).

31. Id. at 412.

32. 12 Stat. 432 (1862).

33. 12 Stat. 319 (1861); 12 Stat. 589 (1862). See Silvana R. Siddall, From Property to Person: Slavery and the Confiscation Acts, 1861–1862 (2005).

34. 12 Stat. 354 (1862).

35. Id. at 617 (1862).

36. Id. at 376.

vetoing some bills before agreeing to sign them.[37] His proclamation proceeded through three stages: a July 22, 1862, draft presented to the Cabinet, a revised proclamation of September 22, 1862, and the final official version released on January 1, 1863.[38]

Congress passed the Thirteenth Amendment to abolish slavery. It was ratified on December 6, 1865. The Fourteenth Amendment provided for the equality of whites and blacks before the law. Ratification came in 1868. The Fifteenth Amendment, effective in 1870, gave blacks the right to vote. The express language of those amendments empowered Congress to enforce them "by appropriate language."

The Fourteenth Amendment had been foreshadowed by the Civil Rights Act of 1866. After passage of the Thirteenth Amendment, some southern states enacted "black codes" to keep newly freed slaves in a subordinate status: economically, politically, and culturally. Congress declared that all persons born in the United States, excluding Indians not taxed, are citizens of the United States. Citizens "of every race and color" would have the same right in every state and territory "to make and enforce contracts, to sue, be parties, and give evidence, to inherit, purchase, lease, sell, hold, and convey real and personal property, and to full and equal benefit of all laws and proceedings for the security of person and property, as is enjoyed by white citizens." President Andrew Johnson vetoed the bill, claiming it invaded state authority. Congress quickly overrode him.[39]

Congressional Safeguards, Judicial Opposition

In 1870 and 1871, Congress passed what are called the force acts. The purpose of the first was to enforce the rights of citizens to vote in the states, "without distinction of race, color, or previous condition of servitude; any constitution, law, custom, usage, or regulation of any State or Territory, or by or under its authority, to the contrary notwithstanding."[40] To administer the statute, Congress extended jurisdiction to federal courts assisted by federal district attorneys and marshals.[41] Congress acted to prevent state courts from nullifying the statute. It also authorized the President "to employ such part of the land or naval forces of the United States, or of the

37. John Hope Franklin, The Emancipation Proclamation 16–19 (1995 ed.).
38. Harold Holzer, Emancipating Lincoln: The Proclamation in Text, Context, and Memory 34–35, 88, 129 (2012).
39. 14 Stat. 27, sec. 1 (1866).
40. 16 Stat. 140, sec. 1 (1870).
41. Id. at 142, sec. 8.

militia, as shall be necessary to aid in the execution of judicial process under this act."[42]

The second force act, known as the Ku Klux Klan Act, marked an effort by Congress to enforce the provisions of the Fourteenth Amendment. The statute provided criminal penalties to individuals who conspired to act against the national government "by force, intimidation, or threat to prevent, hinder, or delay the execution of any law of the United States."[43] As with the 1870 statute, Congress authorized the President to use military force to carry out the statutory objectives and prosecute violators in federal courts. The statute authorized the President to suspend the privilege of the writ of habeas corpus to act against rebellion.[44] President Ulysses S. Grant used that authority to suppress a rebellion in South Carolina.[45]

As with other congressional initiatives to carry out the purpose of the Civil War Amendments, the Supreme Court repeatedly undermined efforts to protect the rights of blacks. With regard to the Enforcement Act of 1870, enacted to guarantee blacks the right to vote in state elections, the Court used a strict dual-federalism model to hold that the statute was not appropriate legislation under the Fifteenth Amendment. Remarkably, it said the Amendment "does not confer the right of suffrage upon any one."[46]

On Easter Sunday, April 13, 1873, armed white men attacked blacks who had assembled at a courthouse in Colfax, Louisiana. More than a hundred blacks were murdered. Federal prosecution under the 1870 statute signaled an effort to fulfill the Civil War Amendments. However, the Supreme Court decided that the counts in the indictments against the white defendants were too vague. The Court again promoted the doctrine of dual federalism, establishing a pure separation between federal and state powers: "The powers which one possesses, the other does not."[47] Under this interpretation, jurisdiction and sovereignty to bring indictments under the statute rested solely with the states, precisely what Congress denied by passing the statute. Judicial opposition to extending rights to blacks continued when lawmakers passed legislation to provide equal access to public accommodations.

42. Id. at 143, sec. 13.
43. 17 Stat. 13, sec. 2 (1871).
44. Id. at 15, sec. 4.
45. 9 Richardson 4090.
46. United State v. Reese, 92 U.S. 214, 217 (1876).
47. United States v. Cruikshank, 92 U.S. 542, 550 (1876).

Public Accommodations Legislation

In 1875, members of Congress took another step to close the gap between the Declaration of Independence and the Constitution. The preamble to the statute read: "Whereas, it is essential to just government we recognize the quality of all men before the law."[48] Although the Civil War Amendments officially elevated blacks to the status of citizen, in many states they were denied access to public facilities. Under the 1875 statute, all persons in the United States were entitled to the "full and equal enjoyment of the accommodations, advantages, facilities, and privileges of inns, public conveyances [transportation] on land and water, theaters, and other places of public amusement."[49]

The statute did not identify the constitutional provision on which Congress relied. Because the Thirteenth Amendment abolished slavery, it could be argued that denying blacks access to public accommodations represented a "badge of slavery." The Fourteenth Amendment, another possible source of authority, provides that no state "shall make or enforce any law which shall abridge the privileges or immunities of citizens of the United States; nor shall any State deprive any person of life, liberty, or property, without due process of law; nor deny to any person within its jurisdiction the equal protection of the laws."

During House debate, Benjamin Butler of Massachusetts defended the authority of Congress to safeguard constitutional rights left unprotected by some of the states. As chairman of the Judiciary Committee and Republican floor leader, he denied that Congress was attempting to impose a national standard of "social equality" among blacks and whites. The issue, instead, was one of law: "The colored men are either American citizens or they are not. The Constitution, for good or evil, for right or wrong, has made them American citizens; and the moment they were clothed with that attribute of citizenship, they stood on a political and legal equality with every other citizen, be he whom he may."[50]

Law had nothing to do, he said, with social equality. Everyone has a right to pick their own friends and associates. Those choices bore no relationship with access to public accommodations. He explained that the men and women riding in the cars "are not my associates." Although he preferred not to sit next to many white men and white women, they had a right to ride in the cars. The same applied to going to a theater, inn, and tavern. Butler felt no obligation to speak to anyone at those public accommodations. In stating that the bill did not require whites to associate with blacks, he added:

48. 18 Stat. 335 (1875).
49. Id. at 336.
50. 3 Cong. Rec. 939–40 (1875).

There is not a white man at the South that would not associate with the negro—all that is required by this bill—if that negro were his servant. He would eat with him, suckle from her, play with her or him as children, be together with them in every way, provided they were slaves. There never has been an objection to such an association. But the moment that you elevate this black man to citizenship from a slave, then immediately he becomes offensive.[51]

The bill passed the House 161 to 79 and the Senate 38 to 26.[52] There was some question whether President Grant would veto the bill because originally it provided equal access to schools. After that language was stripped from the bill he signed it into law.[53]

The statute now faced the prospect of judicial review. In the *Slaughter-House Cases* of 1873, the Supreme Court had expressed its support for independent state powers. It upheld a Louisiana law that granted an exclusive right to a corporation to supervise slaughterhouses in New Orleans. The Court held that the statute, granting the corporation an exclusive privilege for twenty-five years, did not violate the Thirteenth and Fourteenth Amendments. The majority rejected interpretations of the Civil War Amendment that would "fetter and degrade the State governments by subjecting them to the control of Congress."[54] Similar decisions were issued concerning the Colfax slaughter in *Cruikshank* in 1876. Four years later, in *Ex parte Virginia*, the Court upheld a provision in the Civil Rights Act of 1875 that resulted in the prosecution of a state judge in federal court. To the Court, the purpose of the Thirteenth and Fourteenth Amendments was to recognize "limitations of the power of the States and enlargements of the power of Congress."[55]

The Court accepted the need in *Ex parte Virginia* to eliminate racial discrimination in the selection of jurors. How would it respond to congressional legislation that ensured equal access by blacks to public accommodations? That law, challenged in five states (California, Kansas, Missouri, New York, and Tennessee), did not reach the Court until 1882. The following year, in the *Civil Rights Cases*, the Court declared the federal public accommodations statute an encroachment on the states and an interference with private relationships. As to the reach of the Fourteenth Amendment, the Court said that Congress could regulate only "state action," not discrimination by private

51. Id. at 940.
52. Id. at 991, 1870.
53. Bertram Wyatt-Brown, "The Civil Rights Act of 1875," 18 West. Pol. Q. 763 (1965).
54. 83 U.S. (16 Wall.) 36, 78 (1873).
55. 100 U.S. 339, 345 (1880).

parties: "Individual invasion of individual rights is not the subject-matter of the amendment."[56]

Only one Justice dissented: John Marshall Harlan. It is one of the finest dissents ever written. In meticulous fashion, he explained why the statute did not invade individual rights. Instead, the public accommodations at issue were activities that had been promoted, subsidized, and licensed by the state. His close legal analysis would guide the Court eight decades later, in the 1960s, when it upheld congressional legislation on equal accommodations.

Harlan began with a general proposition. The Civil War meant that states should not be left free "to make or allow discriminations against that race, as such, in the enjoyment of those fundamental rights which by universal concession, inhere in a state of freedom."[57] The burdens and "badges of slavery and servitude" that survived the Civil War required congressional remedies, including the Civil Rights Act of 1866 and the Civil War Amendments.[58]

In analyzing the difference between state action and private discrimination, Harlan reviewed the history of public conveyances on land and water. Railroads became public highways established by the state for public use. Even if controlled and owned by private corporations, railroads were able to extend their operations only after the state seized land through the power of eminent domain. Moreover, states regulated railroads by prescribing speed and safety standards. To Harlan, it was artificial to now regard railroads as purely private operations.[59]

He acknowledged that private owners had built inns and taverns without the level of state assistance given to railroads. Did that permit the owners to discriminate on the basis of race and previous condition of servitude? Harlan explained that inns were not the same as a boardinghouse. An innkeeper offered lodging to travelers and wayfarers seeking shelter for the night. Under law existing for centuries, it was the duty of an innkeeper to take all travelers and provide them with room and food if they could pay for it. Inns had no legal right to accept one traveler and exclude another. To that extent, an innkeeper was a public servant.[60]

What about places of public amusement? They did not receive state assistance (as with railroads), and there was no question of needing shelter or food for the night (as with inns). Could owners of a place of public amusement therefore discriminate on the basis of race? Harlan pointed out that places of public amusement are established and licensed under the law. The authority

56. Civil Rights Cases, 109 U.S. 8, 11 (1883).
57. Id. at 34.
58. Id. at 35.
59. Id. at 38–39.
60. Id. at 40–41.

to create and maintain them comes from the public. A license from the public "imports, in law, equality of right, at such places, among all the members of that public."[61]

Toward the end of his dissent, Harlan reminded the Court that *Ex parte Virginia* held that the Fourteenth Amendment was aimed not merely at "States" but at any "agency of the State." Anyone who acted for the state "is clothed with the State's power."[62] His understanding of the relationship between "state action" and private parties, enabling the federal government to act against race discrimination, would be later followed by the Supreme Court in the 1960s, as explained in the section on the Civil Rights Act of 1964.

Also in 1883, the Court reviewed the constitutionality of an Alabama law that prohibited unmarried individuals from living together. For couples of the same color, the first conviction led to a fine not less than $100 and possible imprisonment for not more than six months. For mixed couples, the first conviction meant a prison term for not less than two nor more than seven years.[63] In a decision less than two pages in length, a unanimous Court found no conflict with the Constitution even though it prescribed penalties more severe for those of mixed color than the same color. The concluding clause of the first section of the Fourteenth Amendment declares that no state shall "deny to any person within its jurisdiction the equal protection of the laws."

From *Plessy* to *Brown v. Board*

From 1865 to the *Civil Rights Cases* of 1883, the Supreme Court issued a number of decisions that weakened the promise and commitment of the Civil War Amendments. Those rulings provided the legal framework used by the Court when it analyzed Louisiana's "separate but equal" doctrine in *Plessy v. Ferguson* in 1896. In the years following the Civil War, there was no consistent practice in the South about segregating whites and blacks in transportation systems. Sometimes they traveled in the same railroad car. Southern transportation "was not rigidly segregated in the quarter-century after the Civil War."[64] By the 1880s, many southern states began passing Jim Crow transportation laws to separate blacks and whites.[65] The timing

61. Id. at 41.
62. Id. at 58, citing Ex parte Virginia, 100 U.S. at 346–47.
63. Pace v. Alabama, 106 U.S. 583 (1883).
64. Charles A. Lofgren, The Plessy Case: Legal-Historical Interpretation 9 (1987). See also id. at 11–13.
65. Id. at 21.

here is significant. Those laws appeared after the Supreme Court in the *Civil Rights Cases* invalidated the equal accommodations statute passed by Congress in 1875.

In *Plessy*, the Court divided 7 to 1 in upholding a law that Louisiana enacted in 1890. The statute required railway companies to provide equal but separate accommodations for white and black passengers, either by having them placed in separate coaches or by using a partition in a coach to divide the races. Passengers who refused to follow that policy faced fines and imprisonment. The Court held that Louisiana's law did not conflict with the Thirteenth and Fourteenth Amendments.[66] The statute allowed for one exception. It did not apply to "nurses attending children of the other race."[67]

Train officials had to distinguish between white and black passengers, made sometimes difficult with children from mixed marriages. The petitioner in the case, Homer Plessy, was "seven eighths Caucasian and one eighth African blood."[68] The conductor ordered him to leave the white coach and go to the black coach. When he refused, a police officer removed him, and he was imprisoned.[69]

Justice Henry Billings Brown, writing for the majority, first examined the Thirteenth Amendment's prohibition of slavery and involuntary servitude (except for conviction of a crime). He regarded the lack of conflict between the state law and the constitutional amendment as "too clear for argument," reaching that conclusion by citing the *Civil Rights Cases*. The restrictions against blacks in gaining equal access to public facilities, including railroads, "cannot be justly regarded as imposing any badge of slavery or servitude."[70] The Court was relying not on the intent of a constitutional provision but on its previous interpretation, or misinterpretation. The *Civil Rights Cases* provided a natural building block for *Plessy*.

Proceeding further, Justice Brown reasoned that when a statute merely implies a legal distinction between "the white and colored races—a distinction which is founded in the color of the two races, and which must always exist so long as white men are distinguished from the other race by color," there is "no tendency to destroy the legal equality of the two races, or establish a state of involuntary servitude."[71] Could he have made that statement had Louisiana distinguished whites from other races, including Hispanics and Asians? Those races, or colors, were allowed to sit with whites.

66. Plessy v. Ferguson, 163 U.S. 537 (1896).
67. Id. at 541.
68. Id. at 538.
69. Id.
70. Id. at 542.
71. Id. at 543.

Turning to the Fourteenth Amendment, Justice Brown sought guidance from the *Slaughter-House Cases* of 1873, which greatly undermined national authority under the Civil War Amendments. He said this about the Fourteenth Amendment: "The object of the amendment was undoubtedly to enforce the absolute equality of the two races before the law, but in the nature of things it could not have been intended to abolish distinctions based upon color, or to enforce a social, as distinguished from political equality, or a commingling of the two races upon terms unsatisfactory to either."[72] The purpose of the Fourteenth Amendment was never a "commingling" of the two races or forced social equality but rather political and legal equality. He denied that Louisiana's law implied "the inferiority of either race to the other."[73] There could be little doubt that Louisiana passed the law because whites did not want to be in the company of blacks.

Brown looked for support to the establishment of separate schools for white and colored children, "held to be a valid exercise of the legislative power even by courts of States where the political rights of the colored race have been longest and most earnestly enforced."[74] He spent more than a page discussing state decisions to provide separate schools for blacks and whites, including his home state of Massachusetts.[75] Among the laws he cited were those forbidding interracial marriage, which had no direct relevance to the case before him.[76]

To Justice Brown it was a question whether Louisiana's law "is a reasonable regulation, and with respect to this there must necessarily be a large discretion on the part of the legislature."[77] The Court extended no such deference to Congress when it passed the Civil Rights Act of 1875, providing for equal accommodations, even when Congress was acting to enforce the Civil War Amendments. In one area, Justice Brown did defer to Congress when it passed legislation "requiring separate schools for colored children in the District of Columbia, the constitutionality of which does not seem to have been questioned, or the corresponding acts of state legislatures."[78] From these remarks, it appears that the Court in *Plessy* was concerned that if it struck down the Louisiana law the next step in race relations might be integrated schools.

Justice Brown closed with this thought: if blacks became the "dominant power" in the state legislature and enacted a law separating blacks and whites

72. Id. at 544.
73. Id.
74. Id.
75. Id. at 544–45.
76. Id. at 545.
77. Id. at 550.
78. Id. at 551.

in railroad cars, whites would not assume their race was placed in "an inferior position."[79] He counseled that legislation "is powerless to eradicate racial instincts or to abolish distinctions based upon physical differences."[80] Still further: "If one race be inferior to the other socially, the Constitution of the United States cannot put them upon the same plane."[81] The Louisiana case had nothing to with social equality. It had to do with equal access to public railways. As with the *Civil Rights Cases*, the sole dissenter was Justice Harlan. He predicted that *Plessy* would "prove to be quite as pernicious as the decision made by this tribunal in the *Dred Scott* case."[82]

The Court's desegregation decision in *Brown v. Board of Education* (1954) probably represents, in the minds of many, a dramatic example of the judiciary protecting minority rights. It held that "separate educational facilities are inherently unequal."[83] In some estimates, *Brown* "is simply the greatest of the great cases," the Supreme Court's "finest hour," and "a seismic event in the Court's and the nation's history."[84] Several caveats, however, are in order. First, the Court had to reconsider and reverse its own racist policy in *Plessy* that guided courts and the country for a half century. *Brown* itself (involving public schools) did not reverse *Plessy* (racial discrimination in railroads). It took a series of cases after *Brown* to completely remove racial segregation from such public facilities as beaches and bathhouses;[85] golf courses, parks, playgrounds, and community centers;[86] and bus terminal restaurants.[87] The case that explicitly overruled *Plessy* concerned buses.[88]

Second, the principal force for this reversal was not the Court. As political scientist John Denvir has pointed out: "It was overturned because a group of citizens refused to accept the Supreme Court's interpretation of the Fourteenth Amendment and engaged in a long, arduous, and ultimately successful struggle to have the Court correct its error."[89] Substantial credit goes to those who decided to file lawsuits to initially attack the most vulnerable area: segregated education in law schools and graduate schools. In one case, black applicants were denied admission to the law school at the University of Mary-

79. Id.
80. Id.
81. Id. at 552.
82. Id. at 559.
83. 347 U.S. 483, 495 (1954).
84. Bloom, Do Great Cases Make Bad Law?, at 215, 234.
85. Dawson v. Mayor, 220 F.2d 386 (4th Cir. 1955), aff'd, 350 U.S. 877 (1955).
86. Holmes v. City of Atlanta, 223 F.2d 93 (5th Cir. 1955), aff'd, 350 U.S. 879 (1955); Watson v. Memphis, 373 U.S. 526 (1963).
87. Boynton v. Virginia, 364 U.S. 454 (1960).
88. Browder v. Gayle, 142 F. Supp. 707 (M.D. Ala. 1956), aff'd, 352 U.S. 903 (1956).
89. John Denvir, Democracy's Constitution: Claiming the Privileges of American Citizenship 16 (2001).

land. A unanimous Maryland appellate court ruled that this policy violated the Equal Protection Clause. The court reasoned that blacks would encounter greater costs traveling to another state and paying additional living expenses. Moreover, an education outside the state would not adequately prepare blacks who intended to practice law in Maryland.[90]

In Missouri, the state offered to pay black students their tuition costs for a law school education in an adjacent state. In 1938 the Supreme Court, divided 7–2, held that this policy violated the Equal Protection Clause by creating a privilege for white law students (able to attend the Missouri law school) that was denied to blacks.[91] The next effort by states to comply with *Plessy* was to create a separate law school for blacks within the state. A unanimous Court in 1950 concluded that the proposed school for blacks did not satisfy the separate-but-equal doctrine. The University of Texas Law School, attended by whites, was superior in terms of its professional staff, library, law review, moot court facilities, scholarship funds, distinguished (and wealthy) alumni, tradition, and prestige.[92]

Oklahoma agreed to admit blacks to the state university but insisted on separating them from white students. Blacks had to sit in a special seat in the classroom, a special table in the library, and a special table in the cafeteria. A unanimous Court in 1950 found this a violation of the Equal Protection Clause. Restrictions on the black student impaired and inhibited "his ability to study, to engage in discussions and exchange views with other students, and, in general, to learn his profession."[93]

Third, international pressures pushed against racial discrimination in the United States. In Europe, racism in Nazi Germany led to the extermination of millions of Jews. In the early 1950s, some of the Justices linked racism in the United States to "Hitler's creed."[94] The Soviet Union and Communists pointed to America's racist policy as evidence that it was not a beacon of democracy, human rights, and individual freedom. In its brief to the Supreme Court in *Brown*, the Justice Department emphasized that the United States "is under constant attack in the foreign press, over the foreign radio, and in such international bodies as the United Nations because of various practices of discrimination against minority groups in this country."[95]

90. Pearson v. Murray, 182 A. 593 (Md. 1936).
91. Missouri ex rel. Gaines v. Canada, 305 U.S. 337 (1938). For similar cases, see Sipuel v. Board of Regents, 332 U.S. 631 (1948) and Fisher v. Hurst, 333 U.S. 147 (1948).
92. Sweatt v. Painter, 339 U.S. 629 (1950).
93. McLaurin v. Oklahoma State Regents, 339 U.S. 637 (1950).
94. Michael J. Klarman, From Jim Crow to Civil Rights 303, 316, 447 (2004).
95. Brief for the United States as Amicus Curiae, Brown v. Board of Education, 49 Landmark Briefs 122 (quoting letter from the Secretary of State). See also Mary L. Dudziak, "Desegregation as a Cold War Imperative," 41 Stan. L. Rev. 61, 103–5 (1988).

Fourth, although *Plessy*'s days seemed numbered, in 1952 and through most of 1953, the Court appeared split down the middle on the constitutionality of segregated schools. Only four Justices (Black, Douglas, Burton, and Minton) were ready to overrule *Plessy*.[96] Five (Vinson, Reed, Frankfurter, Jackson, and Clark) either supported *Plessy* or were loath to abandon it. Matters changed slightly on September 8, 1953, with the death of Chief Justice Vinson and his replacement by Earl Warren.[97] There now appeared to be 5–4 majority to reverse *Plessy*. Clark indicated he was ready to shift sides, giving Warren a 6–3 majority, but it was important to reverse *Plessy* by a much larger margin, preferably by a unanimous vote. What could Warren do to attract the votes of Reed, Frankfurter, and Jackson?

Two of the southerners (Clark and Reed) indicated they might join a unanimous opinion if enforcement could be carried out in different ways and times by the states. Jackson and Frankfurter also wanted a flexible remedy. Frankfurter recalled a phrase from Justice Holmes and used it to argue that states could enforce the Court's decision, in *Brown v. Board of Education*, with the oxymoron "all deliberate speed." That vague formulation produced two opinions in *Brown v. Board of Education*, a unanimous—and misleading—opinion in 1954 announcing firm liberal principles on racial integration, followed by the more cautious and conservative implementing opinion in *Brown v. Board of Education* a year later.[98]

This two-step compromise invited minimal compliance by the states. Lucas Powe, in a book largely sympathetic to the Warren Court, concluded that neither *Brown I* nor *Brown II* "was long on legal reasoning" and that the two decisions marked "an ugly political compromise trying to pass itself off as something attractive."[99] *Brown II* provided guidelines for implementing the 1954 ruling. How quickly were states required to make the transition to integrated schools? The Court's answer: No great hurry. The Court largely deferred to local school authorities in determining the appropriate course, leaving to federal lower courts the duty of considering whether school authorities were acting in good faith to comply with desegregation. Several phrases from the Court in *Brown II*—including "practical flexibility," "as soon as practicable,"

96. Klarman, From Jim Crow to Civil Rights, 292–312.

97. For the division within the Court on *Plessy*, see S. Sidney Ulmer, "Earl Warren and the *Brown* Decision," 33 J. Pol. 689, 691–92 (1971); Richard Kluger, Simple Justice 589–614, 682–87, 696–99, 742–45 (1975); William O. Douglas, The Court Years 113 (1980); Bernard Schwartz, Super Chief 72–127 (1983); Philip Elman, "The Solicitor General's Office, Justice Frankfurter, and Civil Rights Litigation, 1946–1960: An Oral History," 100 Harv. L. Rev. 817, 842–43 (1987).

98. Brown v. Board of Education, 347 U.S. 483 (1954); Brown v. Board of Education, 349 U.S. 294 (1955).

99. Lucas A. Powe, Jr., The Warren Court and American Politics 56–57 (2000).

"a prompt and reasonable start," followed by "all deliberate speed"—gave a green light to state obstruction and procrastination. Michael Klarman, in his comprehensive study of civil rights in America, offered this assessment: "That *Brown II* was a mistake from the Court's perspective was quickly apparent. The justices' conciliatory gesture inspired defiance, not accommodation."[100]

Fifth, from 1954 to 1964, the Court's only involvement in school desegregation was a decision in 1958 to strike down the effort of Arkansas Governor Orval Faubus to block school integration to Little Rock.[101] As Klarman notes: "The justices backed off after *Brown II*. With the notable exception of the Little Rock case, they distanced themselves from school desegregation for the next eight years."[102] By the time the Justices reentered the field in 1963–1964, "they were following, not leading, national opinion."[103] In 1964, the Court complained there "has been entirely too much deliberation and not enough speed" in enforcing *Brown I*.[104] A federal appellate court remarked in 1966: "A national effort, bringing together Congress, the executive and the judiciary may be able to make meaningful the right of Negro children to equal educational opportunities. *The courts acting alone have failed.*"[105] Three federal statutes, passed in 1957, 1960, and 1964, put the nation on course to eliminate segregation in public facilities.

Congress acted under pressure from private citizens willing to pay a price to confront racial discrimination. In December 1955, a black woman named Rosa Parks refused to get up and give her bus seat to a white man. She was tired from working all day but also tired of the daily humiliations of living in a racist society. For her action she was jailed.[106] There soon followed the decision of fifty thousand blacks in Montgomery, Alabama, to refuse to ride on segregated buses. They chose to walk.[107] These and other protests led to the Civil Rights Act of 1957, marking the first civil rights measure passed since 1875. It established a Commission on Civil Rights to investigate allegations of discrimination, authorized the President to appoint an additional Assistant Attorney General to head a new Civil Rights Division in the Justice Department, and set fines for those convicted in cases arising from this statute.[108]

100. Klarman, From Jim Crow to Civil Rights, at 320.
101. Cooper v. Aaron, 358 U.S. 1 (1958).
102. Klarman, From Jim Crow to Civil Rights, at 321.
103. Id. at 343.
104. Griffin v. School Bd., 377 U.S. 218, 229 (1964).
105. United States v. Jefferson County Board of Education, 372 F.2d 836, 847 (5th Cir. 1966) (emphasis in original).
106. Charles and Barbara Whalen, The Longest Debate: A Legislative History of the 1964 Civil Rights Act xv (1985).
107. Id. at xvi.
108. 71 Stat. 634 (1957).

The broad investigative powers of the Commission were upheld by the Supreme Court in 1960.[109]

Continued action by civil rights activists led to the Civil Rights Act of 1960. It strengthened existing laws on obstruction of court orders, provided criminal penalties for acts of violence and destruction, and authorized court-appointed "referees" to monitor voting rights.[110] Throughout this period, congressional efforts were delayed by filibusters in the Senate and efforts by the chairman of the House Rules Committee, Howard Smith of Virginia, to block any action.[111] The decisive legislative step came with the Civil Rights Act of 1964, the most far-reaching civil rights statute since the Reconstruction Era.

The Civil Rights Act of 1964

Public pressure for legislative action came from sit-ins, demonstrations, picketing, and boycotts. Americans throughout the country, blacks and whites, put their lives and liberties at stake to end racial segregation. In the spring of 1963, Martin Luther King, Jr., led a march in Birmingham, Alabama, to protest segregated lunch counters and other forms of racial discrimination. In full view of television cameras and photographers from newspapers, the police turned on the protesters with billy clubs, police dogs, and fire hoses, using force against school children between the ages of six and sixteen.[112] Demonstrations in Birmingham and other cities put pressure on the elected branches to act.

During this period, litigation had begun to cut ground from under the *Civil Rights Cases* of 1883. Justice Harlan's dissent in that case had pointed to the close relationship between "state action" and private parties. His position now found acceptance by the Supreme Court in 1961. In a building owned by the state of Delaware, a restaurant refused to serve blacks. The building had been constructed with public funds for public purposes and was owned and operated by the state. A privately owned restaurant leased space in the building. To the Court, the state was therefore a joint participant in operating the restaurant. The Court applied the Fourteenth Amendment to prohibit racial discrimination by the restaurant.[113]

109. Hannah v. Larche, 363 U.S. 420 (1960).
110. 74 Stat. 86 (1960).
111. Loevy, Robert D., The Civil Rights Act of 1964: The Passage of the Law That Ended Racial Segregation 34, 60–61, 150–54, 159 (1997).
112. Whalen, The Longest Debate, at xvii–xix.
113. Burton v. Wilmington Pkg. Auth., 365 U.S. 715 (1961).

After his inauguration on January 20, 1961, President John F. Kennedy did little to advocate equal access for blacks to public accommodations. Early in his first year he issued Executive Order 10925 to establish the Committee on Equal Opportunity but decided against any civil rights initiatives with respect to housing or other areas. For two years he bided his time. Prompted by outside pressures and congressional action, by 1963 he was ready to support legislation on equal accommodations.[114]

The Kennedy administration recognized that the *Civil Rights Cases* of 1883 remained a hurdle because it had never been overturned. For that reason, it chose to rely on both the Fourteenth Amendment and the Commerce Clause. American society, Kennedy argued, had become more mobile and economic life increasingly interdependent: "Business establishments which serve the public—such as hotels, restaurants, theatres, stores and others—serve not only the members of their immediate communities but travelers from other States and visitors from abroad."[115] During testimony before the Senate Commerce Committee, Attorney General Robert F. Kennedy explained that "much of the force" of the *Civil Rights Cases* no longer existed, but it was prudent to defend the legislation on both grounds, including the commerce power.[116]

In reporting the bill, the Senate Commerce Committee concluded that the commerce power provided sufficient constitutional authority.[117] The House Judiciary Committee justified the public accommodations provision on both "state action" (Fourteenth Amendment) and the commerce power.[118] Congressional action attracted top-heavy majorities of 289–126 in the House and 73–27 in the Senate. Bipartisan support was solid. The House voted 153–91 Democrat and 136–35 Republican. The party split in the Senate: 46–21 for Democrats and 27–6 for Republicans. Private groups lobbied for the bill, creating a political base that helped educate citizens and build public support. The rights of blacks were secured far better through this majoritarian process than through judicial action. In two unanimous opinions, the Supreme Court relied on the commerce power to uphold the public accommodations title.[119]

Any thought of relying on judicial power alone to desegregate public schools is dispelled by the poor judgment of the Court to order school busing,

114. Ted Sorensen, Counselor: A Life at the Edge of History 273–74, 282 (2008).

115. Public Papers of the Presidents, 1963, at 485–87.

116. "Civil Rights—Public Accommodations" (Part 1), hearings before the Senate Committee on Commerce, 88th Cong., 1st Sess. 23 (1963).

117. S. Rept. No. 872, 88th Cong., 2d sess. 12–14 (1964).

118. H. Rept. No. 914, 88th Cong., 1st Sess. 2–3, 20–22, 98–101 (1963); H. Rept. No. 914 (Part 2), 88th Cong., 1st Sess. 1–2, 7–9 (1963).

119. Heart of Atlanta Motel v. United States, 379 U.S. 241, 250 (1964); Katzenbach v. McClung, 379 U.S. 294 (1964).

beginning in 1971.[120] The policy spread throughout the country, moving from the South to the West and North, requiring busing between cities and suburbs. Black and white families opposed this judicial initiative. A combination of dissenting Justices, public opposition, and congressional restrictions eventually forced the courts to abandon busing as a remedy. J. Harvie Wilkinson III, a federal judge with the Fourth Circuit, remarked: "The Supreme Court, for all its eminence, cannot disdain political moods. If the public profoundly disagrees with a judgment of the Court, that judgment will not stand."[121]

The Continuing Dialogue

The 1965 Voting Rights Act underscores the impact of private citizens and elected government on constitutional rights. On March 7, 1965, a peaceful group of six hundred protesters in Selma, Alabama, marched against the continuing denial of black voting rights. State troopers used tear gas, clubs, whips, and ropes while some spectators cheered.[122] Television coverage brought this brutality into the homes of Americans. A voting rights bill introduced by President Lyndon B. Johnson sought to prevent state officials from circumventing the Fifteenth Amendment. States could no longer use literacy tests and other methods to disenfranchise blacks. To prevent discriminatory voting practices, most Southern states were required to have changes in voting laws "precleared" by the Justice Department or the D.C. Circuit. The result was a sharp increase in minority registration and voting. The number of elected black officials rose from well under a hundred in 1964 to 963 a decade later.[123]

In 1966, the Supreme Court upheld Justice Department preclearance authority as well as the prohibition on literacy tests.[124] That policy continued over the decades, with the Voting Rights Act reauthorized in 1970, 1975, 1982, with the latter statute reaching to 2007. In 2006, it was reauthorized for an additional twenty-five years. In *Shelby County v. Holder* (2013), a 5–4 Court held the preclearance formula to be unconstitutional. To the Court, matters had changed "dramatically" from conditions in 1965, and Congress

120. Swann v. Charlotte-Mecklenburg Bd. of Ed., 402 U.S. 1 (1971).

121. J. Harvie Wilkinson III, From Brown to Bakke: The Supreme Court and School Integration: 1954–1978, at 20 (1979).

122. Leon Daniel, "Troopers Rout Selma Marchers," Wash. Post, March 8, 1965, at A1.

123. U.S. Commission on Civil Rights, "The Voting Rights Act: Ten Years After," at 40, 49 (1975).

124. South Carolina v. Katzenbach, 383 U.S. 301 (1966); Katzenbach v. Morgan, 384 U.S. 641 (1966).

had failed to provide contemporary evidence to support the need for preclearance.[125]

A dissent by Justice Ginsburg, joined by Breyer, Sotomayor, and Kagan, concluded that Congress had provided sufficient information that the threat to voting rights justified continued use of the preclearance procedure. She noted that the reauthorization in 2006 attracted a vote of 390 to 33 in the House and 98 to 0 in the Senate. In support of the bill, the House and Senate held twenty-one hearings. Congress found there were more Justice Department objections between 1982 and 2004 (626) than between 1965 and the 1982 reauthorization (490). The issue is now in the hands of Congress, which has full authority to assemble a legislative record to justify preclearance review. There is no need or reason to defer to the judicial result in *Shelby County*. The Court has the final word on this issue only if Congress fails to act.

125. Shelby County v. Holder, 570 U.S. ___ (2013).

4

THE RIGHTS OF WOMEN

After the Civil War, women began to receive medical and legal training and pursue other professions historically assigned to men. On a regular basis, they found legal support not from courts but from legislative bodies. What accounts for the capacity of lawmakers to respond positively (and quickly) to women who sought their support, and the inability of judges, at both the state and federal level, to recognize and protect those rights? Judicial failings were conspicuous immediately after the Civil War, but court decisions adverse to the rights of women continue to this day.

Blackstone's Doctrine of Coverture

William Blackstone, the British legal scholar who wrote in the late 1700s, provided an authoritative source for those trained in the law. Without any ambiguity, he placed women in a subordinate role by developing the doctrine of "coverture." In marriage, husband and wife were "one person in law: that is, the very being or legal existence of the woman is suspended during the marriage, or at least is incorporated and consolidated into that of the husband: under whose wing, protection, and *cover*, she performs everything."[1]

The legal status of married women inspired a scene in Charles Dickens's *Oliver Twist* (1867). Mr. Bumble, after trying to dissociate himself from his wife's theft, was told that he was "the more guilty of the two, in the eye of the law; for the law supposes that your wife acts under your direction." Bumble could not contain himself: "If the law supposes that, the law is a ass—a idiot. If that's the eye of the law, the law is a bachelor; and the worst I wish the law is, that his eye may be opened by experience—by experience."[2] Experience has had a greater impact on legislative bodies than on courts.

When the Framers proclaimed in the Declaration of Independence that "all men are created equal," they meant men literally, and not even all men. Blacks were excluded from equal treatment, as were white males who lacked property. Challenges to stereotypes about men and women were expressed at

---

1. 2 William Blackstone, Commentaries on the Laws of England *442 (1783) (emphasis in original).
2. Charles Dickens, Oliver Twist 463 (New American Library ed., 1980).

a meeting in Seneca Falls, New York, in 1848. A Declaration of Sentiments relied on the Declaration of Independence as a model. In referring to "the course of human events," it held "these truths to be self-evident: that all men and women are created equal; that they are endowed by their Creator with certain unalienable rights; that among these are life, liberty, and the pursuit of happiness." The historical record reflected "repeated injuries and usurpations on the part of man toward women": prohibiting females to vote, have a right in property, or pursue educational opportunities.[3]

Myra Bradwell's Effort to Practice Law

After studying law, Myra Bradwell applied for admission to the Illinois bar in 1869. She needed the approval of a panel of all-male judges to practice law in the state. They rejected her application solely because she was a woman. Her appeal to the Supreme Court of Illinois failed.[4] Of her qualifications the court remarked: "We have no doubt."[5] The court took initial direction not from the U.S. Constitution or the state constitution but from British law and custom. Female attorneys "were unknown in England, and a proposition that a woman should enter the courts of Westminster Hall in that capacity, or as a barrister, would have created hardly less astonishment than one that she should ascend the bench of Bishops, or be elected to a seat in the House of Commons."[6]

If British law, guided by Blackstone, seemed insufficient to block the professional advancement of women, the Illinois court invoked another, even higher, authority: "That God designed the sexes to occupy different spheres of action, and that it belonged to men to make, apply and execute the laws, was regarded as an almost axiomatic truth."[7] Axiomatic. No further thinking required. The court advised that if changes were required, "let it be made by that department of the government to which the constitution has entrusted the power of changing the laws."[8] A legislative body could decide if allowing women to "engage in the hot strifes of the bar, in the presence of the public, and with momentous verdicts the prizes of the struggle, would not tend to destroy the deference and delicacy with which it is the pride of our ruder sex to treat her."[9]

3. Miriam Schneir, ed., Feminism: The Essential Historical Writings 77–80 (1972).
4. In re Bradwell, 55 Ill. 535 (1869).
5. Id. at 536.
6. Id. at 539.
7. Id.
8. Id. at 540.
9. Id. at 542.

Taking the court's advice, Bradwell turned to the state legislature. It passed a bill in 1872 stating that no person "shall be precluded or debarred from any occupation, profession or employment (except military) on account of sex."[10] The statute added some qualifications. Nothing in it was to be construed "as requiring any female to work on streets or roads, or serve on juries."[11] Those issues would be dealt with in future years, but Bradwell and other women could now practice law within the state.

After this legislative success, Bradwell decided to take the issue to the U.S. Supreme Court to establish a national right for women to practice law. The attorney who handled her case, Matthew H. Carpenter, assured the Court he was only trying to defend a woman's right to practice law, not to vote. The latter issue, he explained, was highly emotional if not irrational. The issue of female suffrage, he said, "draws to itself, in prejudiced minds," the fear that doing justice to women's rights in any particular "would probably be followed by the establishment of the right of female suffrage, which, it is assumed, would overthrow Christianity, defeat the ends of modern civilization, and upturn the world."[12]

In a brief opinion, the Court examined Bradwell's claim that the Privileges and Immunities Clause of the Fourteenth Amendment included the right of women to practice law. The Court agreed that certain privileges and immunities belong to citizens of the United States, but "the right to admission to practice in the courts of a State is not one of them."[13] The Court acknowledged that many individuals who were not U.S. citizens or of any state had been permitted to practice in federal and state courts. However, it concluded that the right to control and regulate the granting of a license to practice law in a state court was not a power vested in the national government.[14]

A concurrence by Justice Joseph P. Bradley provided additional reasons why women should not be permitted to practice law. He insisted that the civil law, "as well as nature herself, has always recognized a wide difference in the respective spheres and destinies of man and woman." Echoing Blackstone's doctrine of coverture, he said that man "is, or should be, woman's protector and defender." The "natural and proper timidity and delicacy" of women made them "unfit" for many occupations, including law. Reaching to a higher plane, he asserted that a "divine ordinance" commanded that a woman's primary mission in life is centered in the home. While many women

10. Illinois Laws, 1871–1872, at 578.

11. Id.

12. "Argument for Plaintiff in Error," Bradwell v. State of Illinois, U.S. Supreme Court, December Term 1871, No. 67, at 2.

13. Bradwell v. State, 83 U.S. (16 Wall.) 130, 139 (1883).

14. Id.

never marry, he nonetheless decided that a general rule imposed on women the "paramount destiny and mission" to fulfill the offices of wife and mother. "This is the law of the Creator."[15]

Other litigation during this period reflected similar positions by judges regarding the right of women to practice law. An 1875 case involved a request by Lavinia Goodell to practice law before the Wisconsin Supreme Court. Unlike Myra Bradwell, she was not married. The Wisconsin Supreme Court denied her motion, explaining that the "law of nature" destined women to bear and nurture children, take care of the custody of homes, and love and honor their husbands.[16] Chief Justice Ryan agreed that many employments are "not unfit for female character." Law, however, was not one of them: "The peculiar qualities of womanhood, its gentle graces, its quick sensibilities, its tender susceptibility, its purity, its delicacy, its emotional impulses, its subordination of hard reason to sympathetic feeling, are surely not qualifications for forensic strife."[17] Nature, he said, had tempered women as little for the conflicts of the courtroom "as for the physical conflicts of the battlefield."[18]

Warming to the task, Ryan explained that "Womanhood is moulded for gentler and better things." It is not "the saints of the world who chiefly give employment to our profession. It has essentially and habitually to do with all that is selfish and malicious, knavish, and criminal, coarse and brutal, repulsive and obscene, in human life." It would be "revolting to all female sense of the innocence and sanctity of their sex, shocking to man's reverence for womanhood and faith in woman, on which hinge all the better affections and humanities of life, that woman should be permitted to mix professionally in all the nastiness of the world which finds its way into courts of justice."[19]

Ryan identified the kinds of "unclean issues" that found their way into the courtroom: sodomy, incest, rape, seduction, fornication, adultery, pregnancy, bastardy, legitimacy, prostitution, lascivious cohabitation, abortion, infanticide, obscene publications, libel and slander of sex, impotence, and divorce. A variety of social "vices and infirmities," he said, pressed on the legal profession and filled judicial reports "which must be read for accurate knowledge of the law." He then pronounced: "This is bad enough for men." The type of discussions that took place in a courtroom "are unfit for female ears."[20]

15. Id. at 141.
16. In re Goodell, 39 Wis. 232, 245 (1875).
17. Id.
18. Id. at 245–46.
19. Id. at 246.
20. Id.

Belva Lockwood Goes to Congress

In the 1870s, the Supreme Court adopted a rule to prohibit women from practicing before it. Belva Lockwood, who had been admitted to the District of Columbia bar in 1873, drafted legislation to overturn that rule. Her bill provided that when any woman had been admitted to the bar of the highest court of a state, or of the D.C. supreme court, and was otherwise qualified as set forth in the bill (three years of practice and a person of good moral character, as with male attorneys), women may be admitted to practice before the U.S. Supreme Court. She took her draft to members of Congress to seek their support.

What were the odds of an all-male legislative body at that time treating her proposal seriously? Would Congress react in the same manner as federal and state courts, concluding that the natural delicacy of women made them unfit for the law? Lockwood's bill became law within one year, underscoring the striking difference between the legal atmosphere of the legislative and judicial branches during that period. British law and William Blackstone were powerful forces in the judiciary and would continue to be highly influential for many decades to come. They played little role in Congress.

The bill reached the House floor on February 21, 1878, and passed 169 to 87. Benjamin Butler, chairman of the Judiciary Committee, said the committee's report unanimously supported the bill.[21] On March 18, the Senate Judiciary Committee voted against the bill, reasoning that "ever since the foundations of the Government" the Supreme Court and every other federal court were authorized "to make its own rules regulating the admission of persons to practice." Each federal court possessed the discretion to admit or bar women. To the committee, the bill "would make a distinction in favor of women, instead of removing a disability. There is no disability now whatever."[22] The committee adopted a purist view of separation of powers, arguing that if the judicial branch adopted a rule barring women from practicing before it, Congress had no authority to interfere.

Senator Aaron Sargent, who played a leading role in getting the bill enacted, offered an amendment to delete the text of the bill and replace it with: "That, no person shall be excluded from practicing as an attorney and counselor at law from any court of the United States on account of sex."[23] Instead of debating practices dating back to the beginning of government, he spoke about contemporary values. The District of Columbia and a number of states (including California, Illinois, Michigan, Minnesota, Missouri, North

21. 7 Cong. Rec. 1235 (1878).
22. Id. at 1821.
23. Id. at 2704.

Carolina, Utah, and Wyoming) had admitted women to the bar. It seemed
absurd to Sargent to ask a woman to handle a case in state court and be forced
to transfer it to a male attorney if it entered federal court. At that point the
chair of the Judiciary Committee promised to report the bill.[24]

A month later, the committee recommended the indefinite postpone-
ment of the bill on the ground it was unnecessary. But the committee then
learned that the Chief Justice of the Supreme Court appeared to be waiting
for Congress to pass legislation to clarify the law. Goodbye to strict separation of powers! At that point the bill was placed on the legislative calendar for
consideration.[25] On May 29, the bill reached the floor for debate. Sargent's
amendment failed on a tie vote, 26 to 26. With twenty-four Senators absent,
Sargent announced he would try again.[26]

Senate debate continued on February 7, 1879. When the Senate Judiciary
Committee continued to oppose the bill, Sargent reviewed the progress made
by women in various professions, including medicine and surgery. He reminded his colleagues that it was once improper in England for a woman to
appear on stage. Female roles had to be filled with men. In America, he said,
no man "has a right to put a limit to the exertions or the sphere of woman.
That is a right which only can be possessed by that sex itself." Here he spoke
to the present and the future, not solely to the past, as was customary in
federal and state courts that decided cases involving the right of women to
practice law:

> I say again, men have not the right, in contradiction to the intentions,
> the wishes, the ambition, of women, to say that their sphere shall be cir-
> cumscribed, that bounds shall be set which they cannot pass. The enjoy-
> ment of liberty, the pursuit of happiness in her own way, is as much the
> birthright of woman as of man. In this land man has ceased to dominate
> over his fellow [male slaves]—let him cease to dominate over his sister;
> for he has no higher right to do the latter than the former. It is mere
> oppression to say to the bread-seeking woman, you shall labor only in
> certain narrow ways for your living, we will hedge you out by law from
> profitable employments, and monopolize them for ourselves.[27]

Lawmakers debated whether the Supreme Court should be left to decide
for itself who could practice there. Although Senator George Hoar expressed
"the greatest respect for that tribunal," he insisted that the "law-making and

24. Id. at 2705.
25. Id. at 3558–59.
26. Id. at 3889–90.
27. 8 Cong. Rec. 1084 (1879).

not the law-expounding power in this Government" ought to determine that question.[28] On this occasion, the bill passed the Senate 39 to 20. Of the twenty-four absent on the earlier tie vote of 26 to 26, fifteen voted in favor and four opposed. The statute provided than any woman who shall have been a member of the bar of the highest court of any state or territory, or of the D.C. supreme court, for at least three years, and shall have maintained a good standing before such court and a person of good moral character, "shall, on motion, and the production of such record, be admitted to practice before the Supreme Court of the United States."[29]

Judicial Rulings from 1875 to 1971

Within two years of *Bradwell*, the Supreme Court delivered another setback to the rights of women. In a lawsuit, Virginia Minor argued she was a "citizen" within the meaning of the Fourteenth Amendment and entitled to vote as one of its privileges and immunities. A unanimous Court agreed that women are citizens but denied that the Fourteenth Amendment added substantive rights to previous privileges and immunities. To the Court, Section 2 of the Fourteenth Amendment limited voting to men. It pointed out that it took the Fifteenth Amendment to give male blacks the right to vote. The Court concluded that women, like children, were "citizens" and "persons" in the constitutional sense, but that status did not confer the right to vote.[30] A number of states and territories had permitted women to vote, but the national right to vote did not come until the Nineteenth Amendment, ratified in 1920.

In the early decades of the twentieth century, a number of judicial rulings might have appeared—on the surface—to favor women. However, they were premised not on the equality of women but on their inferiority. They covered what was called "protective legislation": statutes that singled out women for special treatment and relief. In 1908 the Supreme Court unanimously upheld Oregon's ten-hour day for women because they were not considered capable of working as long as men. Justice Brewer remarked: "Still again, history discloses the fact that woman has always been dependent upon man. He established his control at the outset by superior physical strength, and this

28. Id.

29. 20 Stat. 292 (1879). See Mary L. Clark, "The First Women Members of the Supreme Court Bar, 1879–1900," 36 San Diego L. Rev. 87 (1999); D. Kelly Weisberg, "Barred from the Bar: Women and Legal Education in the United States 1870–1890," 28 J. Legal Ed. 485 (1977); Alice L. O'Donnell, "Women and Other Strangers before the Bar," Yearbook 1977, Supreme Court Historical Society, at 59–62, 114.

30. Minor v. Happersett, 88 U.S. (21 Wall.) 162 (1875).

control in various forms, with diminishing intensity, has continued to the present."[31] Although women had made some gains, he said "it is still true that in the struggle for subsistence she is not an equal competitor with her brother." Legislation might remove some limitations on a woman's personal and contractual rights, but "there is that in her disposition and habits of life which will operate against a full assertion of those rights."[32]

After ratification of the Nineteenth Amendment, giving women the right to vote, the Court in 1923 decided that protective legislation for women was no longer justified.[33] Yet the Court continued to uphold certain types of legislation. The following year it sustained a New York law that prohibited women in large cities from working between 10 p.m. and 6 a.m.[34] The Court divided 5 to 4 in 1936 in striking down a New York minimum wage law for women and minors.[35] A year later, the Court again split 5–4 in accepting minimum wage legislation for women. It reasoned that states were entitled to consider "the fact that they are in the class receiving the least pay, that their bargaining power is relatively weak, and that they are the ready victims of those who would take advantage of their necessitous circumstances."[36]

By 1948, judicial attitudes about the rights of women seemed not to have advanced very far from the days of William Blackstone. The Supreme Court upheld a Michigan law that prohibited women from serving as bartenders. unless they were the wife or daughter of the male owner. A 6–3 Court decided that the law did not violate the constitutional meaning of equal protection. Writing for the majority, Justice Felix Frankfurter began with smug assurance: "Beguiling as the subject is, it need not detain us for long. To ask whether or not the Equal Protection of the Laws Clause of the Fourteenth Amendment barred Michigan from making the classification the State has made between wives and daughters of owners of liquor places and wives and daughters of non-owners, is one of those rare instances where to state the question is in effect to answer it."[37] Three dissenters, finding the issue far more complex, concluded that the state law arbitrarily discriminated between men and women.

In 1960, Justice Frankfurter wrote for a 6–3 Court to reject the "medieval view" that husband and wife are one person with a single will and, therefore, legally incapable of entering into a criminal conspiracy. He pointed out that legitimate business enterprises between husband and wife had been "commonplace

31. Muller v. Oregon, 208 U.S. 412, 421 (1908).
32. Id. at 422.
33. Adkins v. Children's Hospital, 261 U.S. 525, 553 (1923).
34. Radice v. New York, 264 U.S. 292 (1924).
35. Morehead v. N.Y. ex rel. Tipaldo, 298 U.S. 587 (1936).
36. West Coast Hotel Co. v. Parrish, 300 U.S. 379, 398 (1937).
37. Goesaert v. Cleary, 335 U.S. 464, 465 (1948).

in our time."[38] To the extent that coverture rested on a legal fiction, the three dissenters preferred that the matter be corrected by Congress, not the judiciary. Medieval thinking triumphed the next year when a unanimous Court agreed that women could be largely exempted from jury service because they are "still regarded as the center of home and family life."[39] Elements of coverture survived in the Supreme Court as late at 1966.[40] Three Justices dissented in this case, wondering why the Court "should exalt this archaic remnant of a primitive caste system to an honored place among the laws of the United States."[41]

Although Congress had passed legislation in 1879 rejecting a Supreme Court rule that prohibited women from practicing there, it was not until 1971 that the Court issued an opinion striking down sex discrimination. A unanimous Court declared invalid an Idaho law that preferred men over women in administering estates.[42] A study published that year condemned the judicial record on women's rights: "Our conclusion, independently reached, but completely shared, is that by and large the performance of American judges in the area of sex discrimination can be succinctly described as ranging from poor to abominable."[43]

Equal Rights Amendment

Frustration with judicial attitudes about women's rights led members of the House of Representatives on August 10, 1970, to support the Equal Rights Amendment (ERA). The basic purpose was to ensure that equality of rights under the law "shall not be denied or abridged by the United States or by any State on account of sex."[44] Representative Martha Griffiths, a leading force behind the amendment, explained that the amendment would have no effect on situations where separation of the sexes is necessary for compelling public interests, such as separate restroom facilities in public buildings, nor would it apply to criminal acts capable of commission by only one sex, including rape and prostitution.[45] A more difficult issue, she admitted, was whether women along with men would be subject to military draft.[46]

38. United States v. Dege, 364 U.S. 51, 52 (1960).
39. Hoyt v. Florida, 368 U.S. 57, 62 (1961).
40. United States v. Yazell, 382 U.S. 341, 343, 346, 351, 352–53 (1966).
41. Id. at 361.
42. Reed v. Reed, 404 U.S. 71 (1971).
43. John D. Johnson, Jr., & Charles L. Knapp, "Sex Discrimination by Law: A Study in Judicial Perspective," 46 N.Y.U. L. Rev. 675, 676 (1971).
44. 116 Cong. Rec. 28004 (1970).
45. Id. at 28005.
46. Id.

The first equal rights amendment was introduced in 1923 by Senator Charles Curtis of Kansas. It read: "Men and women shall have equal rights throughout the United States and every place subject to its jurisdiction."[47] Representative Griffiths noted that an equal rights amendment had been introduced in Congress for forty-seven consecutive years, and for twenty-six years both parties in their political conventions endorsed it. However, for the last twenty-two years the House Judiciary Committee had not held a hearing on it.[48] The first step therefore was to discharge the amendment from the committee. That motion passed overwhelmingly, 333 to 22.[49] The amendment then passed the House, 352–15.[50]

During debate in the House, proponents of the amendment drew attention to the failure of the Supreme Court to protect the rights of women. Griffiths said "this is not a battle between the sexes—nor a battle between this body and women. This body and State legislatures have supported women. This is a battle with the Supreme Court of the United States."[51] She added that states legislatures "and frequently their courts or Federal district courts have shown more sense than the Supreme Court ever has."[52] What the equal rights amendment attempted to do, she said, "is to say to the Supreme Court, 'Wake up! This is the 20th century. Before it is over, judge women as individual human beings.'"[53]

When the issue moved to the Senate in October 1970, several amendments were offered. The House version did not stipulate the number of years set aside for ratification of the amendment. An amendment by Senator James B. Allen of Alabama stipulated that the ERA would have to be ratified by the legislatures "within seven years" after being submitted to the states.[54] A second amendment by Allen gave each state sole and exclusive authority to administer public schools. No federal officer or court could impair or infringe on those rights reserved to the states.[55] He later said this amendment was not to the ERA but existed as a free-standing constitutional amendment that would go to the states for ratification.[56]

47. S. J. Res. 21, 65 Cong. Rec. 150 (1923). A companion constitutional amendment (H. J. Res. 75) was introduced in the House by Representative Daniel R. Anthony, Jr., 65 Cong. Rec. 285 (1923).
48. 116 Cong. Rec. 27999.
49. Id. at 28004.
50. Id. at 28036.
51. Id.
52. Id. at 28005.
53. Id. at 35323.
54. Id. at 35621.
55. Id. at 35622.
56. Id. at 35962. For some details on this amendment, which covered such issues as federal controls over school busing and school curricula, see 115 Cong. Rec. 6578–80 (1969).

In the House, on October 12, two committee amendments were rejected. The first would have inserted "of any person" after the word "rights." It was defeated 104–254.[57] The second stated that the ERA "shall not impair the validity of any law of the United States which exempts a person from compulsory military service or any other law of the United States or any State which reasonably promotes the health and safety of the people." It was rejected, 87–265.[58] The House passed the ERA, which now contained language requiring ratification within seven years, by a vote of 354–24.[59]

Also on October 12, the Senate began consideration of the ERA by disposing of several amendments, several of them irrelevant. One, by Senator Allen, concerned the right of states to assign students to public schools under a "freedom of choice" system, as a means of avoiding school integration.[60] It was rejected 17–57.[61] An amendment by Senator Sam Ervin of North Carolina stating that the ERA shall not impair the validity of any federal law that exempts women from compulsory military service was accepted, 36–33.[62] The Senate debated an amendment by Senator Howard Baker of Tennessee to permit nondenominational prayer in public buildings. It passed, 50–20.[63] Because of the amendments by Ervin and Baker, Senator Birch Bayh offered a substitute constitutional amendment: "Neither the United States nor any State shall on account of sex, deny to any person within its jurisdiction, the equal protection of the laws."[64] The Senate adjourned without taking further action on an ERA.[65]

In 1971, by a vote of 354–24, the House passed the ERA with this language: "Equality of rights under the law shall not be denied or abridged by the United States or by any State on account of sex. The Congress shall have the power to enforce, by appropriate legislation, the provisions of this article."[66] Debate in the Senate throughout 1972 successfully produced a constitutional amendment to provide equal rights for men and women.[67] The final vote for the House-passed ERA was 84–8.[68]

57. 116 Cong. Rec. 35782-84.
58. Id. at 35784–813.
59. Id. at 35815.
60. Id. at 36272.
61. Id. at 36278.
62. Id. at 36300–36313, 36448–51.
63. Id. at 36478–81, 36482–505.
64. Id. at 36863.
65. "Equal Rights for Women Amendment Dropped in Senate," 1970 CQ Almanac, at 706–9.
66. 117 Cong. Rec. 35815 (1971). For House debate, including the rejection of two committee amendments: id. at 35782–814.
67. 118 Cong. Rec. 8899–911, 9080–106, 9314–72, 9517–40 (1972).
68. Id. at 9598.

By the end of 1972, twenty-two of the necessary thirty-eight states had ratified the ERA. Eight more states added their support in 1973. By the end of 1977, nearing the seven-year deadline for ratification, only thirty-five states had approved the ERA, and some states were beginning to rescind their ratifications.[69] In late 1977, legislation was introduced to extend the deadline seven years to March 22, 1986.[70] The final version, agreed to on October 20, 1978, extended the deadline three years to June 30, 1982.[71] On December 23, 1981, a federal district court held that Idaho had the power and right to rescind its prior ratification.[72] With an insufficient number of states agreeing to ratify the ERA, it died on June 30, 1982.

In her study of the ERA, Jane Mansbridge pointed out that had the amendment been ratified it "would have had much less substantive effect than either proponents or opponents claimed."[73] The ERA applied only to the federal and state governments, not to private businesses and corporations. Debate on the ERA, particularly criticism of failings by the Supreme Court to protect the rights of women, appeared to have an impact on the federal judiciary. It is often said the Court supplies a check on majoritarian pressures from the elected branches. An article by Leslie Friedman Goldstein concluded that, instead, the Court has "been heeding quite carefully the policies endorsed by the majoritarian branches of government."[74] The ERA encountered many problems in the states, including the issue of abortion and women serving in the military. ERA proponents tried to keep abortion as a separate issue, but the Supreme Court's decision in *Roe v. Wade* (1973) seemed to link ERA with the pro-choice movement.

Abortion Rights

The question before the Supreme Court in 1973, in *Roe v. Wade*, was complex and politically charged. How could abortions be performed within a legal structure that satisfied the competing values of those who wanted abortion on demand and those who believed equally strongly in an embryo's right to life? Various states wrestled with the issue. It became a national controversy when the Court attempted to "settle" it for the entire country. The decision

69. Alan P. Grimes, Democracy and the Amendments to the Constitution 153 (1978).

70. Leslie W. Gladstone, "The Proposed Equal Rights Amendment," Congressional Research Service, Dec. 27, 1982, at 8.

71. 92 Stat. 3799 (1978).

72. State of Idaho v. Freeman, 529 F. Supp. 1107 (D. Idaho 1981).

73. Jane J. Mansbridge, Why We Lost the ERA 2 (1986).

74. Leslie Friedman Goldstein, "The ERA and the U.S. Supreme Court," 1 Research in Law and Policy Studies 145, 154–55 (1987).

THE RIGHTS OF WOMEN

represented a serious political and institutional miscalculation. As Linda Greenhouse noted, the manner in which the Court handled the issue deeply split the nation and gave "rise to the religious Right,"[75] a political development that continues to this day.

Justice Blackmun wrote for a 7–2 Court, with Justices White and Rehnquist in dissent. Concurrences were written by Justices Stewart and Douglas and Chief Justice Burger. The Court struck down a Texas statute that prohibited abortion except on medical advice for the purpose of saving the woman's life. The Court held that a woman's right to privacy, whether found in the Fourteenth Amendment or the Ninth Amendment, "is broad enough to encompass a woman's decision whether or not to terminate her pregnancy."[76] It disagreed that a woman "is entitled to terminate her pregnancy at whatever time, in whatever way, and for whatever reason she alone chooses."[77] It accepted as "reasonable and appropriate" a state's right to decide at some point how to legislate to protect the health of the mother and potential human life.[78]

The Court attempted to draw precise boundaries: "the common law found greater significance in quickening," a stage when the fetus is beginning to move and the woman is about to deliver.[79] Whatever existed in common law, centuries ago, did not reflect medical knowledge in 1973. Justice Blackmun defined the stage at which a fetus may survive (viability) "as usually placed at about seven months (28 weeks) but may occur earlier, even at 24 weeks."[80] He placed the "compelling" point for a woman, in "light of present medical knowledge," at approximately the end of the first trimester.[81] Reference to "present medical knowledge" underscored that the Court could not possibly decide the issue with any finality.

Blackmun placed the state's compelling interest "at viability," which he took to mean the ability of a fetus to survive "outside the mother's womb."[82] Medical technology rapidly changed the concept of viability, with the fetus able to survive outside the mother's womb at much earlier stages. After the first trimester, Blackmun said, the state "retains a definite interest in protecting the

75. Linda Greenhouse, The U.S. Supreme Court: A Very Short Introduction 78 (2012). For the different parties and organizations that publicly debated abortion, see Linda Greenhouse & Reva B. Siegel, eds., Before Roe v. Wade: Voices That Shaped the Abortion Debate before the Supreme Court's Ruling (2010).
76. Roe v. Wade, 410 U.S. 113, 153 (1973).
77. Id.
78. Id. at 159.
79. Id. at 160.
80. Id.
81. Id. at 163.
82. Id.

woman's own health and safety when an abortion is proposed at a late stage of pregnancy."[83]

In dissent, Rehnquist objected that "the conscious weighing of competing factors" by the Court opinion "is far more appropriate to a legislative judgment than to a judicial one."[84] The Court's decision "to break pregnancy into three distinct terms and to outline the permissible restrictions the State may impose in each one . . . partakes more of judicial legislation than it does a determination of the intent of the drafters of the Fourteenth Amendment."[85] White, in a dissent printed in a companion case, remarked: "As an exercise of raw judicial power, the Court perhaps has authority to do what it does today; but in my view its judgment is an improvident and extravagant exercise of the power of judicial review that the Constitution extends to this Court."[86]

The Court's decision drew rebukes from both conservative and liberal camps. An early critique of *Roe v. Wade* by John Hart Ely identified some of its principal weaknesses. Blackmun's decision consisted of "drawing lines with an apparent precision one generally associates with a commissioner's regulations. On closer examination, however, the precision proves largely illusory."[87] He noted that the concept of viability "will become even less clear than it is now as the technology of birth continues to develop."[88] To Ely, "the problem with *Roe* is not so much that it bungles the question it sets itself, but rather that it sets itself a question the Constitution has not made the Court's business."[89]

Support for the trimester framework continued to erode, in part because Sandra Day O'Connor joined the Court in 1981. In a lengthy dissent two years later, she objected that the trimester or "three-stage" approach was "completely unworkable."[90] The *Roe* framework "is clearly on a collision course with itself."[91] In 1986, Rehnquist replaced Burger as Chief Justice, and Antonin Scalia took Rehnquist's seat as Associate Justice, adding another opponent of *Roe*. After Anthony Kennedy replaced Justice Powell in 1988, the Court was in a position to overhaul and possibly overrule *Roe*.

The changed composition of the Court was evident in a 1989 decision, which reviewed a Missouri statute that imposed a number of restrictions on

83. Id. at 150.

84. Id. at 173 (Rehnquist, J., dissenting).

85. Id. at 174.

86. Doe v. Bolton, 410 U.S. 179, 222 (1973) (White, J., dissenting).

87. John Hart Ely, "The Wages of Crying Wolf: A Comment on *Roe v. Wade*," 82 Yale L.J. 920, 922 (1973).

88. Id. at 924.

89. Id. at 943.

90. Akron v. Akron Center for Reproductive Health, 462 U.S. 416, 454 (1983) (O'Connor, J., dissenting).

91. Id. at 458.

a woman's decision to have an abortion. Without overruling *Roe*, a plurality opinion by Rehnquist, White, and Kennedy rejected the trimester framework.[92] Scalia would have repealed all of *Roe*.[93] O'Connor continued to consider the trimester framework as "problematic."[94] In 1992, the Court finally abandoned the framework. An opinion by O'Connor, Kennedy, and Souter specifically rejected it.[95] Stevens and Blackmun disagreed with the rejection. In their separate opinion, Rehnquist, White, Scalia, and Thomas stated that *Roe* "was wrongly decided," apparently rejecting the framework without expressly saying so.[96] Scalia, in an opinion that concurred in the judgment and dissented in part, joined by Rehnquist, White, and Thomas, discussed deficiencies of the entire *Roe* decision.[97]

What was learned from *Roe v. Wade*? Writing in 1985 while serving on the D.C. Circuit, Ruth Bader Ginsburg said the decision became a "storm center" and "sparked public opposition and academic criticism," in part "because the Court ventured too far in the change it ordered and presented an incomplete justification for its action."[98] In 1992, after the Court rejected the trimester framework and she was confirmed as Associate Justice, Ginsburg explained that judges "play an interdependent part in our democracy. They do not alone shape legal doctrine, but . . . they participate in a dialogue with other organs of government, and with the people as well. . . . Measured motions seem to me right, in the main, for constitutional as well as common law adjudication."[99] A "less encompassing" decision, she said, "might have served to reduce rather than to fuel controversy."[100]

Congress responded to *Roe v. Wade* and other judicial rulings with several statutes. In 1976, as an amendment to the Labor-HEW appropriations bill, Representative Henry J. Hyde offered language to prohibit any federal funds "to pay for abortions or to promote or encourage abortions." His amendment passed, 199–165. After action by the Senate and conference committee, the enacted language read: "None of the funds contained in this Act shall be used to perform abortions except where the life of the mother would be

---

92. Webster v. Reproductive Health Services, 492 U.S. 490, 517–20 (1989).
93. Id. at 537 (Scalia, J., concurrence).
94. Id. at 525, 529 (O'Connor, J., concurrence).
95. Planned Parenthood of Southeastern Pa. v. Casey, 505 U.S. 833, 869–79 (1992).
96. Id. at 944 (Rehnquist, C.J., joined by White, J., Scalia, J., and Thomas, J.).
97. Id. at 982–1002.
98. Ruth Bader Ginsburg, "Some Thoughts on Autonomy and Equality in Relation to *Roe v. Wade*," 63 N.C. L. Rev. 375, 376 (1985).
99. Ruth Bader Ginsburg, "Speaking in a Judicial Voice," 67 N.Y.U. L. Rev. 1185, 1198 (1992).
100. Id. at 1199.

endangered if the fetus were carried to term."[101] That language was altered in 1979 by permitting public funds "for the victims of rape or incest when such rape or incest has been reported promptly to a law enforcement agency or public health service."[102]

In 1980, by a 5–4 vote, the Supreme Court upheld the Hyde Amendment. The Court concluded that the amendment, by encouraging childbirth except in the most urgent circumstances, was rationally related to legitimate governmental objectives of protecting potential life.[103] In a companion case, *Harris v. McRae*, the Court (again split 5–4) upheld the right of state legislatures to limit public funds for abortions.[104] When the issue of public funding is framed entirely as a state matter to be decided under the state constitution, the results can differ from the Court's decision in *Harris v. McRae*.[105]

In 1996, President Clinton vetoed a bill that would have prohibited late-term abortions except to save the life of a woman. He said he opposed late-term abortions but insisted on a provision to cover adverse health consequences. Although the House overrode the veto, the Senate fell nine votes short. In 1997, Clinton vetoed a similar bill, and Congress failed to override. A Nebraska law, banning "partial birth abortions," was struck down by the Supreme Court in *Stenberg v. Carhart* (2000).[106] Divided 5–4, the Court was split in many directions: an opinion written by Justice Breyer, separate concurrences by Stevens, O'Connor, and Ginsburg, and dissenting opinions by Rehnquist, Scalia, Kennedy, and Thomas.

Responding to *Stenberg v. Carhart*, Congress in 2002 passed the Born-Alive Infants Protection Act, which provided that the words "person," "human being," "child," and "individual" shall include every infant born alive at any stage of development. "Born alive" was defined as covering a child who after expulsion or extraction "breathes or has a beating heart, pulsation of the umbilical cord, or definite movement of voluntary muscles."[107] Congress then passed the Partial-Birth Abortion Ban Act of 2003, stating that a moral, medical, and ethical consensus exists that the practice of performing a partial-birth abortion "is never medically necessary and should be prohibited."[108] The statute permitted

101. 90 Stat. 1434, sec. 209 (1976).
102. 93 Stat. 926, sec. 109 (1979).
103. Harris v. McRae, 448 U.S. 297 (1980).
104. Williams v. Zbaraz, 448 U.S. 358 (1980).
105. For example, see Committee to Defend Reprod. Rights v. Myers, 625 P.2d 779 (Cal. 1981); Right to Choose v. Byrne, 450 A.2d 925 (N.J. 1982); Moe v. Secretary of Administration, 417 N.Ed.2d 387 (Mass. 1981); Planned Parenthood Ass'n v. Dept. of Human Res., 663 P.2d 1247 (Or. App. 1983); Doe v. Maher, 515 A.2d 134, 143 (Conn. Super. 1986).
106. Stenberg v. Carhart, 530 U.S. 914 (2000).
107. 116 Stat. 926 (2002).
108. 117 Stat. 1201, sec. 2 (2003).

partial-birth abortion when "necessary to save the life of a mother whose life is endangered by a physical disorder, physical illness, or physical injury, including a life-endangering physical condition caused by or arising from the pregnancy itself."[109] In 2007, the Supreme Court upheld the statute, divided 5–4. It distinguished the federal statute from the Nebraska law at issue in *Stenberg*.[110]

Equal Pay Legislation

Advances in women's rights come primarily from the elected branches, demonstrating a much greater capacity than courts to recognize sex discrimination and propose remedies. On December 14, 1961, President John Kennedy established a Commission on the Status of Women. It focused on employment practices of the federal government and affirmative steps to provide for equal pay.[111] The Commission report noted that twenty-four states required that women "who do the same or comparable work as men in the same establishment be paid at the same rates."[112] In practice, however, women were paid substantially less than men for performing the same job.

Relying on its constitutional power to regulate commerce, Congress debated legislation to provide equal pay for women. The bill exempted a number of jobs in agriculture, hotels, motels, restaurants, and laundries, with heavy concentrations of female employees.[113] Lawmakers who supported taking action did so with the understanding that it was only the first of many steps needed to secure the principle of equal pay. The bill passed both chambers by voice vote and became law on June 10, 1963.[114]

Title VII of the Civil Rights Act of 1964 made it illegal for any employer to discriminate against anyone with respect to "compensation, terms, conditions, or privileges of employment" because of the person's sex.[115] However, total elimination of gender-based discrimination would make it impossible to address the special needs of pregnant workers. A California law paid benefits to persons temporarily disabled from working and not covered by worker's compensation. No payment was made for certain disabilities attributed to pregnancy. The Supreme Court upheld that statute in 1974.[116] Building on that precedent, two

109. Id. at 1206, sec. 3.
110. Gonzales v. Carhart, 550 U.S. 124 (2007).
111. Public Papers of the President, 1961, 799–80.
112. American Women," Report of the President's Commission on the Status of Women, 1963, at 37.
113. 109 Cong. Rec. 9193 (1963) (statement by Representative St. George).
114. 77 Stat. 56 (1963).
115. 78 Stat. 241, 255, sec. 703(a)(1) (1964).
116. Geduldig v. Aiello, 417 U.S. 484 (1974).

years later the Court supported a disability plan by General Electric that gave benefits for nonoccupational sickness and accidents but not for inability to work arising from pregnancy. The Court decided the plan did not violate Title VII of the 1964 Civil Rights Act. Three Justices dissented.[117]

As part of the ongoing dialogue between the legislative and judicial branches regarding individual rights, Congress held hearings. The Senate Committee on Human Resources concluded that the Court in the General Electric case had improperly interpreted Title VII.[118] The Senate passed a pregnancy discrimination bill by a vote of 75 to 11.[119] A report by the House Committee on Education and Labor agreed that the dissenting Justices in *General Electric* "correctly interpreted" Title VII.[120] The Pregnancy Discrimination Act of 1978 amended Title VII to prohibit employment discrimination on the basis of pregnancy and to require fringe benefits and insurance plans to cover pregnant workers.[121]

In the late 1980s, after Anthony Kennedy replaced Lewis Powell on the Supreme Court, the Court began to backtrack on some earlier rulings that had upheld civil rights. That pattern continued in the spring of 1989 when the Court shifted the burden to employees to prove that racial disparities at work resulted from employment practices and were not justified by business needs.[122] In response, Congress passed legislation to reverse or modify *nine* Court rulings dealing with employment discrimination. When President George H. W. Bush vetoed the bill, lawmakers lacked sufficient votes for an override. Congress revised the bill slightly in 1991, and this time Bush, facing a likely override, signed the Civil Rights Act of 1991.[123]

The Lilly Ledbetter Case

In 2007, the Supreme Court split 5 to 4 in deciding that Lilly Ledbetter had filed an untimely claim against Goodyear Tire for pay discrimination. She had worked there from 1979 to 1998. In July 1998, she filed a formal charge for

117. General Electric Co. v. Gilbert, 429 U.S. 125 (1976).
118. S. Rept. No. 95-331, 95th Cong., 1st Sess. (1977).
119. 123 Cong. Rec. 29664 (1977).
120. H. Rept. No. 95-948, 950th Cong., 2d Sess. 2 (1978).
121. 92 Stat. 2076 (1978).
122. Wards Cove Packing Co. v. Atonio, 490 U.S. 642 (1989). For other Supreme Court decisions adverse to employees: Independent Fed. of Flight Attendants v. Zipes, 491 U.S. 754 (1989); Lorance v. AT&T Technologies, Inc., 490 U.S. 900 (1989); Patterson v. McLean Credit Union, 491 U.S. 164 (1989).
123. For further details on the Civil Rights Act of 1991, see Louis Fisher & Katy J. Harriger, American Constitutional Law 825–26 (10th ed., 2013).

sex discrimination under Title VII and also a claim under the Equal Pay Act of 1963. A district court dismissed the latter claim but allowed the Title VII claim to proceed to trial, where Ledbetter prevailed and won over $3.8 million in back pay and damages. Goodyear maintained that the evaluations had been nondiscriminatory and that her claims were barred for any pay decision made before September 26, 1997, or 180 days before she filed her complaint. She insisted that evaluations during that 180-day period reflected discriminatory actions from previous years. The Eleventh Circuit held that she could not maintain her suit based on past discrimination because she failed to file timely charges during those periods.

Writing for a 5–4 Court, Justice Alito agreed with the Eleventh Circuit.[124] He explained that Ledbetter in March 1998 submitted a questionnaire to the Equal Employment Opportunity Commission (EEOC) alleging certain acts of sex discrimination. In July of that year she filed a formal EEOC charge and took early retirement in November 1998. At that point she brought her action. Justice Alito stated that anyone filing a Title VII charge with the EEOC must file within a specified period, either 180 or 300 days (depending on the state) after the alleged unlawful employment practice occurred. The shorter period applied to Ledbetter.[125]

Ledbetter argued that her paychecks were unlawful because they would have been larger had she been evaluated in a nondiscriminatory manner *before* she filed with EEOC. In that sense, earlier discriminatory actions "carried forward" with subsequent paychecks.[126] To Justice Alito, "current events alone cannot breathe life into prior, uncharged discrimination." In his judgment, she should have filed with the EEOC within 180 days "after each allegedly discriminatory pay decision was made and communicated to her."[127]

Of course Goodyear had not communicated to Ledbetter discriminatory pay decisions. She did not learn until many years later that she had been paid less than men for the same work. Alito pointed to the value of statutes of limitations. Employers need to be put on notice about an unlawful action so they can properly defend themselves. The EEOC deadline protects employers from having to defend claims arising from company decisions that are long past.[128] The purpose of the 180-day deadline in Ledbetter's case was to encourage employees to promptly file claims of pay discrimination.[129] But Ledbetter could not file a claim unless she had knowledge of

124. Ledbetter v. Goodyear Tire & Rubber Co., 550 U.S. 618 (2007).
125. Id. at 623–24.
126. Id. at 624–25.
127. Id. at 628.
128. Id. at 630.
129. Id.

what Goodyear had done years before, information the company withheld from her.

A footnote in Justice Alito's opinion states that Ledbetter claimed that her pay discrimination resulted from a supervisor who retaliated against her when she rejected his sexual advances in the early 1980s and again in the mid-1990s. By the time of trial he had died. "A timely charge," Alito said, "might have permitted his evidence to be weighed contemporaneously."[130] She did not file earlier because she lacked necessary information.

In a dissent joined by three colleagues, Justice Ruth Bader Ginsburg noted the disparity between Ledbetter's monthly salary as area manager and those of her male counterparts for the end of 1997. The latter group ranged from a high of $5,236 to a low of $4,286. Her monthly salary for that time period was $3,727. As to Ledbetter's failure to file discrimination charges before 1998, Ginsburg explained that comparative pay information was withheld from Ledbetter, as with other employees. Also, initial pay discrepancies, even if modest in size, have the effect of accumulating over time. Recalling the Civil Rights Act of 1991 that overturned in whole or part nine decisions of the Supreme Court, she wrote: "Once again, the ball is in Congress' court. As in 1991, the Legislature may act to correct this Court's parsimonious reading of Title VII."[131]

The Court's decision was released on May 29, 2007. Senator Ted Kennedy responded by saying the Court had "undermined a core protection of Title VII of the Civil Rights Act of 1964."[132] The Court's action was "not only unfair, it sets up a perverse incentive for workers to file lawsuits before they have investigated whether pay decisions are actually based on discrimination." If they waited to receive the information they needed, their complaint could be out of time. As a result, the Court's decision "will create unnecessary litigation as workers rush to beat the clock on their equal pay claims."[133]

In late July, the House of Representatives debated the Lilly Ledbetter Fair Pay Act to reverse the Court's decision. In managing the bill, Representative Jim McGovern of Massachusetts said the "shortsighted and unfortunate recent Supreme Court ruling has forced us to revisit this painful issue from our Nation's past." Although Congress had developed a bipartisan solution by passing Title VII of the Civil Rights Act of 1964, "unfortunately the Supreme Court in one fell swoop, completely, outrageously undermined" that legislative purpose. In her testimony before the House Education and Labor Committee in June, Ledbetter acknowledged that congressional action could

130. Id. at 632, n.4.
131. Id. at 661.
132. 153 Cong. Rec. 14530 (2007).
133. Id. at 14531.

not assist her but hoped "that Congress won't let this happen to anyone else."[134]

Congressional action in passing legislation faced a possible presidential veto. McGovern said that President George W. Bush had announced he would veto the bill if it reached his desk.[135] In support of the legislation, Jerrold Nadler of New York remarked that the Supreme Court "said something truly astonishing," that the only discriminatory act was the initial decision nineteen years earlier to pay Ledbetter less than her male coworkers. Once her employer concealed that fact from her for 180 days "she was out of luck," and Goodyear could pay her less just because she was a woman. "Once again, Congress must correct the Supreme Court and instruct it that when we said discrimination in employment was illegal, we meant it, and we meant for the courts to enforce it."[136]

Voting 225 to 199, the House passed the Ledbetter bill.[137] The legislation amended Title VII of the Civil Rights Act of 1964 and several other statutes. It clarified that a discriminatory pay action occurs each time compensation is paid. Under that procedure, a company could not discriminate, withhold that information from the employee, and be at liberty to continue discriminatory pay actions in the future without fear of litigation.

After the Senate filibustered the bill, no further action was taken until early 2009, when Barack Obama was about to occupy the White House. In House debate on January 9, 2009, John Conyers of Michigan referred to the Supreme Court as "anti-worker, pro-corporate" in denying Ledbetter's claim.[138] Inconsistently, he described courts as "our last line of defense when it comes to protecting the fundamental rights enshrined in our Constitution and in our civil rights laws."[139] As in other cases over the years, the last line of defense would be Congress. The bill passed the House, 247–171.[140]

The Senate debated the bill on January 22, after Obama had taken office. It voted down or tabled several amendments intended to weaken the bill.[141] The bill passed the Senate, 61 to 36.[142] The House voted 250 to 177 to support the Senate bill.[143] As enacted, the bill provides that an unlawful employment practice occurs when a discriminatory compensation decision is adopted.

134. Id.
135. Id.
136. Id. at 21432.
137. Id. at 21929.
138. Id. at 441.
139. Id. at 441–42.
140. Id. at 458–59.
141. Id. at 1369, 1383–84, 1388–89, 1389, 1400.
142. Id. at 1400–1.
143. Id. at 1671.

Nothing in the statute limits an employee's right to introduce evidence of an unlawful employment practice that occurs outside the time for filing a charge of discrimination.[144]

Additional Legislative Activity

Congress has debated other issues dealing with women's rights. In 1975, Congress passed legislation to permit women to enter the service academies: the Military Academy at West Point, the Naval Academy at Annapolis, and the Air Force Academy at Colorado Springs.[145] Job opportunities within the military expanded for women. Before 1970, women could participate in about 35 percent of military jobs. In contemporary times, the percentage is close to 100 percent. Increasingly, women in the military saw combat. In 1993, Congress enacted legislation to repeal the statutory restriction on the assignment of women to combat in the Navy and Marine Corps.[146] Although women entered the service academies at West Point, the Naval Academy, and the Air Force Academy, they were barred from other military academies. In 1996, the Supreme Court held that the exclusion of women from the state-supported Virginia Military Institute (VMI) was unconstitutional. The state had offered a parallel program for women at Mary Baldwin College, but the Court ruled this alternative did not provide equal tangible and intangible benefits.[147] Following this decision, the Citadel (the only other all-male, public military college, located in South Carolina) announced it would begin accepting women.

There have been continuing disputes about the Violence against Women Act (VAWA), passed by Congress in 1994. The Court held that a provision in the statute could not be sustained under the Commerce Clause or Section 5 of the Fourteenth Amendment.[148] The provision permitted victims of rape, domestic violence, and other crimes "motivated by gender" to sue their attackers in federal court. Congress compiled a record to demonstrate that domestic violence and sexual assault cost the economy $5 to $10 billion a year. Split along political lines, the majority consisted of the conservative-moderate wing (Rehnquist, O'Connor, Kennedy, Scalia, and Thomas), while dissents came from moderate-liberals (Stevens, Souter, Ginsburg, and Breyer).

The Court's decision had limited reach because all states have laws prohibiting violence against women. Although the decision blocked congressional

144. 123 Stat. 5 (2009).
145. 89 Stat. 537, sec. 803 (1975).
146. 107 Stat. 1659, sec. 541 (1993).
147. United States v. Virginia, 518 U.S. 515 (1996).
148. United States v. Morrison, 529 U.S. 598 (2000).

policy in one area, nothing prevented Congress from using different sources of authority to regulate violence against women. Congress continued to reauthorize VAWA to combat trafficking in the sex trade, strengthen law enforcement to reduce violence against women, and provide services to victims of violence. Those bills were debated in 2000, 2005, and 2012–2013. This last bill, which passed the Senate 78 to 22 and the House 286 to 138, was signed by President Obama to renew VAWA for a five-year period.

5

THE RIGHTS OF CHILDREN

The legal and constitutional rights available to children extend to many areas, including due process rights for juveniles, standards for search and seizure in public schools, and free speech rights for students. For most of our history, juvenile rights depended on the doctrine of *parens patriae*, with the government at times assuming the role of parent. Juvenile courts were supposed to serve as the guardian for youthful offenders. Procedural rights and protections were considered unnecessary because it was assumed the judge would act in the best interest of the child. In many cases, however, judges acted arbitrarily and harshly toward juveniles, ordering periods of incarceration that exceeded penalties imposed on adults for the same offense.[1] These controversies required the attention of all three branches at the federal and state level.

Two issues are covered in this chapter: legislation on child labor and compulsory flag salutes in public schools. Both issues underscore how the elected branches, private groups, and the general public help shape constitutional rights, often in the face of contrary opinions by the Supreme Court. At no time did Congress, the states, organizations, or individual citizens believe that when the Court decides a constitutional issue it has the final word.

Legislation on Child Labor

Because of industrialization, the factory system, and simplified repetitive processes, child labor increased rapidly after the Civil War. Between 1870 and 1910, census figures revealed a sharp rise in the number of children entering the labor market. By 1900, one child in six between the ages of ten and fifteen was employed, totaling more than 1.75 million child laborers in the United States, much of that on the farm.[2] Concerns about children working in hazardous and poorly supervised jobs led to the formation of the National Child Labor Committee in 1904. Its purpose was to investigate the conditions of

---

1. David S. Tanenhaus, The Constitutional Rights of Children: *In re Gault* and Juvenile Justice (2011); Martin Guggenheim & Alan Sussman, The Rights of Young People (1985).
2. Stephen B. Wood, Constitutional Politics in the Progressive Era: Child Labor and the Law 3–4 (1968).

child labor, inform public opinion, and promote legislative reform at the state level.[3] The committee's effort faced resistance to any type of regulation in the South.[4] Using children as workers lowered wages, allowing states with child labor to gain a competitive advantage over states with stricter regulations.[5] In 1906, Senator Albert Beveridge began to place in the *Congressional Record* facts regarding the serious working conditions inflicted on children.[6]

At that time, prominent individuals opposed any attempt by Congress to pass remedial legislation. Woodrow Wilson, from his position as professor at Princeton University, warned in 1908 that if the congressional power to regulate commerce among the states "can be stretched to include the regulation of labor in mills and factories, it can be made to embrace every particular of the industrial organization and action of the country."[7] William Howard Taft, serving as President and later as Chief Justice of the Supreme Court, offered his views in 1913 while teaching law at Yale University. He said any congressional legislation that attempted to suppress the use of child labor in goods being shipped "would be a clear usurpation of that State's rights."[8]

Political matters took clearer shape in 1916 when party platforms strongly endorsed regulation of child labor by Congress. Democrats backed "speedy enactment of an effective Federal Child Labor Law," while Republicans favored "enactment and rigid enforcement of a Federal child labor law."[9] The Progressive Party also supported child labor reforms.[10] Woodrow Wilson changed his position in 1916 after serving four years as President and campaigning for reelection. Advised that support for the bill would attract female votes in state elections, while failure to pass legislation would be politically costly, he now urged immediate passage of a child labor bill.[11]

3. Id. at 10–13.

4. John R. Vile, Encyclopedia of Constitutional Amendments, Proposed Amendments, and Amending Issues, 1789–2002, at 61 (2d ed., 2003).

5. Alan P. Grimes, Democracy and the Amendments to the Constitution 101 (1978).

6. Richard B. Bernstein, Amending America 179 (1993).

7. Woodrow Wilson, Constitutional Government in the United States 179 (1964 paper ed., originally published in 1908).

8. William Howard Taft, Popular Government: Is Essence, Its Permanence, and Its Perils 143 (1913).

9. National Party Platforms, Volume 1 1840–1956, at 119, 207 (Donald Bruce Johnson, comp., 1978).

10. Wood, Constitutional Politics in the Progressive Era, at 28–29, 41, 65, 78.

11. 37 The Papers of Woodrow Wilson 428–29, 431, 436, 447–48, 451, 463, 469, 522–23 (Arthur S. Link, ed., 1981); 38 The Papers of Woodrow Wilson 14, 61, 63, 123–24, 264–65, 469, 471, 586 (Link, ed., 1982).

Invoking the Commerce Power

In reporting child labor legislation on January 17, 1916, the House Labor Committee concluded that "the entire problem has become an interstate problem rather than a problem of isolated States and is a problem which must be faced and solved only by a power stronger than any State."[12] After listening to various experts, with their statements appended to the report, the committee expressed confidence that its proposed bill "falls properly within the power granted to Congress to regulate commerce among the States, and that such seems to be the strongly prevailing view among students of constitutional law."[13] As reported, the bill prohibited the interstate shipment of the product of any mine or quarry by the labor of children under sixteen, or any product of any mill, cannery, workshop, factory, or manufacturing establishment produced in whole or in part by children under the age of fourteen. The prohibition also applied to the labor of children between fourteen or sixteen who worked more than eight hours in a single day, more than six days in any week, or after 7 p.m. or before 7 a.m.

House debate lasted from January 26 to February 2.[14] In defending the bill, Representative David J. Lewis of Maryland explained that the Supreme Court in *Champion v. Ames* (1903) had upheld the authority of Congress to prohibit lotteries from moving in interstate commerce: "If it can use a regulation of interstate commerce to stop lotteries, surely it can not be denied the power to use the same regulation with the object of stopping the employment of children and women under certain deleterious and forbidden circumstances."[15] Noting that he was employed in the mines of Pennsylvania at the age of nine, he said such work placed serious burdens on children and deprived them of needed education.[16]

Representative Edwin Y. Webb of North Carolina raised the principal objection to the bill: "the constitutional question of State rights." To him, the bill was designed to "rob the several States of their reserved constitutional right to regulate their purely internal affairs."[17] But if the product left the state, it was no longer internal. Webb said that forty-four states had already legislated on child labor and the matter should be left to them.[18] Representative James J. Britt of North Carolina favored "just and proper child-labor

---

12. H. Rept. No. 46, 64th Cong., 1st Sess. 7 (1916).
13. Id. at 13.
14. 53 Cong. Rec. 1568–606, 2007–35 (1916).
15. Id. at 1569.
16. Id.
17. Id.
18. Id.

laws," but the states "are the only competent authority to make them."[19] The bill passed the House 337 to 46.[20]

Senate debate began on February 24 and continued until August 8.[21] Senator William S. Kenyon of Iowa explained the appeal of child labor: "It is to get cheap labor, to increase profits and dividends, the placing of commercialism before humanity."[22] Child labor "reduces the standard of wages; it makes pauperism, crime, disease. Efficient labor must be intelligent labor. Child labor is not intelligent labor."[23] He argued for national legislation because states permitted child labor at different ages and used different systems of inspection and enforcement.[24] A table he presented compared the differences in state child-labor laws and legislation on child labor in thirteen countries.[25]

In a lengthy address, Senator Thomas W. Hardwick of Georgia opposed the bill as an unconstitutional interference with state power.[26] Senator Joe T. Robinson of Arkansas responded: "Nobody claims that Congress has power to enforce State laws. Congress enforces its own laws; but the fact that the States do not enforce their own laws as to matters of this kind might justify Congress, in exercising the power it possesses to regulate commerce, to suppress an evil."[27] Senator Kenyon of Iowa asked Hardwick whether the principle he was espousing would have prevented Congress from using its power over interstate commerce to pass the pure food and drugs act or the white-slave act. The latter statute, enacted in 1910, prohibited the transport from any state or foreign country of any woman or girl for the purpose of "prostitution or debauchery, or for any other immoral purpose."[28] The term "white slave" referred to women being kidnapped, enticed, or compelled to engage in prostitution. Hardwick initially answered: "Well, it depends." After Kenyon pressed the question on the white-slave act, Hardwick admitted he voted against it because he thought the statute unconstitutionally interfered with independent state authority.[29]

On August 8, the Senate passed the House bill with amendments, voting 52 to 12. Thirty-one Senators did not vote. The Senate requested a conference

19. Id. at 1578.
20. Id. at 2035.
21. Id. at 3021–57, 9233, 11281, 12034, 12052–57, 12060–93, 12131–38, 12194–229, 12276–313.
22. Id. at 3023.
23. Id. at 3024.
24. Id. at 3026–27.
25. Id. at 3027–44.
26. Id. at 12071.
27. Id. at 12072.
28. 36 Stat. 825 (1910).
29. 53 Cong. Rec. 12073.

with the House on the Senate's version.[30] On August 18 the House agreed to the conference report, which included several Senate amendments.[31] Three days later the Senate agreed to the conference report, and the bill became law on September 1.[32] It retained the basic intent of the House bill: to use the congressional power over interstate commerce to prevent products of child labor from being shipped to other states or foreign governments. To secure proper enforcement of the statute, the Secretary of Labor could authorize individuals to enter and inspect at any time mines, quarries, mills, canneries, workshops, factories, manufacturing establishments, and other places in which goods were produced or held for interstate commerce.

Within two years the Supreme Court struck down the child labor statute as unconstitutional. The case arose when Roland H. Dagenhart and his two sons—all three employed in a cotton mill in North Carolina—filed a suit claiming the statute was unconstitutional. One son, under the age of fourteen, was discharged from his job as a result of the child labor statute. The other son, between fourteen and sixteen, had his hours curtailed. The father complained that the statute deprived him of funds needed to support and maintain his family.[33]

Divided 5–4, the Court concluded that Congress lacked authority to prohibit the transportation in interstate commerce of manufactured goods produced by child labor. It acknowledged that in previous cases, involving lottery schemes, impure foods, prostitution, and intoxicating liquors, the Court had upheld congressional authority to pass regulatory legislation.[34] In each of those cases the use of interstate regulation by Congress was necessary to prevent harmful results.[35] In the Court's judgment, the goods shipped as a result of child labor "are of themselves harmless."[36] Moreover, the making of goods and the mining of coal "are not commerce."[37] The "production of articles, intended for interstate commerce, is a matter of local regulation."[38] To the majority, the child labor statute impermissibly invaded state authority.

Justice Oliver Wendell Holmes, in a dissent joined by three colleagues, reviewed earlier decisions that had read broadly the authority of Congress to regulate economic conditions within states: "It does not matter whether the supposed evil precedes or follows the transportation. It is enough that in

30. Id. at 12313.
31. Id. at 12845.
32. Id. at 12917–18; 39 Stat. 675 (1916).
33. 18 Landmark Briefs 927 (pages 2–3 of brief for appellees, Hammer v. Dagenhart).
34. Hammer v. Dagenhart, 247 U.S. 251, 270–71 (1918).
35. Id. at 271.
36. Id. at 272.
37. Id.
38. Id.

the opinion of Congress the transportation encourages the evil."[39] Holmes believed that Congress, not the Court, possessed the constitutional authority to determine these policy and moral questions: "It is not for this Court to pronounce when prohibition is necessary to regulation if it ever may be necessary—to say that it is permissible as against strong drink but not against the product of ruined lives."[40] The child labor statute did not interfere with anything belonging to the states: "They may regulate their internal affairs and their domestic commerce as they like," but when "they seek to send their products across the state line they are no longer within their rights."[41]

Turning to the Taxing Power

Congress did not accept the Court's decision as the final word on constitutional authority. Within a matter of days, members of Congress offered legislation to regulate child labor not through the commerce power but the taxing power. An excise tax would be levied on the net profits of persons employing child labor within prohibited ages.[42] In addition, Senator Robert L. Owen reintroduced the identical bill that the Court had just invalidated, adding in plainspoken language: "Any executive or judicial officer who in his official capacity denies the constitutionality of this act shall ipso facto vacate his office."[43] He continued:

> It is said by some that the judges are much more learned and wiser than Congress in construing the Constitution. I can not concede this whimsical notion. They are not more learned; they are not wiser; they are not more patriotic; and what is the fatal weakness if they make their mistakes there is no adequate means of correcting their judicial errors, while if Congress should err the people have an immediate redress; they can change the House of Representatives almost immediately and can change two-thirds of the Senate within four years, while the judges are appointed for life and are removable only by impeachment.[44]

The effort to regulate child labor through the taxing power found ready support in the Senate, 50 to 12. The bill passed the House, 312 to 11, and

39. Id. at 279–80.
40. Id. at 280.
41. Id. at 281.
42. 56 Cong. Rec. 8341, 11560 (1918).
43. Id. at 7432.
44. Id. at 7433.

became law as Title XII of a general revenue act.[45] A federal district court in North Carolina declared the excise tax unconstitutional. When the issue returned to the Supreme Court, Solicitor General James M. Beck advised the Justices to exercise judicial prudence when reviewing legislation that had been adopted by the elected branches. He said the Philadelphia Convention "voted down any proposition that the judiciary should have an absolute revisionary power over the legislature, which as the representative of the people was regarded as the most direct organ of their will."[46] Only when a case, he said, presents an *"invincible, irreconcilable, and indubitable repugnancy"* between a congressional statute and the Constitution should the Court nullify the statute."[47]

Beck denied that federal courts have "an unlimited power to nullify a law if its incidental effect is in excess of the governmental sphere of the enacting body." There exists a large field of political activity "in which the judiciary may not enter."[48] He reminded the Justices of the consequences of *Dred Scott*, "possibly the principal cause, next to slavery itself, in precipitating the greatest civil war in history."[49] The belief that the Court is fully empowered to judge the motives or objectives of the elected branches "is a mischievous one, in that it so lowers the sense of constitutional morality among the people that neither in the legislative branch of the Government nor among the people is there as strong a purpose as formerly to maintain their constitutional form of Government."[50] The idea that the Court "is the sole guardian and protector of our constitutional form of government has inevitably led to an impairment, both with the people and with their representatives, of what may be called the constitutional conscience."[51]

The Court dismissed Beck's warning. In 1922, a majority of 8 to 1 struck down the child labor tax. In a short ten-page opinion for the majority, Chief Justice William Howard Taft agreed that courts are generally reluctant to speculate about legislative motives, but it "must be blind not to see that the so-called tax is imposed to stop the employment of children within the age limits prescribed. Its prohibitory and regulatory effect and purpose are palpable."[52] Allowing the use of the taxing power for this purpose "would be to break down all constitutional limitation of the powers of Congress and

45. 57 Cong. Rec. 609–21, 3029–35 (1918–19); 40 Stat. 1057, 1138 (1919).
46. "Brief on Behalf of Appellants and Plaintiff in Error," Bailey v. George, and Bailey v. Drexel Furniture Co., Supreme Court of the United States, October Term, 1921, Nos. 590, 657, Feb. 1922, reprinted at 21 Landmark Briefs 45 (using page numbers at the top).
47. Id. at 46 (emphases in original).
48. Id. at 47.
49. Id. at 48.
50. Id. at 54.
51. Id.
52. Child Labor Tax Case (Bailey v. Drexel Furniture Co.), 259 U.S. 20, 37 (1922).

completely wipe out the sovereignty of the States."[53] Justice John Clarke dissented, without providing any reasons.

Congress Keeps Trying

Unsuccessful with the commerce power and the taxing power, members of Congress might have decided to surrender to the Court's judgment. They did not. In 1924 Congress passed a constitutional amendment to give it authority to regulate child labor. The language empowered Congress "to limit, regulate, and prohibit the labor of persons under 18 years of age." It further provided that the power of the States "is unimpaired by this article except that the operation of State laws shall be suspended to the extent necessary to give effect to legislation enacted by the Congress."[54] There were never enough states to ratify the amendment.[55]

The House debated the amendment on April 25 and April 26,[56] passing it by a margin of 297 to 69—far in excess of the two-thirds required.[57] Representative Edward E. Denison of Illinois explained why he thought lawmakers should defer to the judiciary on constitutional issues: "The Supreme Court has settled the question as to the power of Congress to enact such legislation under our present constitutional limitations. And I think we should willingly accept their conclusions upon that matter." Congress, he said, "should guard carefully the prerogatives of that court and preserve respect for its decisions and acquiesce in its constructions of our constitutional limitations."[58]

There were several problems with his analysis. First, the Court can change its mind, especially when the composition differs from one period to the next. Second, even without a change in membership it is possible for Justices, upon hearing critical responses to a decision, to change their minds within a year or two. That point is driven home by the flag-salute cases, covered at the end of this chapter. Just as Congress can be persuaded by Court opinions, so can legislative action influence the Court.

53. Id. at 38.
54. 65 Cong. Rec. 7166 (1924).
55. John R. Vile, Encyclopedia of Constitutional Amendments, Proposed Amendments, and Amending Issues, 1789–2002, at 61–63 (2003); David E. Kyvig, Explicit and Authentic Acts: Amending the U.S. Constitution, 1776–1995 (1996); Richard B. Bernstein, Amending America 179–81 (1993); Alan P. Grimes, Democracy and the Amendments to the Constitution 101–4 (1978).
56. 65 Cong. Rec. 7165–206, 7250–95 (1924). Additional House remarks appear at 7295–7321, 7726–27.
57. Id. at 7294–95.
58. Id. at 7296.

The Senate debated the child labor amendment on May 27 and completed action on June 2.[59] Senator Samuel M. Shortridge of California explained the decision to use "labor" instead of "employment" in the amendment, giving Congress the power "to limit, regulate, and prohibit the labor of persons under 18 years of age." The word employment was somewhat uncertain, and cases revealed that its use in a statute led to circumvention and "escape from its terms."[60] A critic of the amendment objected: "Under this idiotic and insane proposition a law could be passed under which a mother could be sent to jail for asking her daughter to assist in the family sewing."[61] Shortridge replied: "I mean to say that we must assume some intelligence, some knowledge, some fidelity to duty, some ordinary, common, horse sense in Congress."[62]

Senators rejected several amendments to the House joint resolution, including efforts to exclude workers engaged in agriculture, horticulture, and outdoor employment; to change the age from eighteen to fourteen or from eighteen to sixteen; and to make the amendment inoperable unless ratified by the states within five years.[63] Having disposed of those amendments, the Senate passed the House joint resolution by a vote of 61 to 23, more than two-thirds of the Senators present and voting.[64] The constitutional amendment attracted the support of a number of states, but it looked unlikely that it would reach the required three-fourths majority. How would the Supreme Court prevail in this legislative-judicial conflict?

By 1937, only twenty-eight of the necessary thirty-six states had ratified the child labor amendment.[65] Throughout much of the 1930s, the Court remained a conservative bulwark against legislative initiatives by Congress and President Franklin D. Roosevelt, but there were signs that some Justices would retire and give Roosevelt his first opportunity to nominate replacements. Ironically, this opportunity occurred soon after Roosevelt lost decisively in his 1937 effort to pack the Court, increasing the number of Justices from nine to fifteen. The Senate Judiciary Committee, controlled by Democrats supposedly loyal to Roosevelt, denounced his proposal and methodically shredded its premises, structure, content, and motivation.[66]

59. Id. at 10142. For Senate debate: 65 Cong. Rec. 9597–98, 9600–03, 9858–64, 9866–68, 9962–77, 9991–10012, 10073–104, 10105–29, 10139–42.

60. Id.

61. Id. at 10089 (Senator Reed of Missouri).

62. Id. at 10096.

63. Id. at 10106–42.

64. Id. at 10142.

65. Vile, Encyclopedia of Constitutional Amendments, at 61–63.

66. S. Rept. No. 711, 75th Cong., 1st Sess. 3 (1937). See William E. Leuchtenburg, The Supreme Court Reborn: The Constitutional Revolution in the Age of Roosevelt (1995).

Shortly before Roosevelt offered his ill-starred proposal, the Court had begun to modify some of its earlier rulings. On March 29, 1937, it upheld a state law establishing a minimum wage law for women, basically reversing a decision handed down ten months earlier.[67] This reversal occurred because of a change in position by Justice Owen Roberts, leading some to refer to the "switch in time that saved nine." However, Roberts had already broken with his laissez-faire colleagues. In 1934, he wrote the opinion for a 5–4 Court in *Nebbia v. New York*, upholding a New York price-setting statute.[68] With his support, the Court was prepared to sustain minimum wage legislation in the fall of 1936 but delayed the ruling because of Justice Stone's illness. Late in 1936, Roberts voted with the liberals to affirm a state unemployment insurance law.[69]

In early 1937, Congress passed legislation to provide full judicial pay during retirement. With that enticement, Justice Van Devanter stepped down on June 2, 1937, giving Roosevelt his first chance in more than four years to nominate a Justice to the Supreme Court. He chose Hugo Black. In 1938, Justice Sutherland retired, replaced by Stanley Reed. The retirements of Justices Brandeis and Cardozo led to the appointments of William Douglas and Felix Frankfurter in 1939. The next year, Justice Butler's death permitted Roosevelt to place Frank Murphy on the Court. In 1941, with the retirement of Charles Evans Hughes as Chief Justice, Roosevelt nominated Justice Stone for that position. Robert Jackson filled Stone's slot as Associate Justice. Justice McReynolds retired and was replaced by James Byrnes. Of the 1933 Court, only two Justices remained: Stone and Roberts.

In 1937, Congress debated a wage and hour bill that included provisions to regulate child labor. The purpose was to eliminate from interstate commerce the products of "oppressive child labor." The term applied to work by a child under sixteen employed in any occupation, except farming, or a condition of work for a child between sixteen and eighteen in an occupation hazardous or detrimental to his health.[70] One amendment, accepted by the House, stated

67. West Coast Hotel Co. v. Parrish, 300 U.S. 379 (1937), overturning Adkins v. Children's Hospital, 261 U.S. 525 (1923) but "distinguishing" (in fact reversing) Morehead v. New York ex rel. Tipaldo, 298 U.S. 587 (1936).

68. 291 U.S. 502 (1934).

69. W. H. H. Chamberlin, Inc. v. Andrews, 299 U.S. 515, decided Nov. 23, 1936. The Court was equally divided. For Roberts's vote, see John W. Chambers, "The Big Switch: Justice Roberts and the Minimum-Wage Cases," 10 Labor Hist. 44, 57 (1969). See also Felix Frankfurter, "Mr. Justice Roberts," 104 U. Pa. L. Rev. 311 (1955); 2 Merlo J. Pusey, Charles Evans Hughes 757 (1963). For a challenge to Roberts's recollection of key events in 1936, see Clement E. Vose, Constitutional Change: Amendment Politics and Supreme Court Litigation since 1900, at 228–34 (1972).

70. 82 Cong. Rec. 1798 (1937), statement by Representative Fitzgerald of Connecticut. Further debate on the child-labor provisions appears at 1775–83, 1821–24, 1829.

that child-labor restrictions did not apply to any child engaged in profes-sional acting in motion pictures.[71] At the end of the debate, on December 17, the House voted 216 to 198 to recommit the bill to the House Labor Committee.[72]

On May 23, 1938, Congress resumed debate on the wage and hour bill, and this time the provision for child labor prevailed. The motion to discharge the bill from the House Rules Committee passed 322 to 73.[73] No child under the age of sixteen could be employed other than by a parent or a person stand-ing in place of a parent, except by special certificate issued by the Chief of the Children's Bureau. Children between sixteen and eighteen may not work in occupations deemed hazardous by the Children's Bureau.[74] As to pros-pects for judicial review, Representative George J. Schneider of Wisconsin re-marked that "this method of child-labor control is not likely to meet with any objection of the Supreme Court."[75] The House passed the bill 314 to 97.[76]

The bill went to conference and the Senate agreed to it by voice vote.[77] The child labor provisions were identical to the House bill.[78] On agreeing to the conference report, the House voted 291–39.[79] The Fair Labor Standards Act of 1938 defined "oppressive child labor" to apply to anyone under sixteen who works for an employer (other than a parent or a person standing in place of a parent, employing his own child or one in his custody, other than manu-facturing or mining), or any employee between sixteen and eighteen who works in an occupation declared by the Chief of the Children's Bureau to be "particularly hazardous" or "detrimental to their health or well-being." The Bureau could also decide that oppressive child labor for employees between fourteen and sixteen, other than for manufacturing and mining, would not exist if the Bureau determined that such employment "is confined to periods which will not interfere with their schooling and to conditions which will not interfere with their health and well-being."[80] The statute prohibited any producer, manufacturer, or dealer from shipping in commerce any goods pro-duced in a U.S. establishment by oppressive child labor.[81] The statute did not

71. Id. at 1779–80.
72. Id. at 1834–35.
73. 83 Cong. Rec. 7278–79 (1938).
74. Id. at 7280. This floor statement says that no child under fourteen "may be employed at all other than by a person standing in place of a parent or a parent, or except in agriculture." That language does not appear in the statute.
75. Id. at 7400. For further House debate on child labor: id. at 7441–42.
76. Id. at 7449–50.
77. Id. at 9178.
78. Id. at 9257.
79. Id. at 9266–67.
80. 52 Stat. 1061, sec. 3(1) (1938).
81. Id. at 1067, sec. 12 (a).

apply to any employee who works in agriculture "while not legally required to attend school, or to any child employed as an actor in motion pictures or theatrical productions."[82]

In 1940, a district court in Georgia held the statute to be unconstitutional because the activity within the state was not "interstate commerce" subject to the control of Congress. The court accepted the Supreme Court's position in *Hammer v. Dagenhart* that the "manufacture" of goods is not commerce.[83] A year later, a reconstituted (and chastened) Supreme Court reversed the district court and not only upheld the child labor provision but did so *unanimously*. A brief opinion by Justice Harlan Fiske Stone noted that "while manufacture is not of itself interstate commerce, the shipment of manufactured goods interstate is such commerce and the prohibition of such shipment by Congress is indubitably a regulation of the commerce."[84] What was struck down by a 5–4 Court in 1918 was now—without the slightest doubt—constitutional. Stone deferred fully to the judgment of members of Congress.

Stone remarked that a broad reading of the commerce power, in place since *Gibbons v. Ogden* in 1824, had been upended "by a bare majority" of the Court in *Hammer v. Dagenhart*.[85] He said the reasoning advanced in *Dagenhart* "was novel when made and unsupported by any provision of the Constitution" and has "long since been abandoned."[86] His statement stands as a striking repudiation to both judicial finality and judicial competence. A 5–4 decision in *Dagenhart* found no support from any provision in the Constitution. To Stone, the "conclusion is inescapable" that *Dagenhart* "was a departure from the principles which have prevailed in the interpretation of the Commerce Clause both before and since the decision and that such vitality, as a precedent, as it then had has long since been exhausted. It should be and now is overruled."[87] The capacity of the Court to reverse itself, after issuing a ruling that provokes intense criticism in the public arena, is apparent in the flag-salute cases of 1940 and 1943.

Compulsory Flag Salutes

Flag-salute ceremonies in American public schools are a product of wartime. The first mandatory salute was adopted in New York in 1898, one day after

82. Id. at 1068, sec. 13 (c).
83. United States v. F. W. Darby Lumber Co, 32 F. Supp. 734, 736 (S.D. Ga. 1940).
84. United States v. Darby, 312 U.S. 100, 113 (1941).
85. Id. at 115.
86. Id. at 116.
87. Id. at 116–17.

the United States declared war on Spain.[88] Only five states enacted flag-salute laws before World War I, but by 1935 eighteen states had adopted such laws and hundreds of local school boards in other states did the same.[89] In Nazi Germany, Jehovah's Witnesses objected to compulsory flag salutes and the raised-palm Fascist salute, considering them a violation of their religious beliefs not to bow down to secular objects. On Hitler's orders, the Witnesses were banned, and more than ten thousand were sent to concentration camps. Because of that prosecution, the leader of American Witnesses denounced the compulsory flag salute in 1935.[90]

In 1940, a commanding 8–1 majority of the Supreme Court upheld a compulsory flag salute in Pennsylvania that forced children in public schools to violate their religious beliefs. The case originated when the children of a Jehovah's Witnesses family objected that the flag salute violated their interpretation of this biblical provision in Exodus 20:4–5: "Thou shalt not make unto thee any graven image, or any likeness of any thing that is in heaven above, or that is in the earth beneath, or that is in the water under the earth. Thou shalt now bow thyself to them, nor serve under them."

In the Lower Courts

In 1937, a federal district court declared the Pennsylvania law unconstitutional. The case involved two public school students: Lillian Gobitas and her brother William. The family name, incorrectly spelled Gobitis early in the litigation, retained the misspelling at every stage thereafter and will be followed here.[91] Their refusal to salute the flag led school authorities to charge them with insubordination and order their expulsion. Their father told the court he was financially unable to pay for the expense of private schooling.[92]

The Pennsylvania Constitution, drawing from the state's rich tradition of religious liberty, provided this guiding principle: "All men have a natural and infeasible right to worship Almighty God according to the dictates of their own consciences; . . . no human authority can, in any case whatever, control of

88. David R. Manwaring, Render unto Caesar: The Flag-Salute Controversy 3 (1962).

89. Peter Irons, The Courage of Their Convictions: Sixteen Americans Who Fought Their Way to the Supreme Court 16 (1988).

90. Id.; Manwaring, Render unto Caesar, at 30–31. See also Leonard A. Stevens, Salute! The Case of the Bible vs. the Flag (1973).

91. Shawn Francis Peters, Judging Jehovah's Witnesses: Religious Persecution and the Dawn of the Rights Revolution 19 (2000).

92. Gobitis v. Minersville School Dist., 21 F. Supp. 581, 583 (E.D. Pa. 1937).

interfere with the rights of conscience."[93] To the district court, the individual "must be the judge of the validity of his own religious beliefs. Liberty of conscience means liberty for each individual to decide for himself what is to him religious." That personal judgment must be accepted by the state unless it appeared to raise questions of public safety, health, morals, property, or personal rights, which the court said the state had not shown. Allowing public officers to override the individual "would be to sound the death knell of religious liberty."[94] The court pointed to religious intolerance that was "again rearing its ugly head in other parts of the world," including the policy of anti-Semitism in Nazi Germany.[95]

In upholding this decision in 1939, the Third Circuit agreed that children "can and have been forced to learn Latin," but it found no grounds for compelling a flag salute, which could cancel "the very affection sought to be instilled." Students of educational psychology, it said, warned against "overemphasis of the flag salute."[96] The Third Circuit was unable to detect "the essential relationship between infant patriotism and the martial spirit."[97]

The Supreme Court accepted the case on March 4, 1940.[98] Attorneys for the school district argued that the flag salute was designed only to "inculcate patriotism" and had no relationship to any religious observance. Saluting the flag merely acknowledged "the *temporal* sovereignty of this nation and has nothing whatsoever to do with a person's religious feelings."[99] The school district noted that when the Gobitis children and their father were in court "they arose and stood at attention at the opening and closing of court," without claiming that such conduct offended their religious beliefs.[100] However, they did not *salute* the court.

The brief for the Jehovah's Witnesses objected that the "form of the salute is very much like that of the Nazi régime in Germany."[101] Compelling citizens to violate their conscience "is one of the chief rules enforced by the Corporate or Totalitarian States."[102] In Europe in the 1930s, the policy of "saluting flags

93. Id. at 584.
94. Id.
95. Id. at 586. See also Gobitis v. Minersville School Dist., 24 F. Supp. 271 (E.D. Pa. 1938).
96. Minersville School Dist. v. Gobitis, 108 F.2d 683, 691 (3d Cir. 1939).
97. Id. at 692.
98. Minersville School Dist. v. Gobitis, cert. granted, March 4, 1940, 309 U.S. 645 (1940).
99. Petitioners' Brief in Support of Petition for Writ of Certiorari; 37 Landmark Briefs 323–25 (emphasis in original).
100. Brief for Petitioners, 37 Landmark Briefs 363.
101. Respondents' Brief, Landmark Briefs 375.
102. Id. at 384.

and 'heiling' men is a movement to compel the people to recognize the State as before or superior to Almighty God."[103] The brief did not question the need for loyalty: "Should not all citizens be loyal to the country in which they live? Emphatically yes."[104] Two briefs filed by the American Civil Liberties Union and the American Bar Association concluded that school authorities had violated the children's sincerely held religious belief.[105]

Given political conditions in the country, particularly the looming war in Europe, Witnesses feared that their objection to the flag salute would expose them to persecution from groups who considered them unpatriotic. During the spring of 1940, with the German army moving across Europe, the Justice Department received reports of hundreds of attacks against Jehovah's Witnesses in America from June 12 to June 20.[106] On May 23, a mob in Del Rio, Texas, assaulted three Witnesses as supposed Nazi agents.[107]

The Supreme Court Decides

On June 3, 1940, on the last day of the Court's term, Justice Frankfurter upheld the school board. Joined by seven colleagues, he began with this general principle: "Certainly the affirmative pursuit of one's convictions about the ultimate mystery of the universe and man's relation to it is placed beyond the reach of law. Government may not interfere with organized or individual expression of belief or disbelief."[108] He proceeded to undermine that principle on the following page: "But to affirm that the freedom to follow conscience has itself no limits in the life of a society would deny that very plurality of principles which, as a matter of history, underlies protection of religious toleration."[109]

The task of the Court, he said, was to "reconcile two rights in order to prevent either from destroying the other." In safeguarding conscience, "we are dealing with interests so subtle and so dear, every possible leeway should be given to the claims of religious faith."[110] As his analysis unfolded, there would be no reconciliation and no leeway to individual rights. Government had a right to subordinate religious liberty to the claimed needs of the state.

103. Id. at 391–92.
104. Id. at 398.
105. Id. at 413–504.
106. Victor W. Rotnem & F. G. Folsom, Jr., "Recent Restrictions upon Religious Liberty," 36 Am. Pol. Sci. Rev. 1053, 1061 (1942).
107. Francis H. Heller, "A Turning Point for Religious Liberty," 29 Va. L. Rev. 440, 447 (1943).
108. Minersville School District v. Gobitis, 310 U.S. 586, 593 (1940).
109. Id. at 594.
110. Id.

He relied on several principles. First, religious liberty "has never excluded legislation of general scope not directed against doctrinal loyalties of particular sects." Second, conscientious scruples have never relieved the individual from obeying laws "not aimed at the promotion or restriction of religious beliefs." Third, the possession of religious convictions that conflict with "the relevant concerns of a political society does not relieve the citizen from the discharge of political responsibilities." Fourth, religious beliefs could not prevent government from passing laws "essential to secure and maintain that orderly, tranquil, and free society without which religious toleration itself is unattainable."[111]

Frankfurter concluded that the Gobitis children had no right to be excused from conduct "required of all the other children in the promotion of national cohesion." The Court was dealing "with an interest inferior to none in the hierarchy of legal values. National unity is the basis of national security."[112] Under his analysis, the flag salute was essential for national cohesion, and national security depended on national unity. National security therefore trumped religious freedom.

Frankfurter turned to a question posed by President Abraham Lincoln: "Must a government of necessity be too *strong* for the liberties of its people, or too *weak* to maintain its own existence?"[113] To Frankfurter, all activities of government "presuppose the existence of an organized political society," and the "ultimate foundation of a free society is the binding tie of cohesive sentiments." He viewed the American flag as the "symbol of national unity, transcending all internal differences, however large, within the framework of the Constitution." From a 1907 Supreme Court decision, he said the flag signified government resting on "the consent of the governed; liberty regulated by law; the protection of the weak against the strong; security against the exercise of arbitrary power; and absolute safety for free institutions against foreign aggression."[114]

For the Gobitis children, the compulsory flag salute did not rest on the consent of the governed or protect the weak against the strong. Furthermore, the 1907 ruling had no application to religious beliefs. It concerned a Nebraska law that punished the use of the American flag to advertise the sale of products, in this case a company that printed the flag on a bottle of beer. Frankfurter's reference to Lincoln was misleading. Lincoln did not subordinate religious liberty to national security. As explained in the next chapter, when Jews during the Civil War objected to a statute that required military

111. Id. at 594–95.
112. Id. at 595
113. Id. at 596 (emphases in original).
114. Id., citing Halter v. Nebraska, 205 U.S. 34, 43 (1907).

chaplains to be from a "Christian denomination," Lincoln recognized the error in the statute. Congress changed it to "some religious denomination" to permit Jewish military units to have a chaplain of their own faith.

Frankfurter attempted to minimize judicial authority. The wisdom of training schoolchildren to follow patriotic impulses "is not for our independent judgment."[115] But it was. In another effort at judicial modesty: "the courtroom is not the arena for debating issues of educational policy."[116] If so, why not sidestep the case by calling it a political question best left to the elected branches? Frankfurter added: "The preciousness of the family relation, the authority and independence which give dignity to parenthood, indeed the enjoyment of all freedom, presuppose the kind of ordered society which is summarized by our flag."[117] Translation: the state may override family and parental values.

In closing, Frankfurter said that although judicial review represented a fundamental part of the constitutional system, "to the legislature no less than to courts is committed the guardianship of deeply-cherished liberties."[118] As this book underscores, individual liberties left unprotected in the courts have often been safeguarded by legislative activity, at both the national and state levels. Justice McReynolds concurred "in the result," without saying why.[119] Perhaps he wanted to distance himself from some of the reasons advanced by Frankfurter.

Justice Stone penned the only dissent. Several other Justices had substantial misgivings about Frankfurter's opinion but initially kept silent. Stone conceded that the constitutional guarantees of personal liberty "are not always absolute" and that government may compel citizens to serve in the military.[120] But it was "a long step, and one which I am unable to take, to the position that government may, as a supposed educational measure and as a means of disciplining the young, compel public affirmations which violate their religious conscience."[121] Even if one believed the flag salute contributes to national unity, "there are other ways to teach loyalty and patriotism which are the sources of national unity, than by compelling the pupil to affirm that which he does not believe and by commanding a form of affirmance which violates his religious convictions."[122]

115. Id.
116. Id.
117. Id. at 600.
118. Id.
119. Id. at 601.
120. Id. at 602.
121. Id.
122. Id. at 6503–4.

Stone warned: "History teaches us that there have been but few infringements of personal liberty by the state which have not been justified, as they are here, in the name of righteousness and the public good, and few which have not been directed, as they are now, at politically helpless minorities."[123] He objected to Frankfurter's belief that such matters are best left to the political process outside the courts: "This seems to me no less than the surrender of the constitutional protection of the liberty of small minorities to the popular will."[124]

Despite the vigor of Stone's dissent, it had little impact on the other Justices. According to his law clerk, Allison Dunham, Stone entered the conference room intending to defend the religious freedom of the Jehovah's Witnesses but did not reveal his position, nor did he circulate his dissent sufficiently early to attract votes to his side.[125] Had he spoken up at conference and expressed his dissenting views, he might have drawn some allies.[126] As relative newcomers to the Court, Hugo Black, William Douglas, and Frank Murphy decided to defer to Frankfurter. By the time they saw Stone's dissent, they felt it was too late to abandon Frankfurter.[127] Initially, Murphy drafted a dissent but did not circulate it.[128] Had Stone articulated his views at conference, Murphy might have joined him.[129] It has been well said that *Gobitis* "presents a case study in judicial misperceptions and breakdown in communication among the Justices."[130]

Having Second Thoughts

Far from accepting the Court's decision as the exclusive and final word on the meaning of individual rights, Frankfurter's opinion was excoriated by law journals, the press, religious organizations, and the general public. The *New Republic*, which Frankfurter helped found, warned that the country was "in great danger of adopting Hitler's philosophy in the effort to oppose Hitler's legions." The Court was imperiling "religious liberty in the interest of the

123. Id. at 604.
124. Id. at 606.
125. Alpheus Thomas Mason, Harlan Fiske Stone: Pillar of the Law 527–28 (1956). See also asterisked note on page 528.
126. Alice Fleetwood Bartee, Cases Lost, Causes Won: The Supreme Court and the Judicial Process 64 (1984).
127. William O. Douglas, The Court Years, 1939–75, at 45 (1981).
128. J. Woodford Howard, Jr., Mr. Justice Murphy: A Political Biography 251 (1968); Peters, Judging Jehovah's Witnesses, at 65–66.
129. Bartee, Cases Lost, Causes Won, at 65.
130. Id. at 53.

American state," coming "dangerously close to being a victim of [war] hysteria."[131] A separate article added some sarcasm: "Already Mr. Justice Frankfurter has been heroically saving America from a couple of school children whose devotion to Jehovah would have been compromised by a salute to the flag."[132] Out of thirty-nine law reviews that discussed *Gobitis*, thirty-one were critical, while newspapers condemned the Court for violating individual rights and buckling to popular prejudices and war hysteria.[133] Editorials in 171 newspapers tore apart Frankfurter's reasoning.[134]

Following release of the Court's decision, Jehovah's Witnesses were subjected to a wave of violence. By one estimate, the persecution of Witnesses from 1941 to 1943 marked the greatest outbreak of religious intolerance in twentieth-century America.[135] Branded as disloyal, they were subjected to arrests, forced marches, threats, beatings, vandalism, arson, and destruction of their buildings and property.[136] Black, Douglas, and Murphy came to regret joining the majority without forming—and voicing—independent views. Toward the end of the summer, Douglas told Frankfurter that Black was having second thoughts about his vote. With satire, Frankfurter asked whether Black had been reading the Constitution. "No," Douglas replied, "he has been reading the papers."[137]

According to another account, "the rush of work at the term's close prevented the justices' looking at [Stone's] dissent until after the opinion came down."[138] Black told an obituary writer in 1967 that "we knew we were wrong, but we didn't have time to change our opinions. We met around the swimming pool at Murphy's hotel and decided to do so as soon as we could."[139] The author of this account said that, "over a half century later, Black's excuse still sounds lame. He never needed anyone to join him to take a stand he believed in."[140]

Given the criticism leveled at *Gobitis*, state courts in New Hampshire, New Jersey, and Kansas dismissed Frankfurter's opinion and offered greater protection to schoolchildren who cited religious reasons for not saluting the flag.[141]

---

131. "Frankfurter v. Stone," New Republic, June 24, 1940, at 843–44.

132. Walton Hamilton & George Braden, "The Supreme Court Today," New Republic, Aug. 5, 1940, at 180.

133. Manwaring, Render unto Caesar, at 158–60; Heller, "A Turning Point for Religious Liberty," at 452–53.

134. Mason, Harlan Fiske Stone, at 532.

135. John T. Noonan, Jr., The Believer and the Powers That Are 251 (1987).

136. Peters, Judging Jehovah's Witnesses, at 72–123.

137. H. N. Hirsch, The Enigma of Felix Frankfurter 152 (1981).

138. Roger K. Newman, Hugo Black: A Biography 284 (1997).

139. Id.

140. Id. at 284–85.

141. State v. Lefebvre, 20 A.2d 185 (N.H. 1941); In re Latrecchia, 26 A.2d 881 (N.J. 1942); State v. Smith, 127 P.2d 518 (Kans. 1942).

In 1942, Justices Black, Douglas, and Murphy publicly announced that *Gobitis* was "wrongly decided."[142] The 8–1 majority now fell to 5–4. Chief Justice Hughes had retired in 1941, succeeded by Stone. Two Justices who had joined with Frankfurter (Byrnes and Roberts) were replaced with Wiley Rutledge and Robert H. Jackson. Rutledge's opinions on the D.C. Circuit suggested he would vote against Frankfurter.[143]

Legislation passed by Congress on June 22, 1942, further undermined *Gobitis*. When pledging allegiance to the flag, the statute required individuals to stand "with the right hand over the heart; extending the right hand, palm upward, toward the flag at the words 'to the flag' and holding this position until the end, when the hand drops to the side." Congress also provided an alternative: "civilians will always show full respect to the flag when the pledge is given by merely standing at attention, men removing the headdress."[144] In citing this statute to demonstrate that *Gobitis* had lost its authority, the Justice Department emphasized that Witnesses had no objection to standing at attention during a flag-salute exercise.[145] Moreover, compliance with the statute was wholly voluntary. It provided rules and customs pertaining "to the display and use of the flag, without penalty for violations."[146]

By the time the flag-salute issue returned to the Court in the fall of 1942, *Gobitis* continued to lose credibility in the lower courts. A federal district court in West Virginia ruled that the state could not compel the children of Jehovah's Witnesses to salute the flag in public schools. It rejected *Gobitis* "as binding authority" for this reason: "Of the seven Justices now members of the Supreme Court who participated in that decision, four have given public expression to the opinion that it is unsound."[147]

On June 14, 1943, for a 6–3 majority, Justice Jackson held that the mandatory flag salute for public school children violated the First and Fourteenth Amendments.[148] In reversing *Gobitis*, Jackson skillfully and eloquently defended individual freedom and religious liberty, but credit for the reversal also belongs to individuals who refused to accept Frankfurter's analysis. Citizens around the country told the Court it did not understand the Constitution, minority rights, or religious freedom. Their independent voices

142. Jones v. Opelika, 316 U.S. 584, 624 (1942).
143. Busey v. District of Columbia, 129 F.2d 24, 38 (D.C. Cir. 1942).
144. 56 Stat. 380, sec. 7 (1942). The alternative did not appear in the original House bill; it was added by the Senate. 88 Cong. Rec. 3722 (sec. 5), 5212 (sec. 7), and S. Rept. No. 1477, at 2 (1942).
145. Rotnem & Folsom, "Recent Restrictions upon Religious Liberty," at 1064.
146. 88 Cong. Rec. 3721 (1942), statement by Representative Hobbs.
147. Barnette v. West Virginia State Board of Ed., 47 F. Supp. 251, 253 (D. W.Va. 1942).
148. West Virginia Board of Education v. Barnette, 319 U.S. 624 (1943).

persuaded Black, Douglas, and Murphy to reconsider their position and switch sides.

Jackson began his decision by examining Frankfurter's dependence on this question from Lincoln: "Must a government of necessity be too *strong* for the liberties of its people, or too *weak* to maintain its own existence?" To Jackson, it "may be doubted whether Mr. Lincoln would have thought that the strength of government to maintain itself would be impressively vindicated by our confirming power of the State to expel a handful of children from school."[149] Routinely siding with government to protect its existence "would resolve every issue of power in favor of those in authority and would require us to override every liberty thought to weaken or delay execution of their policies."[150]

He then examined the "very heart" of *Gobitis*: that "national unity is the basis of national security," that government authorities have "the right to select appropriate means for its attainment," and that compulsory measures toward "national unity" are constitutional.[151] If using more moderate means to attain unity falls short, greater government pressure will be applied, "so strife becomes more bitter." The "ultimate futility" to compel coherence recalled for Jackson the Roman drive to "stamp out Christianity as a disturber of its pagan unity, the Inquisition, as a means of religious and dynastic unity," and other efforts of totalitarian regimes. Those who begin coercive elimination of dissent "soon find themselves exterminating dissenters." Compulsory uniformity of opinion "achieves only the unanimity of the graveyard."[152]

To Jackson, the belief that patriotism will not flourish if patriotic ceremonies "are voluntary and spontaneous instead of a compulsory routine is to make an unflattering estimate of the appeal of our institutions to free minds."[153] Freedom to differ "is not limited to things that do not matter much." That would be "a mere shadow of freedom." The test of the right to differ is "to things that touch the heart of the existing order."[154]

Jackson's opinion, while widely admired, has some limitations. He said the very purpose of a Bill of Rights "was to withdraw certain subjects from the vicissitudes of political controversy, to place them beyond the reach of majorities and officials and to establish them as legal principles to be applied by the courts."[155] Further: "One's right to life, liberty, and property, to free

149. Id. at 636.
150. Id.
151. Id. at 640.
152. Id. at 641.
153. Id.
154. Id. at 642.
155. Id. at 638.

speech, a free press, freedom of worship and assembly, and other fundamental rights may not be submitted to vote; they depend on the outcome of no elections."[156] This is the language of judicial monopoly, placing the ultimate protection of all individual rights not with elected government but with the Supreme Court. The record, however, demonstrates that many freedoms of blacks, women, children, and other minorities were secured by the elected branches, not the courts.

Another Jackson passage is frequently praised: "If there is any fixed star in our constitutional constellation, it is that no official, high or petty, can prescribe what shall be orthodox in politics, nationalism, religion, or other matters of opinion or force citizens to confess by word or act their faith therein. If there are any circumstances which permit an exception, they do not now occur to us."[157] In a democracy, there is much to be said for that sentiment, but often the Supreme Court attempts to decide what is orthodox when it pretends to release a decision that presents the final and exclusive word on the Constitution. The 8–1 ruling in Gobitis failed, as have many other decisions, including *Dred Scott*, the 1883 *Civil Rights Cases*, *Plessy*, *Lochner*, the 1918 and 1922 child-labor cases, and the trimester framework announced in *Roe v. Wade*. The true lesson of *Gobitis* is that no official—including those in the judiciary—may prescribe what is orthodox for the country.

In the 1943 flag-salute case, Justices Roberts and Reed adhered to *Gobitis*, without providing additional views.[158] Justices Black and Douglas concurred in Jackson's opinion, stating they were "substantially" in agreement without identifying parts they found inadequate or unpersuasive. Their main purpose was to explain why they initially joined *Gobitis*. Similarly, a concurrence by Justice Murphy shed light on why he now thought the 1940 decision was defective: "Reflection has convinced me that as a judge I have no loftier duty or responsibility than to uphold that spiritual freedom to its farthest reaches."[159]

The dissent by Justice Frankfurter is intensely personal, starting with a statement about being Jewish: "One who belongs to the most vilified and persecuted minority in history is not likely to be insensible to the freedoms guaranteed by our Constitution." He said if it were purely a matter of personal attitudes he would have "wholeheartedly associated" himself with the Court's opinion, "but as judges we are neither Jew nor gentile, neither Catholic nor agnostic."[160] He was not justified "in writing my private notions of policy into the Constitution, no matter how deeply I may cherish them or how

156. Id.
157. Id. at 642.
158. Id. at 642–43.
159. Id. at 645.
160. Id. at 646–47.

mischievous I may deem their disregard."[161] But where did Frankfurter find the
principle that guided him in *Gobitis*: that in order to have national security we
need national unity, and in order to have national unity we need to compel
children to salute the flag? If that wasn't a private notion, what was it?[162]

Two scholars in 2004 analyzed the flag-salute cases to understand how the
Court could deliver over a period of three years such contradictory rulings. As
they note, seldom in history has a constitutional controversy "generated such
antipathy within the Court, such widespread civil violence directly attribut-
able to a judicial decision, such anticipatory public recanting by individual
justices," and such "a daring switch of rationale."[163] In part they say: "Majoritarian institutions cannot always be counted on to respect the 'freedom
of mind and spirit.'"[164] That has been true at times of Congress and other
legislative bodies, but it was true about the Supreme Court in 1940, deliver-
ing a majority decision of eight Justices with only one dissent.

161. Id. at 647.
162. See Richard Danzig, "Justice Frankfurter's Opinions in the Flag Salute Cases: Blending
Logic and Psychologic in Constitutional Decisionmaking," 36 Stan. L. Rev. 675, 678 (1984).
163. Vincent Blasi & Seana V. Shriffin, "The Story of *West Virginia State Board of Education
v Barnette*: The Pledge of Allegiance and the Freedom of Thought," in Michael C. Dorf, ed.,
Constitutional Law Stories 433 (2004).
164. Id. at 442.

6

PROTECTING RELIGIOUS LIBERTY

Securing an individual's right to believe or not believe in religion has occurred largely outside the courtroom. Though it may seem counterintuitive, the regular political process has safeguarded the religious freedom of minorities as well as—and often better than—the courts. Citizens, legislators, and executive officials have acted jointly to support minority rights left unprotected by the courts. At times, checks to misguided federal court decisions come from rulings by state courts that are more generous to religious freedom. Individual rights are best protected by society as a whole, operating through the political process, aided by vigorous exchanges between federal and state courts.[1]

Constitutional Principles

On June 8, 1789, James Madison told his colleagues in the House of Representatives that he would offer a list of amendments to the Constitution. Among his suggestions was this language, to be inserted in Article I, Section 8, between Clauses 3 and 4: "The civil rights of none shall be abridged on account of religious belief or worship, nor shall any national religion be established, nor shall the full and equal rights of conscience be in any manner, or on any pretext, infringed."[2] Next he proposed language to be inserted in Article I, Section 10, between Clauses 1 and 2: "No State shall violate the equal rights of conscience, or the freedom of the press, or the trial by jury in criminal cases."[3]

The House debated the religion clauses on August 15. The language, reworked by a select committee, read: "No religion shall be established by law, nor shall the equal rights of conscience be infringed."[4] After some initial debate, Madison interpreted the language in this manner: "Congress should not establish a religion, and enforce the legal observation of it by law, nor compel

---

1. For a more detailed analysis of constitutional principles and broad political efforts to protect religious freedom, see Louis Fisher, Religious Liberty in America: Political Safeguards (2002).
2. 1 Annals of Cong. 434 (1789).
3. Id. at 435.
4. Id. at 729.

men to worship God in any manner contrary to their conscience." He said that some of the state conventions looked to the power of Congress to make all laws "necessary and proper" but expressed concern that Congress might make laws "of such a nature as might infringe the rights of conscience, and establish a national religion." To Madison, the amendment was designed to prevent such actions.[5] A motion by Samuel Livermore, altering the language to read that Congress "shall make no laws touching religion, or infringing the rights of conscience," passed on a vote of 31 to 20.[6]

Madison's effort to protect an individual's conscience faced major obstacles. The two chambers resolved their differences and produced language that became the First Amendment: "Congress shall make no law respecting an establishment of religion, or prohibiting the free exercise thereof; or abridging the freedom of speech, or of the press, or the right of the people peaceably to assemble, and to petition the Government for a redress of grievances." House language, prohibiting infringing on the rights of conscience, had been deleted by the Senate.

Conscientious Objectors

Since colonial times, Americans have presented a mix of religious and ethical reasons for refusing to serve in the military. Ethical objectors rely on personal judgments, not a religious or sectarian moral code. However, this constitutional value is often shared broadly within a community. The branch that initially recognized the right of conscientious objectors was the legislature, not the judiciary. Courts arrived late to this constitutional issue, offering rulings that upheld or developed what had already been expressed in statutes and state constitutions. Some Presidents and executive officials came to play important roles in protecting conscientious objectors.

In requiring citizens to serve in the militia, colonies and early state governments granted exceptions for individuals who presented religious objections. Massachusetts in 1661, Rhode Island in 1673, and Pennsylvania in 1757 passed legislation to allow conscientious objectors to perform noncombatant services. A Pennsylvania law provided that all "Quakers, Mennonites, Moravians, and others conscientiously scrupulous of bearing arms" were entitled, upon the call to arms, to assist by extinguishing fires, suppressing the insurrection of slaves and other persons, caring for the wounded, and performing other services.[7] In 1775, the Assembly of Pennsylvania passed legisla-

5. Id. at 730.
6. Id. at 731.
7. U.S. Selective Service System, Conscientious Objection (Special Monograph No. 11, Vol. I) 30 (1950).

tion to create a militia but recognized that "many of the good people of this Province are conscientiously scrupulous of bearing of arms" and urged those willing to join the militia to "bear a tender and brotherly regard toward this class of their fellow-subjects and Countrymen."[8]

On July 18, 1775, while preparing for war against England, the Continental Congress debated plans for a militia. It recommended that all able-bodied men, between the ages of sixteen and fifty, form regular companies. It then announced: "As there are some people, who, from religious principles, cannot bear arms in any case, this Congress intend no violence to their consciences, but earnestly recommend it to them, to contribute liberally in this time of universal calamity, to the relief of their distressed brethren in the several colonies, and to do all other services to their oppressed Country, which they can consistently with their religious principles."[9]

After the Declaration of Independence, a number of state constitutions specifically recognized the rights of conscientious objectors. The 1776 constitution of Pennsylvania provided: "Nor can any man who is conscientiously scrupulous of bearing arms, be justly compelled thereto, if he pay such equivalent."[10] The Vermont Constitution of 1777 stated that no one "conscientiously scrupulous of bearing arms, [may] be justly compelled thereto."[11] The New Hampshire Constitution of 1784 contained language similar to Pennsylvania's.[12] The Maine Constitution of 1819 identified the religious sects entitled to exemption: Quakers and Shakers, "but no other person . . . shall be exempted, unless he shall pay an equivalent, to be fixed by law."[13]

On June 8, 1789, during House consideration of constitutional amendments, Madison offered language on what would be the Second Amendment. His draft language: "The right of the people to keep and bear arms shall not be infringed; a well armed and well regulated militia being the best security of a free country: but no person religiously scrupulous of bearing arms shall be compelled to render military service in person."[14] By August 17, after changes in the draft, the language about conscientious objectors remained.[15]

Elbridge Gerry of Massachusetts objected that the language was too broad, preferring that such persons belong to a particular "religious sect scrupulous

8. Id. at 33. See Lillian Schlissel, ed., Conscience in America: A Documentary History of Conscientious Objection in America, 1757–1967, at 34, 36 (1968).
9. 2 Journals of the Continental Congress 189 (1905).
10. Pa. Const. of 1776, VIII; 8 Swindler 278.
11. Vt. Const. of 1777, Ch. I, IX; 9 Swindler 490.
12. N.H. Const. of 1784, Art. I. XIII; 6 Swindler 345.
13. Me. Const. of 1819, Art. VII, Sec. 5; 4 Swindler 323.
14. 1 Annals of Cong. 434 (1789).
15. Id. at 749.

of being arms." James Jackson of Georgia thought Gerry exaggerated the danger. He did not expect that "all the people of the United States would turn Quakers or Moravians." For those who chose not to participate in the militia, he suggested they pay "an equivalent, to be established by law."[16] Egbert Benson of New York wanted to eliminate the exception for religious objectors, leaving to the "benevolence" of the legislature to grant this privilege by statute. His motion to delete the language failed, 22 to 24.[17] The House language included an exception for persons "religiously scrupulous of bearing arms."[18] As ratified, the Second Amendment provides no exemption for conscientious objectors.

The next year, during debate on the militia bill, Congress again considered an exemption for conscientious objectors, allowing them to pay a certain amount in lieu of military service.[19] Unlike other legislators, Madison did not restrict the exemption to a particular denomination, such as the Quakers. He allowed exceptions for "persons conscientiously scrupulous of bearing arms." William Giles of Virginia spoke against the exemption for Quakers, insisting that every individual had an obligation to contribute to the protection of society. What criteria, he asked, would determine whether someone in good faith operated under the principle of conscience?[20]

On December 23, Madison proposed language to exempt "all persons religiously scrupulous of bearing arms, who shall make a declaration of the same before a civil magistrate, . . . but be liable to a penalty of _____ dollars."[21] On the following day, a majority of lawmakers decided to leave the issue to the states.[22]

The issue of conscientious objection resurfaced during the Civil War. In an 1863 debate on a conscription bill, Senator Ira Harris of New York proposed that all persons "who, being from scruples of conscience averse to bearing arms, are by the constitution of any State excused therefrom."[23] Some states recognized exemptions from military service for Shakers and Quakers in their statutes, but not other individuals. After several Senators raised objections, Harris withdrew his amendment.[24] In the House, lawmakers wanted to exclude conscientious objectors who seemed to be late converts just to avoid military service. A proposal to require that someone be religiously scrupulous

16. Id. at 750.
17. Id. at 749–51.
18. 1 Senate Journal 63–64 (1789).
19. 1 Annals of Cong. 1869–73 (1790).
20. Id. at 1871–73.
21. Id. at 1874.
22. Id. at 1875.
23. Cong. Globe, 37th Cong., 3d Sess. 994 (1863).
24. Id.

for a set period of time, such as one year or three years, was voted down, 18 to 95.[25] A Senate amendment required someone seeking an exemption to petition a federal judge. If granted an exemption, the individual would have to contribute toward "any public hospital or charitable service, a peace offering in accordance with his means." That proposal failed, 8 to 32.[26]

The conscription bill that gained passage made no mention of conscientious objection.[27] However, Quakers and other individuals could seek relief under another section of the law. Any person drafted and notified to appear for military service may "furnish an acceptable substitute to take his place in the draft" or pay an amount not to exceed $300. Those who found a substitute or paid cash "shall be discharged from further liability under that draft."[28] Quakers had long opposed slavery but did not believe that war was the proper remedy. The Society of Friends drafted language that Quakers could present to draft boards, relying on this provision of the law.[29]

Quakers met with members of Congress to discuss national policy toward military service. Legislation enacted in 1864 dealt specifically with conscientious objectors. An exemption applied to members of "religious denominations" who by oath or affirmation declare conscientious opposition to the bearing of arms and "are prohibited from doing so by the rules and articles of faith and practices of said religious denomination." Through this process they became noncombatants. The Secretary of War could assign them to duty in hospitals or to the care of freedmen, or they "shall pay the sum of three hundred dollars" to be applied to the "benefit of the sick and wounded soldiers."[30]

Those safeguards for religious minorities came from the regular political process, reached by majority vote, with no input from the courts. Quakers and other religious groups learned they could meet with members of Congress and executive officials to shape national policy. President Lincoln, when pressed to compel Quakers, Mennonites, and other conscientious objectors to take up arms, refused: "No, I will not do that. These people do not believe in war. People who do not believe in war make poor soldiers. Besides, the attitude of these people has always been against slavery. If all our people held the same view about slavery as these people there would be no war. . . . We will leave them on their farms where they are at home and where they will make their contributions better than they would with a gun."[31]

25. Id. at 1261, 1292.
26. Id. at 1389–90.
27. 12 Stat. 731 (1863).
28. Id. at 733, sec. 13.
29. Edward Needles Wright, Conscientious Objectors in the Civil War 15–16, 69–70 (1931).
30. 13 Stat. 9, sec. 17 (1864).
31. U.S. Selective Service System, Conscientious Objection, at 42–43.

Pacifism after World War I

America's entry into World War I in 1917 ushered in a new period of debate over conscientious objectors. Unlike the conscription statutes for the Civil War, Congress did not allow citizens to hire substitutes or pay a set fee. However, the rights of conscientious objectors were recognized from the start, with distinctions drawn between combatant and noncombatant duties. The National Defense Act of 1916 identified various exemption from military duty, including acquiring the status of noncombatant for all persons of religious belief "if the conscientious holding of such belief by such person shall be established under such regulations as the President shall prescribe." It added: "no person so exempted shall be exempt from militia service in any capacity that the President shall declare to be noncombatant."[32]

In the bill reported by the House Committee on Military Affairs in 1916, the section on conscientious objection did not require membership in a religious group. It read: "all persons who because of religious beliefs are exempted by the laws of the respective States and Territories shall be exempt from militia duty without regard to age."[33] Later versions of the bill distinguished between combatant and noncombatant duties.[34] After the United States entered World War I in April 1917, Congress required conscientious objectors to be a member "of any well-recognized religious sect or organization at present organized and existing and whose existing creed or principles forbid its members to participate in war in any form."[35]

During congressional debate on this provision, several lawmakers objected to language requiring conscientious objectors to belong to a religious sect. They offered broader language to permit anyone conscientiously opposed to military service to be exempt from serving. Those efforts in the House and Senate failed.[36] The accompanying committee reports did not elaborate on the section on religious exemption.[37]

Instead of fully deciding national policy on conscientious objectors, Congress left many issues to the President and his advisers. On March 20, 1918, President Woodrow Wilson issued an executive order establishing guidelines

32. 39 Stat. 197, sec. 59 (1916).
33. H.R. 12766, 64th Cong., 1st Sess. 49 (lines 8–10), as reported by the House Committee on Military Affairs.
34. H. Rept. No. 695, 64th Cong., 1st Sess. 38 (1916); S. Doc. No. 442, 64th Cong., 1st Sess. 38 (1916).
35. 40 Stat. 78, sec. 4 (1917).
36. 55 Cong. Rec. 1473, 1476–79, 1528–33 (1917).
37. H. Rept. No. 17, 65th Cong., 1st Sess. (1917); H. Rept. No. 49, 65th Cong., 1st Sess. (1917); H. Rept. No. 52, 65th Cong., 1st Sess. (1917); H. Rept. No. 53, 65th Cong., 1st Sess. (1917).

for the kinds of noncombatant duties to be available to conscientious objectors. Duties included service in the Medical Corps, the Quartermaster Corps, and the engineer service. Section 3 of Wilson's order broadened the category of conscientious objectors to include those "who profess religious or other conscientious scruples." This created two categories: "religious objector" and "individual objector."[38] For the latter, persons would serve in noncombatant positions. Sentences imposed by court-martial included confinement in Disciplinary Barracks but not in a penitentiary.[39]

Harlan F. Stone, later to serve on the Supreme Court as Associate Justice and Chief Justice, wrote an article in 1919 describing his experience with the board that reviewed claims by men who refused military service on grounds of conscience. At that time he served as dean of the Columbia Law School. He began his article by saying that until 1917 "we knew little of the conscientious objector in this country."[40] In fact, from colonial times forward, much was known about conscientious objectors in the United States. Stone used harsh terms for those who objected to military service on grounds of conscience: "sheer stupidity," "cowards and slackers," "sublime egoists," "glib talkers," "loose-thinking," "wild-talking," and "muddle-headed."[41] For those from such religious sects as Dunkards, Mennonites, and Hutterites, he described them as "bovine-faced."[42]

One of the conscientious objectors who appeared before Stone's board wrote to him later when he was Associate Justice, posing various challenges to Stone's views on religious liberty. Stone replied that "inasmuch as I must live in and be a part of organized society, the majority must rule."[43] Did Stone believe in a society and a Constitution that made no room for minority rights and individual conscience? As explained in chapter 5, he later rejected that position in the compulsory flag-salute case in 1940.

With World War I, the issue of conscientious objection began to reach federal courts in a number of cases. The 1917 draft law faced challenges on the ground that the exemption for conscientious objectors was repugnant to the First Amendment by establishing or interfering with religion. A year later, a unanimous Supreme Court found no merit to the complaint. Chief Justice White merely said he found the argument so strained that "its unsoundness is too apparent to require us to do more."[44] In 1918, the Second Circuit

38. Walter Guest Kellogg, The Conscientious Objector 22 (1919).
39. Executive Order 2823 (March 20, 1918).
40. Harlan F. Stone, "The Conscientious Objector," 21 Colum. U. Q. 254 (1919).
41. Id. at 254, 264–65, 266, 269.
42. Id. at 262.
43. Alpheus Thomas Mason, Harlan Fiske Stone: Pillar of the Law 105 (1956).
44. Selective Draft Law Cases, 245 U.S. 366, 389–90 (1918).

decided the case of someone who had been convicted after asserting that the status of conscientious objector applied as much to a nonreligious objector as to a religious objector. The court affirmed his conviction.[45]

That judicial position found little support in society. In preparation for World War II, American churches defended the right of their members to object to participating in wars, and individuals understood they could be conscientious objectors without belonging to a religious organization.[46] In 1940, Raymond Wilson, a Quaker, testified at a House hearing that the statutory phrase "well-recognized religious sect" benefited his denomination but he did not believe they had "any right of preferential treatment." Wilson urged consideration "on the basis of conscience rather than on the basis of membership."[47] Amos Horst, a Mennonite, asked the House to use the words "any person" to cover someone conscientiously opposed to participating in war.[48] Other religious organizations wanted the exemption to military service to apply to individuals, not members of particular sects.[49]

The Selective Training and Service Act of 1940 contained exemptions for military service, including anyone who "by reason of religious training and belief, is conscientiously opposed to war in any form." Unlike the language of the World War I statutes, it was not necessary to be a member of a religious organization. If an individual opposed military service, he could be assigned to work "of national importance under civilian direction."[50]

As to judicial involvement, the Supreme Court in 1931 upheld the government's action in denying an application for U.S. citizenship by someone who promised to bear arms only if he believed the war to be morally justified.[51] On that issue the Court split 5–4. Relying on that case in 1945, the Court divided 5–4 once again when it upheld a state's refusal to admit an individual to the bar after he refused, on religious grounds, to take an oath to support the state constitution if that required a willingness to serve in the state militia in time of war.[52] A year later, a 5–3 Court held that a Seventh Day Adventist could not be denied citizenship for objecting to combatant service while agreeing to serve in a noncombatant role. The Court underscored the respect

45. Fraina v. United States, 255 F. 28 (2d Cir. 1918).

46. 3 Stokes 293–95.

47. National Service Board for Religious Objectors, Congress Looks at the Conscientious Objector 15 (1943).

48. Id. at 74.

49. Id. at 75, 86–89.

50. 54 Stat. 889, sec. 5(g) (1940).

51. United States v. Macintosh, 283 U.S. 605 (1931).

52. In re Summers, 325 U.S. 561, 573 (1945).

shown by Congress over the years "for the conscience of those having religious scruples against bearing arms."[53]

A related issue: Did the exemption for conscientious objector require belief in a "Supreme Being"? A congressional statute in 1948 authorized someone to avoid combatant training and service in the armed forces if that person, "by reason of religious training and belief, is conscientiously opposed to participation in war in any form."[54] It defined religious training and belief to mean "an individual's belief in a relation to a Supreme Being involving duties superior to those arising from any human relation" but did not include "essentially political, sociological, or philosophical views of a merely personal moral code."[55]

In 1965, the Supreme Court reviewed the authority of Congress to confer a special legal benefit on a conscientious objector who professed belief in a Supreme Being. Not every religion is theistic. Could Congress prefer theistic over nontheistic or polytheistic religions? Four years earlier, the Court had struck down a requirement that a notary public take an oath affirming a belief in God. The Court ruled that government may not "aid those religions based on a belief in the existence of God as against those religions founded on different beliefs."[56]

The Court in the 1965 *Seeger* case concluded that when Congress used the expression "Supreme Being" rather than "God," it was "merely clarifying the meaning of religious training and belief so as to embrace all religions and to exclude essentially political, sociological, or philosophical views."[57] It then argued that "the test of belief" in a Supreme Being is whether a given belief that is "sincere and meaningful" occupies a place in the life of an individual parallel to that filled by the orthodox belief in God.[58] In other words, a "Supreme Being" could be some force outside oneself, even if not a traditional deity.[59]

In 1967, Congress revisited the issue and removed the statute's definition of religious training and belief ("an individual's belief in a relation to a Supreme Being involving duties superior to those arising from any human relation").[60]

53. Girouard v. United States, 328 U.S. 61, 66–67 (1946), overruling two earlier decisions requiring individuals to take up arms to defend the country: United States v. Macintosh, 283 U.S. 605 (1931) and United States v. Bland, 283 U.S. 636 (1931).

54. 62 Stat. 612, sec. 5(j) (1948).

55. Id. at 613.

56. Torcaso v. Watkins, 367 U.S. 488, 495 (1961).

57. United States v. Seeger, 380 U.S. 163, 165 (1965).

58. Id. at 166.

59. Id. at 174–75.

60. 81 Stat. 100, 104 (1967).

In reporting the bill, the House Armed Services Committee noted *Seeger* and the controversy that developed. The committee decided to eliminate language that had caused so much trouble.[61]

In subsequent cases, the Supreme Court continued to fine-tune the exemption for conscientious objectors. In 1970, it upheld the claim of someone who could neither affirm nor deny a belief in a "Supreme Being."[62] A year later, it examined the statutory restriction to individuals opposed "to participation in war in any form." In so doing, it denied relief to those who objected in particular to the Vietnam War.[63] The Court may have had good institutional reasons for not challenging Congress on that point, but the objection to particular wars and not all wars has been customary in distinguishing between just and unjust wars.[64]

Chaplains

After deciding to declare independence from England, the Continental Congress received prayers from a Christian chaplain, beginning with Mr. Jacob Duché in 1774.[65] The following year, Congress provided a chaplain to army regiments.[66] No religious denomination was specified for those chaplains, but it was not until 1860 that the House of Representatives invited a rabbi to give the opening prayer. It was delivered by Morris J. Raphall of New York City.[67] With the start of the Civil War, a congressional statute on July 22, 1861, stipulated that each military regiment be assigned a "regular ordained minister of a Christian denomination" to serve as chaplain.[68] Two amendments, to permit the appointment of Catholic and Jewish chaplains, were rejected.[69] Statutory language the following month referred to "some Christian denomination,"[70] apparently to permit the selection of Catholic chaplains.

61. H. Rept. No. 267, 90th Cong., 1st Sess. 31, 61 (1967). See also the conference report: H. Rept. No. 346, 90th Cong., 1st Sess. 15 (1967).

62. Welsh v. United States, 398 U.S. 333, 337 (1970).

63. Gillette v. United States, 401 U.S. 437 (1971).

64. Joseph E. Capizzi, "Selective Conscientious Objection in the United States," 38 J. Church & State 339 (1996); Kent Greenawalt, "All or Nothing at All: The Defeat of Selective Conscientious Objection," 1971 Sup. Ct. Rev. 31.

65. 1 Journals of the Continental Congress, 1774–1789, at 26 (1904).

66. 4 Journals of the Continental Congress, at 61.

67. Cong. Globe, 36th Cong., 1st Sess. 648–49 (1860); a chapter entitled "The First Jewish Prayer in Congress" appears in Bertram Wallace Korn, Eventual Years and Experience 98–124 (1954).

68. 12 Stat. 270, sec. 9 (1861).

69. Cong. Globe, 37th Cong., 1st Sess. 100 (1861).

70. 12 Stat. 288, sec. 7 (1861).

In practice, the chaplains who had previously served with the military were Protestant.[71]

The Sixty-Fifth Regiment of the Fifth Pennsylvania Cavalry had a large number of Jewish soldiers. Apparently unaware that Congress had limited chaplains to Christians, it selected a Jew, Michael Allen, to serve as regimental chaplain. When that fact reached the press, an Army general warned that any chaplain not from a Christian denomination would be discharged. To avoid that action, Allen cited ill health and resigned.[72] A number of newspapers, including the *New York Tribune, New York Journal of Commerce, Philadelphia Sunday Dispatch*, and *Baltimore Clipper*, began to insist that Jewish soldiers in the Union army had a right to a Jewish chaplain.[73] Christians and Jews sent petitions to Congress to remove the sectarian statutory policy.[74]

The next step was to send someone to Washington, D.C., to lobby elected officials. Selected for that task was Rabbi Arnold Fischel of New York City, who met with President Lincoln and members of Congress. Fischel explained the problem to Lincoln on December 11, 1861. Two days later he received a note from Lincoln, acknowledging that the statute was defective and that he would "try to have a new law broad enough to cover what is desired by you in behalf of the Israelites."[75] Fischel also met with lawmakers, including those who served on the Military Affairs Committees of both houses. There was no need to litigate the issue. The elected branches understood the problem and fixed it.[76] Within one year, Congress deleted "Christian denomination" from the statute and inserted "some religious denomination."[77] Acting by majority vote, Congress met the needs of a religious minority and safeguarded a constitutional principle.

The elected branches continue to protect religious diversity among military chaplains. Until 1993, active duty chaplains were either Christians or Jews. Because of an increasing number of Muslims serving in the U.S. military, Captain Abdul-Rasheed Muhammed became the first Muslim chaplain

---

71. Bertram Wallace Korn, American Jewry and the Civil War 56 (1951).

72. Id. at 58.

73. Id. at 65.

74. Id. at 65–68.

75. Id. at 69–70.

76. For House debate on December 20, 1861, to revise the statute to permit Jews to serve as military chaplains: Cong. Globe, 37th Cong., 2d Sess. 157–58 (1861).

77. 12 Stat. 595, sec. 8 (1862). Also on Fischel's efforts: Jonathan D. Sarna & David G. Dalin, Religion and State in the American Jewish Tradition 130 (1997); Albert Issac Slomovitz, The Fighting Rabbis: Jewish Military Chaplains and American History 10–18 (2001 paper ed.). For a history of Jewish chaplains: Louis Barish, Rabbis in Uniform: A Century of Service to God and Country 1862–1962) (1962).

in 1993, and there have been additional Muslim chaplains appointed since that time.[78]

Legislation on Polygamy

During the Civil War, Congress tackled another issue of religious freedom. In 1860, it began debate on legislation to prohibit polygamy in the territories and to annul certain acts of the legislature of Utah that sanctioned multiple marriages. Lawmakers acted under their own constitutional interpretations without assistance or guidance from the courts. A report by the House Judiciary Committee stated that "the whole civilized world regard the marriage of one man to one woman as being authorized by the law of God" and that marriage "is the foundation of civil society." The "law of God" here was clearly sectarian. The Jewish Old Testament recognized multiple marriages; the Christian New Testament did not. The House committee noted that every state treated polygamy as a crime, generally a felony.[79] The legislation passed the House, 149 to 60.[80]

The Senate, acting in 1862, passed the bill 37 to 2.[81] In the statute, Congress reasoned that it was not interfering with religious beliefs or "the dictates of conscience." It was prohibiting certain types of religious *practice*.[82] In 1879, the Supreme Court upheld the statute by drawing the same distinction between belief and practice: "Laws are made for the government of actions, and while they cannot interfere with mere religious belief and opinions, they may with practices."[83] After the Mormon Church refused to comply with national policy, Congress passed legislation in 1882 to make polygamists ineligible to serve on juries, to vote, or to hold territorial or federal office.[84] Part of the purpose was to prevent Mormon jurors from voting to acquit fellow polygamists. The Supreme Court upheld the 1882 statute.[85]

With Mormons continuing to disobey national policy, Congress in 1887 began to confiscate church property and repealed the act that incorporated the church. The statute exempted certain buildings, such as those used exclusively

78. Laurie Goodstein, "Military Clerics Balance Arms and Allah," N.Y. Times, Oct. 7, 2001, at B1.
79. H. Rept. No. 83, 36th Cong., 1st Sess. 1, 2 (1860). For debate, see Cong. Globe, 36th Cong., 1st Sess. 1150–51, 1409–12, 1492–501, 1512–23, 1540–46, 1557–60 (1860).
80. Cong. Globe, 36th Cong., 1st Sess. 1559 (1860).
81. Cong. Globe, 37th Cong., 2d Sess. 2506–7 (1862).
82. 12 Stat. 501, sec. 2 (1862).
83. Reynolds v. United States, 98 U.S. 145, 166 (1879).
84. 22 Stat. 30 (1882). See also 18 Stat. 253 (1874) (part 3 of vol. 18).
85. Murphy v. Ramsey, 114 U.S. 14, 44 (1885).

for the worship of God, parsonages related to those buildings, and burial grounds.[86] The Supreme Court upheld this legislation, citing congressional authority over the territories and the organic statute of the Territory of Utah that reserved to Congress the authority to disapprove and annul the acts of its legislature.[87] In that sense, territorial legislation was subject not to judicial review but congressional review.[88]

Exemptions in Prohibition Statutes

The temperance movement in America began in the early part of the nineteenth century. The consumption of alcohol produced devastating effects on workers, families, women, and children. The Massachusetts Society for the Suppression of Intemperance, founded in 1813, advocated moderation—not abstinence—in the use of alcohol.[89] Initially, efforts were made to abolish the products of distillation (hard liquor), not fermentation (wine and beer).[90] Over time, the movement turned to full prohibition, either by statute or constitutional amendment.

In 1826, evangelical clergymen created the American Society for the Promotion of Temperance—or the American Temperance Society (ATS)—urging total abstinence.[91] Protestant reformers charged that intemperance, by "undermining man's health, impairing his reason, dulling his conscience, and obliterating his fear of God," led to "ungodliness, immorality, disease, and death, destroying both body and soul."[92] Members of the Roman Catholic, Episcopal, and Lutheran Churches were more lenient toward drinking.[93] Because of wine needed for communion and seders, Catholics and Jews generally endorsed temperance, not prohibition.

In 1846, most of the towns and cities in New York banned the licensing of taverns and grogshops. Five years later, the Maine legislature prohibited the manufacture and sale of "spirituous or intoxicating liquors." By 1855,

86. 24 Stat. 635, 637 (sec. 13), 638 (sec. 17) (1887).

87. Mormon Church v. United States, 136 U.S. 1, 42, 44 (1890).

88. See Orma Linford, "The Mormons and the Law: The Polygamy Cases" (Part II), 9 Utah L. Rev. 543, 582–83 (1965), and Fisher, Religious Liberty in America, at 20–27.

89. Jack S. Blocker, Jr., American Temperance Movement: Cycles of Reform 11–12 (1989).

90. Norman H. Clark, Deliver Us from Evil: An Interpretation of American Prohibition 8 (1976).

91. Blocker, American Temperance Movement, at 12.

92. James H. Timberlake, Prohibition and the Progressive Movement, 1900–1920, at 4 (1963).

93. Id. at 5.

similar laws had been adopted in Minnesota, Rhode Island, Massachusetts, Vermont, Michigan, Connecticut, Indiana, Delaware, Iowa, Nebraska, New York, and New Hampshire. Some states permitted wine or beer.[94] The National Temperance Society, drawing on the evangelical Christian tradition, was incorporated in 1866.[95] John Russell, a Methodist clergyman, became the principal spokesman for the Prohibition Party, founded in 1869.[96] Five years later, Protestant women established the Woman's Christian Temperance Union (WCTU).[97] Howard Russell, unrelated to John Russell, built on work as a Congregational minister to help found the Anti-Saloon League in 1893.[98]

To prohibitionists, saloons provided a corrupting environment that permitted urban bosses to control immigrant voters. Saloons attracted prostitution, gambling, and minors. Some of the prohibition campaign carried an anti-Catholic bias, with many Protestants regarding Catholic immigrants as "lower-class, illiterate, and vulnerable to evil habits."[99] The drive for prohibition depended primarily on white, middle-class, rural, Protestant, and native-born citizens.[100] Support also came from urban business leaders, labor leaders, physicians, teachers, and other professionals.[101]

From 1912 to 1919, Congress passed a number of statutes and constitutional amendments to prohibit the manufacture and selling of intoxicating beverages. Each time it granted exceptions for the use of sacramental wines for religious ceremonies. Legislation in 1912, designed to suppress the traffic of intoxicating liquors among Native Americans, made it lawful to introduce and use wines "solely for sacramental purposes, under church authority."[102] Language to suppress the traffic was added as a Senate amendment.[103] The provision for sacramental wine appeared only in the conference report.[104]

A draft constitutional amendment in 1913 prohibited intoxicating beverages but gave Congress authority to provide for the manufacture and sale

94. Clark, Deliver Us from Evil, at 45–49.

95. K. Austin Kerr, Organized for Prohibition: A New History of the Anti-Saloon League 39–41 (1985).

96. Id. at 41–42.

97. Ruth Bordin, Woman and Temperance: The Quest for Power and Liberty, 1873–1900, at 34–36 (1981).

98. Kerr, Organized for Prohibition, at 76–89.

99. Clark, Deliver Us from Evil, at 88. See also Robert Booth Fowler, Religion and Politics in America (1985).

100. Alan P. Grimes, Democracy and the Amendments to the Constitution 83–89 (1978).

101. Clark, Deliver Us from Evil, at 11.

102. 37 Stat. 519 (1912).

103. 48 Cong. Rec. 8603 (1912).

104. H. Rept. No. 1185, 62d Cong., 2d Sess. 15 (1912); H. Rept. No. 1238, 62d Cong., 2d Sess. 14 (1912).

of intoxicating liquors in certain areas, including sacramental wines.[105] The proposal, after attracting committee and floor interest, failed to pass either chamber.[106] The Webb-Kenyon Act of 1913 flatly prohibited the shipment of intoxicating liquors into any state, territory, or the District of Columbia in violation of their laws.[107] Although the statute made no express exception for sacramental wines, floor debate indicated that lawmakers understood there would be exceptions for "sacramental, medicinal, mechanical, pharmaceutical, or scientific purposes, or for use in the arts."[108]

President Taft vetoed the bill on the ground that Congress had somehow delegated to the states its power over interstate commerce.[109] However, Congress in the past prohibited the shipment of many items (impure food, opium, nitroglycerine, etc.) without constitutional dispute. The Senate overrode the veto 63–12; the House override was 246–95.[110] In 1917, the Supreme Court upheld the statute by a vote of 7–2.[111] The argument that the statute delegated interstate commerce to the states "rests upon a mere misconception."[112] The two dissenting Justices, Oliver Wendell Holmes and Willis Van Devanter, provided no reasons.

Federal legislation enacted on February 14, 1917, prohibited the manufacture or sale of alcoholic beverages in the Territory of Alaska. An exception in the statute seemed confined to use of communion wine by Christians. Suppliers were allowed to transport "shipments of wine for sacramental purpose," requiring an "officiating priest or minister" to certify that the wine was to be used solely for sacramental purposes.[113] Other exceptions covered pharmacists who used alcohol for "scientific, artistic, or mechanical purposes" and preparing medicines.[114]

World War I placed great strains on the national economy. In order to prosecute the war, Congress in 1918 passed legislation designed to promote agriculture, feeding animals, and the production of food. It prohibited the use of any grains, cereals, fruit, or other food products for the manufacture of beer, wine, "or other intoxicating malt or vinous liquor for beverage purposes." No beer, wine, or other intoxicating malt or vinous liquor could be

105. 51 Cong. Rec. 615 (1913).
106. Richard F. Hamm, Shaping the Eighteenth Amendment: Temperance Reform, Legal Culture, and the Polity, 1880–1920, at 228–29 (1995).
107. 37 Stat. 699 (1913).
108. 51 Cong. Rec. 615 (1913).
109. 49 Cong. Rec. 4291–92 (1913).
110. Id. at 4291–99, 4434–48.
111. Clark Distilling Co. v. West'n Md. Ry. Co., 242 U.S. 311 (1917).
112. Id. at 326.
113. 39 Stat. 903, 905, sec. 8 (1917).
114. Id. at 903, sec. 2.

sold for drinking except for export.[115] The statute authorized the executive branch to prescribe rules for the manufacture, sale, and distribution of wine for "sacramental, medicinal, or other than beverage uses."[116]

These forces led to the Eighteenth Amendment, passed by Congress in December 1917 and ratified by the states on January 16, 1919. It prohibited the "manufacture, sale, or transportation of intoxicating liquors" within the United States, including importation and exportation. To enforce the amendment, Congress passed the National Prohibition Act of 1919 (the Volstead Act). It prohibited intoxicating beverages and regulated the manufacture, production, use, and sale of high-proof spirits intended for other than beverages. The statute pledged to ensure an ample supply of alcohol for use in industry and scientific research, for the development of fuel and dye, and for other lawful purposes. An exception allowed for liquor in the form of "wine for sacramental purposes."[117] The head of any ecclesiastical jurisdiction would designate "any rabbi, minister, or priest" to manufacture wine for religious ceremonies.[118]

Instead of controlling crime and elevating morality, the Eighteenth Amendment unleashed crime in ever greater force by producing a class of gangsters willing to supply liquor to customers anxious to have it. Representative Manny Celler, Democrat from New York, remarked in 1933: "New York City had 26,000 saloons before prohibition; it now has over 32,000 speakeasies."[119] The cost to the country was so great that the amendment was repealed by the Twenty-First Amendment on December 5, 1933.

The Yarmulke Case

Religious interests often fare well in the political marketplace. On repeated occasions, the majoritarian process supports religious minorities. A particularly vivid illustration is the congressional response to a 1986 Supreme Court decision that upheld an Air Force regulation that prohibited an observant Jew in the military from wearing a skullcap (yarmulke) while on duty. Far from having the last word on this constitutional issue, the Court's opinion was followed by congressional policy that protected religious liberty.

Simcha Goldman, an Orthodox Jew and ordained rabbi, served as a Captain in the Air Force and was assigned to a mental health clinic, where he

115. 40 Stat. 1046 (1918).
116. Id. at 1047.
117. 41 Stat. 305, 308, sec. 3 (1919).
118. Id. at 311, sec. 6.
119. 76 Cong. Rec. 4514 (1933).

worked as a clinical psychologist. While in uniform and on duty, he wore a yarmulke at all times. Orthodox Jewish religious practice requires a Jewish male to keep his head covered. Over a three and a half year period, Goldman wore a yarmulke while in uniform without incident.

Matters changed on May 8, 1981, when the Air Force informed Goldman that wearing a yarmulke violated the military dress code. He could not wear it indoors while in uniform except when working at the regional hospital. His counsel asked the Air Force to permit an exception but was turned down. On June 23, the Air Force ordered Goldman to stop wearing a yarmulke anywhere while in uniform, including at the regional hospital. Because of the dispute over the yarmulke, a previously positive recommendation for Goldman was withdrawn and replaced by a negative one. The Air Force threatened him with court-martial if he continued to wear a yarmulke in uniform.

Why, after three and a half years, did Goldman's wearing of a yarmulke provoke a confrontation? In April 1981, the month before he was warned about wearing the yarmulke, he appeared at a court-martial to testify on behalf of the defense (and therefore against the Air Force). The action against Goldman therefore appeared to have a retaliatory motive.[120]

Having exhausted administrative remedies, Goldman's attorney went to court to enjoin the Secretary of Defense and the Secretary of the Air Force from preventing Goldman from wearing his yarmulke. A federal district court ruled that Goldman was entitled to a preliminary injunction because he was likely to prevail in showing that the Air Force had violated the First Amendment's Free Exercise Clause. The judge noted that the dispute involved a departmental regulation, not a statute passed by a "coequal branch of government."[121] He appeared to make light of the Pentagon's position that allowing Goldman to wear his yarmulke "will crush the spirit of uniformity, which will in turn weaken the will and fighting ability of the Air Force."[122]

In a separate action by another Orthodox Jew who challenged Air Force policy on yarmulkes, a district judge from the same circuit sided with the military. Departures from uniformity, said this court, would adversely affect "the promotion of teamwork, counteract pride and motivation, and undermine discipline and morale, all to the detriment of the substantial compelling governmental interest of maintaining an efficient Air Force."[123]

120. Goldman v. Weinberger, 475 U.S. 503, 511 (1986) (concurrence by Justice Stevens, joined by Justices White and Powell).
121. Goldman v. Secretary of Defense, 530 F. Supp. 12, 15 (D.D.C. 1981).
122. Id. at 16.
123. Bitterman v. Secretary of Defense, 553 F. Supp. 719, 725 (D.D.C. 1982).

When those conflicting opinions reached the D.C. Circuit, all three judges of the appellate panel agreed that the Air Force was justified in adopting and enforcing its regulation, notwithstanding issues of the First Amendment's Free Exercise Clause.[124] The Air Force argued that Jewish law does not require the covering of the head during work. Goldman agreed that some Orthodox Jews do not feel obliged to cover their heads at all times.[125] The Air Force also said that if it accommodated Goldman on the yarmulke it would be under pressure from other military personnel to grant their religious use of turbans, robes, face and body paint, short hair, unshorn hair, badges, rings, amulets, bracelets, jodhpurs, and symbolic daggers.[126]

The D.C. Circuit declined to rehear the case en banc. Three judges, with quite familiar names, dissented from the decision against full bench review. Judge Kenneth Starr, later Solicitor General in the George H. W. Bush administration and independent counsel for the Whitewater investigation involving President Clinton, said the panel's decision "does considerable violence to the bulwark of freedom guaranteed by the Free Exercise Clause."[127] Judges Ruth Bader Ginsburg and Antonin Scalia, now on the Supreme Court, said the military's order to Goldman not to wear his yarmulke suggested "callous indifference" to his religious faith and ran counter to the American tradition of accommodating spiritual needs.[128]

The decision by the D.C. Circuit triggered legislative action in Congress. As an amendment to the defense authorization bill in 1984, Representative Stephen Solarz proposed that members of the armed forces may wear unobtrusive religious headgear, such as a skullcap, if religious observances or practices require the wearing of such headgear. Under this amendment, offered for a one-year trial period, the Defense Department could prohibit the headgear if it interfered with the performance of military duties.[129]

Although Representative William Dickinson warned that "we are flying in the face of a court decision just made," the House accepted the Solarz amendment.[130] Conferees decided to eliminate the amendment but ordered the Defense Department to report on changes in service regulations that would promote the free expression of religion to the greatest extent possible consistent with the requirements of military discipline.[131] This lengthy study,

124. Goldman v. Secretary of Defense, 734 F.2d 1531, 1535 (D.C. Cir. 1984).
125. Id. at 1537.
126. Id. at 1539.
127. Goldman v. Secretary of Defense, 739 F.2d 657, 658 (D.C. Cir. 1984).
128. Id. at 660.
129. 130 Cong. Rec. 14295 (1984).
130. Id. at 14298.
131. H. Rept. No. 98-1080, 98th Cong., 2d Sess. 293–94 (1984); 98 Stat. 2492, 2532–33, sec. 554 (1984).

touching on a broad range of issues, concluded that courts would most likely defer to military service policy regarding the wearing of yarmulkes.[132]

The Supreme Court accepted Goldman's case for review. The brief submitted by Solicitor General Charles Fried, supporting the Defense Department regulation, argued that Goldman's position would force the military to choose between "virtual abandonment of its uniform regulations and constitutionally impermissible line drawing."[133] The "entire purpose of uniform standards would be defeated if individuals were allowed exemptions."[134] To disregard the government's interests in favor of exceptions made on a case-by-case basis "would make a mockery of the military's compelling interest in uniformity."[135] To Fried, the standard for evaluating religious liberty in the civilian sector had no application to the military.[136]

Fried exaggerated the military's policy of uniformity. Defense Department regulations already allowed exceptions for hair styles. Regulations limited facial hair to mustaches, "the corner of which may not extend beyond the mouth," and permitted the wearing of jewelry, rings, and "neat and conservative identification bracelets."[137] Rosary beads and crosses could be worn underneath the uniform.[138] With that understanding, Jews could wear the Star of David under their uniform.

During oral argument in 1986, some Justices appeared uncomfortable about second-guessing military regulations. Justice Rehnquist pointed out to Nathan Lewin, Goldman's attorney, that the religious liberty cases he had cited for support came from civilian life: "We've never applied that balancing test where the military has been involved, have we?" Lewin agreed.[139] Oral argument wandered a bit when Justice White asked whether Goldman could satisfy his religious belief by wearing a toupee. Lewin admitted that a toupee would suffice, but his client wouldn't be interested because "he's not bald." Trying to turn the tables, Lewin said that "on someone who has a full head of hair, wearing a toupee would look somewhat strange." White was fully prepared: "It doesn't in the courtrooms in London where they are required to wear a wig."[140]

132. Joint Service Study on Religious Matters 21, 25 (March 1985).

133. Brief for the Respondents, Goldman v. Weinberger, No. 84-1097, U.S. Supreme Court, October Term, 1985, at 19.

134. Id. at 49.

135. Id. at 49–50.

136. Id. at 20–28.

137. Id. at 3–4.

138. Oral argument, Goldman v. Weinberger, U.S. Supreme Court, Jan. 14, 1986, at 41 (Justice Department attorney Kathryn Oberly).

139. Id. at 5.

140. Id. at 21–24.

Kathryn Oberly from the Justice Department advised the Court to stay out of the battle and leave the dispute to the elected branches: "If Congress thinks that further accom[m]odation is either required or desirable it can legislate it."[141] That marked an impressive understanding by an executive official that all constitutional issues need not be settled by the judiciary. In the event that legislation proved inadequate, Congress could easily amend the statute. If the Court tried to decide mandatory exceptions to the uniform requirements, it would be "far more difficult" to correct what might turn out to mistaken judgment about the effect on discipline and morale.[142]

Divided 5–4, the Supreme Court held that the First Amendment did not prohibit the Air Force regulation even though Goldman's religious belief required the wearing of a yarmulke. The Court accepted the Air Force judgment that the outfitting of military personnel in standardized uniforms "encourages the subordination of personal preferences and identities in favor of the overall group mission."[143] To the Court, the values of uniformity, hierarchy, unity, discipline, and obedience fully justified the regulation.

The majority of five included Justices Stevens, White, and Powell. In their concurrence, they agreed that the Air Force had reason to pursue a single standard of religious apparel because otherwise the military would have to contend with a variety of religious claims, including the wearing of a yarmulke by an Orthodox Jew, a turban by a Sikh, a saffron robe by a Satchidananda Ashram–Integral Yogi, and dreadlocks by a Rastafarian. An exception for yarmulkes, they said, would represent a risky departure from the basic principle of uniformity.[144]

A dissent by Justice Brennan, joined by Justice Marshall, presented inconsistent views on which branch is responsible for protecting individual rights. Brennan first claimed that the Court's decision represented an abdication of its role "as principal expositor of the Constitution and protector of individual liberties in favor of credulous deference to unsupported assertions of military necessity."[145] Yet he later acknowledged that other parts of government have a duty to protect religious freedom: "Guardianship of this precious liberty is not the exclusive domain of federal courts. It is the responsibility as well of the States and the other branches of the Federal Government."[146] His concluding sentence pointed to the institutional remedy: "The Court and the military have refused these servicemen their constitutional rights; we must hope that Congress will correct this wrong."[147]

141. Id. at 45.
142. Id.
143. Goldman v. Weinberger, 475 U.S. 503, 508 (1986).
144. Id. at 512–13.
145. Id. at 514.
146. Id. at 523.
147. Id. at 524.

In dissent, Justice Blackmun concluded that the Air Force "has failed to produce even a minimally credible explanation for its refusal to allow Goldman to keep his head covered indoors."[148] The Air Force "simply has not shown any reason to fear that a significant number of enlisted personnel and officers would request religious exemptions that could not be denied on neutral grounds such as safety, let alone that granting these requests would noticeably impair the overall image of the service."[149] Under these circumstances, judicial deference "seems unwarranted."[150]

A dissent by Justice O'Connor, joined by Justice Marshall, agreed that in order to fulfill its mission, "the military is entitled to take some freedoms from its members."[151] But the government's "asserted need for absolute uniformity is contradicted by the Government's own exceptions to its rule." An Air Force dress code in effect at the time of Captain Goldman's service stated: "Neither the Air Force nor the public expects absolute uniformity of appearance. Each member has the right, within limits, to express individuality through his or her appearance."[152] On the facts of the case, O'Connor "would require the Government to accommodate the sincere religious belief of Captain Goldman."[153]

Congress, acting under its express Article I authority to "make rules for the Government and Regulation of the land and naval Forces," proceeded to protect the religious beliefs of members of the military. Within two weeks of the Court's decision, legislation was introduced to permit members of the armed forces to wear items of apparel not part of the official uniform. Members of the military would have statutory authority to wear any "neat, conservative, and unobtrusive" item of apparel to satisfy the tenets of a religious belief. The Secretary of a military branch could prohibit the wearing of the item only after determining that it "significantly interferes with the performance of the member's military duties."[154] In reporting legislation to extend greater protection to religious liberty in the military, the House Armed Services Committee denied that the wearing of yarmulkes "would necessarily threaten good order, discipline, or morale in the armed forces."[155]

---

148. Id. at 526.
149. Id. at 527.
150. Id.
151. Id. at 531.
152. Id. at 532.
153. Id. at 533.
154. 132 Cong. Rec. 6655 (1986) (Senator Alfonse D'Amato); id. at 7042, 7211 (Senator Frank Lautenberg).
155. H. Rept. No. 99-718, 99th Cong., 2d Sess. 200, 488 (1986). See also 132 Cong. Rec. 20644 (1986).

The House passed this legislation, but the Senate tabled an amendment, 51 to 49, that would have permitted members of the military to wear religious apparel while in official uniform.[156] Conferees dropped the House provision, which the military services strongly opposed.[157] The following year the House again added language to permit the wearing of neat and conservative religious apparel while in uniform, provided it did not interfere with the performance of military duties. No one spoke against the amendment. Senate debate was more spirited, but this time the provision passed 55 to 42.[158]

The Senate's reversal reflected some switches by Senators and the results of the 1986 elections. Six Senators (Rudy Boschwitz, Quentin Burdick, John Danforth, Pete Domenici, Tom Harkin, and John Rockefeller) changed from favoring the 1986 tabling motion to favoring the 1987 amendment. Eight new Senators (Brock Adams, John Breaux, Tom Daschle, Bob Graham, David Karnes, Barbara Mikulski, Harry Reid, and Tim Wirth) voted for the 1987 amendment. Senators Al Gore and Paul Simon, who opposed the 1986 tabling motion, did not vote on the 1987 amendment. Senators Robert Byrd, Don Nickles, and J. Bennett Johnston switched from opposing the 1986 tabling motion to opposing the 1987 amendment. Lobbying against the Senate amendment was fierce, involving the American Legion, the Military Coalition, Secretary of Defense Caspar Weinberger, and the Joint Chiefs of Staff.[159] With President Reagan's signature, the bill became law.[160]

Although the Defense Department did everything it could to defeat the amendment, it has learned to accommodate not only yarmulkes but many other types of religious apparel. An article in 2014 describes a new military regulation that allows the wearing of a turban, scarf, and beard as long as the practices do not interfere with military discipline, order, or readiness. A news release by the Pentagon said it "places a high value on the rights of members of the military services to observe the tenets of their respective religions."[161] Progress in protecting individual rights came from Congress, not the Supreme Court.

The next chapter covers religious liberty for Native Americans, including use of peyote as a sacrament. The issue involved all three branches at the federal and state level, eventually leading to a conflict between the Supreme Court and Congress that led to the Religious Freedom Restoration Act (RFRA) of 1993.

156. 132 Cong. Rec. 19801–8 (1986).
157. H. Rept. No. 1001, 99th Cong., 2d Sess. 474 (1986).
158. 133 Cong. Rec. 25260 (1987).
159. Fisher, Religious Liberty in America, at 121.
160. 101 Stat. 1086–87, sec. 508 (1987). See Dwight D. Sullivan, "The Congressional Response to *Goldman v. Weinberger*," 121 Mil. L. Rev. 125 (1988).
161. Pamela Constable, "Pentagon Loosens Restrictions on Service Members' Religious Articles," Wash. Post, Jan. 23, 2014, A15.

7

THE RIGHTS OF NATIVE AMERICANS

For most of U.S. history, little was done by government to protect the rights of Indians. Initially, they were to be "civilized," assimilated, and acculturated into American society. Later stages led to the exclusion of most Indians from the East Coast, sending them westward to reservations. At that time, few efforts were made to preserve their unique beliefs and customs. Funds were provided to convert Indians to Christianity. Only in recent periods have the national and state governments taken steps to safeguard Indian heritage. That initiative came largely from the elected branches, not the judiciary.

Propagating the Gospel

By the time of the American Revolution, religious missions to the Indians had been operating in the eastern colonies for more than a century.[1] The first Virginia charter of 1606 directed colonists to be active in "propagating of *Christian* religion to such People . . . and may in time bring the Infidels and Savages, living in those parts, to human Civility."[2] The Charter of Massachusetts Bay in 1629 expressed the intention that the natives learn of "the Knowledg and Obedience of the onlie true God and Sauior of Mankinde, and the Christian Fayth."[3]

On February 5, 1776, the Continental Congress resolved that "friendly commerce between the people of the United Colonies and the Indians, and the propagation of the gospel . . . may produce many and inestimable advantages to both." Congress directed the commissioners of Indian affairs to select individuals who would live among the Indians "and instruct them in the Christian religion."[4] In 1785, a special committee received a petition requesting the assistance of Congress to instruct Indians "in reading, writing

---

1. R. Pierce Beaver, Introduction to Native American Church History (1983); R. Pierce Beaver, "Church, State, and the Indians: Indian Missions to the New Nation," 4 J. Church & State 11 (1962).
2. 7 Thorpe 3784 (emphasis in original).
3. 3 Thorpe 1857.
4. 4 Journals of the Continental Congress (1906) (hereafter "Journals").

and the principles of the Christian religion."[5] Those policies carried over to the administration of President George Washington. His Secretary of War, Henry Knox, proposed on July 7, 1789, that missionaries "of excellent moral character" be appointed to live among the Indians. With duties ranging beyond religious instruction, missionaries would supply the implements of husbandry, the necessary stock for a farm, and would serve as "their friends and fathers."[6]

In 1796, Congress passed legislation that set aside three tracts of land for the Society of United Brethren "for propagating the gospel among the heathen."[7] Debate on another bill the following year, concerning trade with the Indians, reveals an understanding among some legislators about the natural rights of Indians and the obligation of Congress to secure those rights.[8] Upon hearing a colleague remark that Indians had no right to their land, Theodore Sedgwick of Massachusetts said he "believed that wherever the natives of a country had possession, there they had a right, and not because they did not dress like us, were not equally religious, or did not understand the arts of civilized life, they were to be deprived of their possessions, but that their rights or their possessions were as sacred as the rights of civilized life. . . . Indians will never submit to be told they have no rights."[9]

President Thomas Jefferson found much among Indians to admire, describing them as brave, moral, responsible, caring of family and friends, and "in body and mind equal to the white man."[10] He gave serious and respectful study to their culture, character, and language, anticipating that Indians "will mix with us by marriage. Your blood will run in our veins, and will spread with us over this great land."[11] Yet it was Jefferson's initiative with the Louisiana Purchase, opening up a vast territory to the west, that set the stage for the forced removal policy of the 1830s and 1840s.[12]

In 1819, Congress enacted legislation "for the purpose of providing against the further decline and final extinction of the Indian tribes." In an effort to introduce among the tribes "the habits and arts of civilization," the statute authorized the President to employ individuals to instruct Indians "in the mode of agriculture suited to their situation," and to teach their children in reading,

5. 28 Journals 374 (1933).
6. 1 American State Papers: Indian Affairs 54 (1834).
7. 1 Stat. 491, sec. 5 (1796).
8. 5 Annals of Cong. 897–98 (Representatives Cooper and Hillhouse).
9. Id. at 901.
10. Anthony F. C. Wallace, Jefferson and the Indians: The Tragic Fate of the First Americans 77 (1999).
11. Id. at 317.
12. Id. at 257, 273–75.

writing, and arithmetic.[13] Although the statute and legislative history make no mention of instructing Indians in the tenets of Christianity, that became a key objective. President James Monroe, and his Secretary of War, John C. Calhoun, used appropriated funds to support the effort of missionaries and religious societies brought in to establish schools for Indian children.[14]

President John Quincy Adams told Congress in 1818 that "it was our policy and our duty to use our influence in converting to Christianity and in bringing within the pale of civilization." By taking their hunting grounds, government had an obligation to teach them "the arts of civilization and the doctrines of Christianity."[15] Religious missions demonstrated little interest or respect for Indian religious beliefs.[16] It would not be until the 1930s that steps were taken to safeguard Indian beliefs and practices.

Indian Removal

Indians on the East Coast gradually lost their lands. The Treaty of Hopewell in 1785 guaranteed the Cherokees their tribal lands, but persistent encroachments by white settlers led to new agreements from 1791 to 1806, each time compensating the Cherokees for land they had ceded to Georgia, Tennessee, and Kentucky. In 1816, the Cherokees ceded all their lands in South Carolina.[17] Beginning in 1816, the governor of Tennessee recommended that the Cherokees be relocated west of the Mississippi. Those that remained would be given 640 to 1,000 acres to develop.[18]

Georgia precipitated a legal crisis by withdrawing rights from Cherokees and seizing their land. The Cherokees and church groups appealed to Congress to reverse Georgia, but remedial legislation did not emerge.[19] The American Board of Commissioners for Foreign Nations, having sponsored

13. 3 Stat. 516 (1819). For legislative history: Annals of Cong., 15th Cong., 2d Sess. 546, 1426, 1427, 1431, 1435 (1819).

14. Margaret Connell Szasz & Carmelita Ryan, "American Indian Education," in William C. Sturtevant, ed., 4 Handbook of North American Indians 284–300 (1988).

15. 3 Richardson 981–82.

16. R. Pierce Beaver, "Protestant Churches and the Indians," in 4 Handbook of North American Indians 439 (Sturtevant, ed., 1988). See also Robert F. Berkhofer, Jr., Salvation and the Savage: An Analysis of Protestant Missions and American Indian Response, 1787–1862 (1965).

17. Donald Grinde, "Cherokee Removal and American Politics," 8 Indian Historian 33, 33–34 (1975).

18. Reginald Horsman, The Origins of Indian Removal, 1815–1824, at 6 (1970).

19. Joseph C. Burke, "The Cherokee Cases: A Study in Law, Politics, and Morality," 21 Stan. L. Rev. 500, 505–6 (1969).

missions to the Cherokees and the Choctaws, prepared a legal suit for the Cherokee Nation.[20]

While this case was being heard, President Andrew Jackson persuaded Congress to pass the Removal Act of 1830, which called for Indians to be moved west of the Mississippi River.[21] The Board took its case to the U.S. Supreme Court. William Wirt, who had served Presidents James Monroe and John Quincy Adams as Attorney General, argued the case for the Cherokees. In 1831, the Court acknowledged that the Cherokee Nation was a state with which the United States had dealt successively by treaty. However, it ruled that the Cherokees were not a "foreign state" and were not entitled to present the case as one of original jurisdiction. Whatever rights the Indians possessed regarding their lands, they were not legally positioned to ask the Court to prevent Georgia from exercising its legislative power.[22]

The dispute returned a year later, with the plaintiff this time being Samuel A. Worchester, a missionary imprisoned by Georgia. In 1830, Georgia had passed legislation prohibiting white persons without a state license from residing in lands occupied by the Cherokees. Worchester, one of seven whites who defied the statute, was imprisoned for four years at hard labor. He argued that he entered the Cherokee Nation in the capacity of a missionary authorized by the American Board and the U.S. President, and that his prosecution by Georgia violated several U.S.-Cherokee treaties. Those treaty rights, he said, could not be interfered with by any state.

Speaking for the Court, Chief Justice John Marshall first determined that congressional statutes gave the Court jurisdiction to hear and decide the case. Furthermore, he said the Indian nations "had always been considered as distinct, independent political communities, retaining their original natural rights, and the undisputed possessors of their soil, from time immemorial."[23] The single exception to that status was their exclusion from intercourse with other nations. The laws of Georgia could therefore have no force on the Cherokees unless with their consent and in conformity with treaties and congressional statutes. The law of Georgia under which Worchester was prosecuted "is consequently void, and the judgment a nullity." The acts of Georgia "are repugnant to the constitution, laws, and treaties of the United States."[24]

Marshall was well aware that political institutions might not comply with his ruling. The Georgia legislature had passed a resolution warning that any attempt by the U.S. Supreme Court to reverse the Georgia Superior Court

20. Beaver, Introduction to Native American Church History, at 69.
21. 4 Stat. 411 (1830).
22. Cherokee Nation v. Georgia, 30 U.S. 1 (1832).
23. Worchester v. Georgia, 32 U.S. 515, 559 (1832).
24. Id. at 561.

"will be held by this State as an unconstitutional and arbitrary interference in the administration of her criminal laws and will be treated as such."[25] After Marshall issued his decision, Georgia ignored it. It is highly unlikely that Jackson said what is widely attributed to him: "Well, John Marshall has made his decision, now let him enforce it."[26] Not until thirty years later did Horace Greeley recall that Jackson supposedly made that statement, at a time when Jackson was not alive to correct the record.[27] Moreover, the judicial process never reached the point of mandating Jackson to do anything.[28] Wirt tried to get Congress to pass legislation to force Jackson's hand but was unsuccessful.[29]

Greeley's recollection seems imaginary for another reason. On the crucial issue of preserving national power over the states, Jackson looked to the Supreme Court as an important ally. If Georgia could thumb its nose at the national government, so could other states. That is what South Carolina did on November 24, 1832, when its legislature passed the Nullification Ordinance, part of which attacked the jurisdiction of the U.S. Supreme Court and promised to treat any judicial interference in state matters as a nullity. Jackson's proclamation of December 10 strongly repudiated South Carolina's position.[30] In a message to Congress on January 16, 1833, Jackson urged legislation giving federal courts additional authority to deal with the threat from South Carolina.[31] At that point, the governor of Georgia issued a pardon to the missionaries and released them from prison.[32]

The removal of Indians was carried out at different times, with different tribes, and in different places over the next decade. Some Cherokees left early. The principal move in 1838 involved about seventeen thousand who were forced into temporary stockades and then marched eighteen hundred miles west. Deaths from illness, inadequate food, exposure, and trauma might have reached as high as eight thousand.[33] Many of the deaths occurred after the

---

25. 1 Charles Warren, The Supreme Court in United States History 754 (1937).

26. Id. at 759–64.

27. Donald B. Cole, The Presidency of Andrew Jackson 114 (1993). For some history on the recollection by Horace Greeley: 1 Warren, The Supreme Court in United States History, at 759, including the footnote.

28. 1 Warren, The Supreme Court in United States History, at 764–65; Burke, "The Cherokee Case," 21 Stan. L. Rev. at 525–27; William F. Swindler, "Politics as Law: The Cherokee Cases," 3 Am. Ind. L. Rev. 7, 16 (1975).

29. Jill Norgren, The Cherokee Cases: The Confrontation of Law and Politics 123–24 (1996).

30. 3 Richardson 1203.

31. Id. at 1192–93.

32. 1 Warren, The Supreme Court in United States History, at 776.

33. Norgren, The Cherokee Cases, at 143. See Grant Foreman, Indian Removal: The Emigration of the Five Civilized Tribes of Indians (1932).

Indians arrived in Indian Territory in present-day Oklahoma.[34] The Choctaws, Chickasaws, Creeks, and Seminoles also suffered huge losses during the
removal. In 1843, the Secretary of War reported that eighty-nine thousand
Indians had been moved west and 22,846 remained east of the Mississippi
River.[35]

Stirrings of Reform

Chronic corruption within the Bureau of Indian Affairs prompted President
Ulysses S. Grant to act. He appointed Ely S. Parker, a Seneca Indian, to serve
as Commissioner of Indian Affairs and removed all but two of the former
superintendents of Indian schools. He relied on Quakers, who had developed
a strong trust among the Indians, to nominate superintendents and agents.[36]
In his first annual message on December 6, 1869, he reminded Congress that
the management of Indian affairs had long been "a subject of embarrassment
and expense." He described the Society of Friends as "well known as having
succeeded in living in peace with the Indians in the early settlement of Pennsylvania," with a reputation for "strict integrity and fair dealings."[37]

For almost a century, Indian tribes had been treated as foreign nations sub-
ject to the treaty-making power of the President and the Senate. However, the
Constitution also empowers Congress to "regulate Commerce with foreign
Nations, and among the several States, and with the Indian Tribes." Partly
because of corruption and mismanagement in the Office of Indian Affairs, the
House of Representatives began to object to the Senate's prerogative in Indian
affairs. In 1869, the Senate added funds to an appropriations bill to fulfill
Indian treaties it had approved, but the House refused to grant the funds.[38]
The House completed its reassertion two years later by enacting this language:
"*Provided*, That hereafter no Indian nation or tribe within the territory of the
United States shall be acknowledged or recognized as an independent nation,
tribe, or power with whom the United States may contract by treaty."[39] The
House now had coequal power with the Senate over Indian affairs.

34. Russell Thornton, "The Demography of the Trail of Tears Period: A New Estimate
of Cherokee Population Losses," in William L. Anderson, ed., Cherokee Removal: Before and
After (1991).

35. John K. Mahon, "Indian–United States Military Situation, 1775–1848," in 4 Handbook of North American Indians 160 (Sturvevant, ed., 1988).

36. Beaver, "Protestant Churches and the Indians," at 443.

37. 9 Richardson 3992–93.

38. Felix Cohen, Handbook of Federal Indian Law 66 (1971).

39. 16 Stat. 566 (1871).

In 1869, Congress appropriated $2 million to enable the President "to maintain the peace among and with the various tribes, bands, and parties of Indians."[40] Friction among Friends, Protestants, and Catholics in administering Indian schools increased.[41] In 1897, the Indian appropriations act stated it to be "the settled policy of the Government to hereafter make no appropriation whatever for education to any sectarian school." Two years later, the Indian appropriations act included what Congress called "the final appropriation for sectarian schools."[42] After the elimination of federal funds, churches continued to operate Indian schools, sometimes relying on tribal trust funds and treaty funds.[43]

Congressional legislation in 1919 granted citizenship to Indians who had served in the military services during World War I and had received, or would receive, an honorable discharge.[44] Five years later, Congress passed legislation giving citizenship to the remaining Indians.[45] In 1928, the Institute for Government Research published a comprehensive work entitled *The Problem of Indian Administration*. The study was highly critical of U.S. policy toward the Indians, noting the "common failure to study sympathetically and understandingly the Indians' own religions and ethics and to use what is good in them as the foundation upon which to build. . . . The attempt blindly to destroy the whole Indian religion may in effect be an attack on some of the very elements of religious belief which the missionary himself espouses and which he hopes the Indian will adopt."[46]

John Collier, former Executive Secretary of the American Indian Defense Association, became Commissioner of Indian Affairs in 1934 and remained in that position until 1945. He helped persuade Congress to repeal a number of obsolete laws that covered Indians.[47] The repeal statute passed Congress without any debate.[48] The major piece of legislation was the Indian

40. 16 Stat. 40, sec. 4 (1869).
41. Louis Fisher, Religious Liberty in America: Political Safeguards 155–56 (2002).
42. 30 Stat. 79 (1897); 30 Stat. 942 (1899). See also Peter J. Rahill, The Catholic Indian Missions and Grant's Peace Policy, 1870–1884 (1953).
43. R. Pierce Butler, "The Churches and President Grant's Peace Policy," 4 J. Church & State 174, 189–90 (1962). In Quick Bear v. Leupp, 210 U.S. 50 (1908), the Supreme Court held that tribal and trust funds, used to compensate Indians for lands they had ceded to the United States, could be used to educate Indians in sectarian schools without violating the Establishment Clause. See also Elsie Mitchell Rushmore, The Indian Policy during Grant's Administration (1914).
44. 41 Stat. 350 (1919).
45. 43 Stat. 253 (1924). The Dawes Allotment Act of 1887 had granted citizenship to Indians who accepted an allotment of land and "adopted the habits of civilized life." 24 Stat. 390, sec. 6 (1887).
46. The Problem of Indian Administration 845–46 (1928).
47. 48 Stat. 487 (1934).
48. 78 Cong. Rec. 7271, 8222, 8351, 8361, 8447–48, 8607 (1934).

Reorganization Act of 1934.[49] Over the past half century, tribal lands had been subdivided to create individual allotments, to give Indians an incentive to work the property they owned. Much of the remaining (or "surplus") land was transferred to the whites.[50] The 1934 statute provided for the return of some surplus lands to tribal ownership.

Protective Legislation

Beginning in 1962, Congress passed a number of bills to protect Indian religious freedom, covering such areas as eagle feathers, Indian civil rights, and an Indian religious freedom statute. One of the first Indian religious issues addressed by Congress concerned legislation to protect eagles. In 1940, Congress passed a law to protect the bald eagle, which the Continental Congress had adopted in 1782 as the national symbol. The 1940 statute prohibited the taking, possession, sale, purchase, export, or import of any bald eagle, but did not specify the religious use of eagle feathers by Indians.[51] Nothing in the sparse legislative record referred to the need to protect Indian religious practices.[52]

The issue returned in 1962. Congress learned that immature bald eagles, similar in appearance to golden eagles, were sometimes killed by persons who confused the two. The legislative history explains the importance of the eagle for many Indian tribes, particularly in the Southwest, that performed ceremonies of religious significance. The eagle, "by reason of its majestic, solitary, and mysterious nature, became an especial object of worship."[53]

The legislation authorized the Secretary of the Interior to issue regulations allowing exceptions for various reasons, including "the religious purposes of Indian tribes."[54] In defining the possession and use of eagles for religious purposes, a regulation issued in 1963 allowed permits to Indians "who are authentic, bona fide practitioners of such religion."[55] Subsequent regulations required an applicant to be "an Indian who is authorized to participate in *bona fide*

49. 48 Stat. 984 (1934).

50. Francis Paul Prucha, American Indian Policy in Crisis: Christian Reformers and the Indian, 1865–1900, at 227–55 (1976).

51. 54 Stat. 250 (1940).

52. H. Rept. No. 2104, 76th Cong., 3d Sess. (1940); 85 Cong. Rec. 6446–47, 7006–7 (1940).

53. H. Rept. No. 1450, 87th Cong., 2d Sess. 4 (1962).

54. 76 Stat. 1246 (1962).

55. 28 Fed. Reg. 976, sec. 11.5 (1963).

tribal religious ceremonies."[56] The statute did not allow Indians to make commercial sales of eagles or eagle parts.[57]

In 1968, as part of an omnibus bill providing penalties for certain acts of violence or intimidation, Congress passed what is called the Indian Civil Rights Act. It reads more like a bill of rights. Federal courts had ruled that in cases of religious liberty, neither the First Amendment nor the Fourteenth Amendment applied to Indian tribal governments, and that Congress had not passed legislation making those constitutional provisions applicable to Indians.[58]

As with any bill of rights, the statute extends protections to individuals and imposes restrictions on government, in this case the tribal governments. Thus, no Indian tribe exercising powers of self-government shall "make or enforce any law prohibiting the free exercise of religion." Because some tribes have a theocratic foundation, an establishment of religion clause was not included. An Establishment Clause might have worked "to the disadvantage of tribal religion."[59] Other rights are listed, prohibiting tribal governments from abridging the freedom of speech or of the press, or the right of people peaceably to assemble and to petition for redress of grievances. Indian tribes may not conduct unreasonable searches and seizures, subject persons for the same offense to be twice put in jeopardy, compel persons in a criminal case to be a witness against themselves, take private property for a public use without just compensation, or take other actions injurious to individual rights.[60]

Much of the statute is directed toward safeguards of criminal proceedings, such as the right to a speedy and public trial, to be informed of the nature and cause of the accusation, to be confronted with witnesses against you, to have compulsory process for obtaining witnesses in your favor, and to have the assistance of counsel. Other provisions prohibit excessive bail, excessive fines, cruel and unusual punishments, the denial of equal protection, deprivation of liberty or property without due process of law, bills of attainder, ex post facto laws, or the denial of a trial by jury of not less than six persons.

In 1978, Congress passed a joint resolution expressing principles of religious freedom for Indians. The resolution, called the American Indian Religious Freedom Act (AIRFA), begins by recognizing that freedom of religion is an "inherent right" for all people and "fundamental to the democratic structure of the United States." Moreover, the individual right to practice religion has produced "a rich variety of religious heritage in this country." Included

56. 50 C.F.R. § 22.22 (c)(2) (Oct. 1, 2000 ed.).
57. United States v. Top Sky, 547 F.2d 486, 487–88 (9th Cir. 1976).
58. Native American Church v. Navajo Tribal Council, 272 F.2d 131 (10th Cir. 1959).
59. Milner S. Ball, "Constitution, Court, Indian Tribes," 1987 Am. Bar Foundation Research J. 1, 132 (1987).
60. 82 Stat. 77–78, sec. 202 (1968).

within this culture are the religious practices of the American Indian, "such practices forming the basis of Indian identity and value systems."[61] The legislative history is quite brief. The resolution passed the Senate by voice vote and by a margin of 337 to 81 in the House.[62]

Religious Use of Peyote

The peyote religion among Indian tribes in the United States began at the end of the nineteenth century, although its use by Indians in other territories dates back much earlier.[63] Peyote grows in small buttons at the top of a spineless cactus and contains a number of alkaloids, including the psychotropic mescaline. With its hallucinogenic properties, peyote offers a supernatural alternative to other religions by establishing an intermediate spirit (peyote, Jesus, or both) and a Supreme Being (the Great Spirit or God).[64] As used by the Native American Church (NAC), the drug is considered a sacrament (like bread and wine) and an object of worship. Prayers are devoted to it just as prayers are devoted to the Holy Ghost. By ingesting peyote, members of the NAC say they enter into direct contact with God. Peyote is not injurious to the Indian religious user, is not addictive or habit-forming, and is often helpful in controlling alcohol abuse among Indian people.[65]

Initially, states reacted to peyote by forbidding its use. In 1899, Oklahoma prohibited use of the mescal bean but repealed the law in 1908.[66] Other states enacted legislation to prohibit the use of peyote: Colorado, Nevada, and Utah in 1917; Kansas in 1920; Arizona, Montana, North Dakota, and South Dakota in 1923; Iowa in 1924; New Mexico and Wyoming in 1929; and Texas in 1937.[67] These laws had little application to the use of peyote on Indian reservations, where states lacked jurisdiction. Enforcement was possible on state property or state highways. In 1926, the Supreme Court of Montana held that under some circumstances the state could enforce the state law prohibiting peyote against an Indian who used it within a reservation.[68]

61. 92 Stat. 469 (1978).

62. S. Rept. No. 95-709, 95th Cong., 2d Sess. (1978); H. Rept. No. 95-1308, 95th Cong., 2d Sess. (1978); 124 Cong. Rec. 8365–66, 21443–46, 21450–52 (1978).

63. Omer C. Stewart, Peyote Religion: A History 16–30 (1987).

64. George de Verges, "Peyote and the Native American Church," 2 Am. Ind. L. Rev. 71 (1974); H. Rept. No. 103-675, 103d Cong., 2d Sess. 3 (1994).

65. H. Rept. No. 103-675, 103d Cong., 2d Sess 3 (1994).

66. Omer C. Stewart, "Peyote and the Law," in Christopher Vecsey, ed., Handbook of American Indian Religious Freedom 60 (1991).

67. De Verges, "Peyote and the Native American Church," at 77, n.14.

68. State v. Big Sheep, 242 P. 1067 (Mont. 1926).

Congress prohibited the sale of intoxicating drinks to Indians in 1897.[69] Lawmakers made an effort in 1913 to provide funds to suppress the use of peyote, but House and Senate conferees deleted the money, explaining that "the Indians claim this peyote is used in their religious worship and would cause a great deal of confusion."[70] The enacted bill did not contain money to suppress peyote.[71]

In 1918, the House Committee on Indian Affairs reported legislation to prohibit the sale of peyote to Indians. The committee, accepting the recommendations of the Indian Bureau and relying on published articles, described peyote as "poison" and referred to "night orgies in a close [sic] tent polluted with foul air."[72] The bureau recognized that peyote was used by Indians "as a substitute for intoxicating liquors," but the committee decided to prohibit peyote.[73] Part of the reason is that the peyote bill was caught up in the national campaign to prohibit the drinking of alcohol, resulting in the Eighteenth Amendment in 1919.

The House passed the committee-reported bill to prohibit the sale of intoxicating liquor, Indian hemp, or peyote to any Indian. After an amendment to permit the sale of peyote when used for religious purposes was rejected, the bill passed.[74] The Senate took no action on the House bill. Instead, it debated an amendment to prohibit the introduction of peyote into Indian territories. The amendment was rejected on a point of order because it constituted general legislation on an appropriations bill.[75] Although this bill did not pass, Interior Department appropriations acts from 1923 to 1934 contained funds to suppress "the traffic in intoxicating liquors and deleterious drugs, including peyote, among Indians."[76]

In the 1950s, states began to relax their laws regarding the use of peyote by Indians in religious services. Montana in 1957 and New Mexico in 1959 amended their narcotics laws to provide that the prohibition against narcotics "shall not apply to the possession, sale or gift of peyote for religious sacramental purposes by a bona fide religious organization incorporated under

69. 29 Stat. 506 (1897).
70. H. Rept. No. 28, 63d Cong., 1st Sess. 6 (1913).
71. 38 Stat. 78 (1913).
72. H. Rept. No. 560, 65th Cong., 2d Sess. 26 (1918).
73. Id. at 2.
74. 56 Cong. Rec. 11113–15 (1918).
75. Id. at 4129–33.
76. 42 Stat. 1182 (1923); 43 Stat. 396 (1924); 43 Stat. 1147 (1925); 44 Stat. 458 (1926); 44 Stat. 939 (1927); 45 Stat. 204 (1928); 45 Stat. 1566 (1929); 46 Stat. 1119 (1931); 47 Stat. 94 (1932); 47 Stat. 824 (1933); 48 Stat. 366 (1934). Funds for suppression of peyote were not included in the 1935 Interior appropriations bill; 49 Stat. 182 (1935).

the laws of the state."[77] In 1959, the Tenth Circuit decided a case brought by the NAC, which sought an injunction against an ordinance adopted by the Navajo Tribal Council making it an offense to introduce peyote into Navajo country. The Navajos entered the house of an NAC member while he conducted religious ceremonies and without a warrant searched the premises and arrested several people. The NAC claimed the ordinance was void because it violated the rights under the First, Fourth, and Fifth Amendments of the U.S. Constitution. The court held that in the absence of a constitutional provision or a congressional statute making the federal Bill of Rights applicable to Indian nations, federal courts lacked jurisdiction over tribal laws or regulations.[78]

In 1960, an Arizona trial court ruled against the state in a case involving a Navajo woman arrested for illegal possession of peyote. The court held that her religious interests outweighed whatever governmental interest the state could present. The judge wrote that the use of peyote was "essential to the existence of the peyote religion. Without it, the practice of the religion would be effectively prevented."[79] The state appealed, but the Arizona Supreme Court affirmed the holding of the trial judge.[80] Several years later, in 1964, the California Supreme Court reached a similar result in *People v. Woody*. State police arrested a group of Navajos who used peyote during a religious ceremony. Their convictions were overturned in court because peyote served a sacramental purpose similar to bread and wine in certain Christian churches. To use peyote for nonreligious purposes, said the court, "is sacrilegious."[81]

Several state cases in the 1970s explored the use of peyote for religious purposes. An appellate court in Arizona in 1972 upheld the use of peyote in a religious ceremony (a wedding) convened by the Native American Church.[82] In 1977, an Oklahoma appellate court supported the right of an Indian to wear a string of peyote buttons around his neck and to keep other peyote buttons wrapped and tied in a handkerchief inside his pocket. Testifying as a member of the NAC, he said he used peyote for religious ceremonies and not for illicit drug purposes.[83]

77. People v. Woody, 394 P.2d 813, 819 (Cal. 1964).
78. Native American Church v. Navajo Tribal Council, 272 F.2d 131 (10th Cir 1959).
79. Carolyn N. Long, Religious Freedom and Indian Rights 18 (2000).
80. Neither decision in this case, Arizona v. Attakai, Criminal No. 4098, Coconino County, was reported, but the case is cited in People v. Woody, 394 P.2d at 813, n.5.
81. People v. Woody, 394 P.2d at 817. See also In re Grady, 394 P.2d 728 (Cal. 1964), in which the Supreme Court of California insisted that the religious use of peyote must be honest and bona fide.
82. State v. Whittingham, 504 P.2d 950, 952 (Ariz. 1972).
83. Whitehorn v. State, 561 P.2d 539, 547 (Okla. 1977). See Robert Johnston, "Whitehorn v. State: Peyote and Religious Freedom in Oklahoma," 5 Am. Ind. L. Rev. 229 (1977).

Federal action during this period supported the religious use of peyote by NAC members. In passing a drug abuse act in 1965, Congress authorized broad discretion on the part of administrative officials to make exemptions for depressant or stimulant drugs. The House bill provided the NAC with a specific exemption for peyote, but the enacted bill left that issue to administrative regulation.[84] A notice in the Federal Register the following year explained that listing peyote as a drug "does not apply to non-drug use in bona fide religious ceremonies of the Native American Church."[85] In 1991, the Fifth Circuit upheld the exemption for the NAC on the grounds that Congress had been given extraordinary authority over Indian matters and the exemption was rationally related to the legitimate governmental objective of preserving Indian culture.[86]

Religious Freedom Restoration Act (RFRA)

A peyote case in Oregon led to a controversial decision by the U.S. Supreme Court, *Employment Division v. Smith* (1990). The case began with Alfred Smith, a Klamath Indian and a member of the NAC who served as a counselor for alcoholics. He worked for ADAPT (Alcohol and Drug Abuse Prevention and Treatment) until his discharge on March 5, 1984. ADAPT required counselors to abstain from alcohol and mind-altering drugs and warned Smith that he could be fired for using peyote, even if part of a religious ceremony. After ingesting peyote during a weekend service conducted by the NAC, he was fired and subsequently denied unemployment benefits because of the drug use.[87]

In 1986, the Supreme Court of Oregon held that the denial of benefits did not violate state constitutional provisions regarding freedom of worship and religious opinion, but it did violate the Free Exercise Clause of the First Amendment of the U.S. Constitution.[88] It relied on the standards announced in 1963 by the U.S. Supreme Court in *Sherbert v. Verner*. The person claiming the free exercise right must show that the application of law "significantly burdens" the free exercise of religion, and the state must show that the constraint

84. 111 Cong. Rec. 14608 (1965); 79 Stat. 226 (1965).

85. 31 Fed. Reg. 4679 (1966); the peyote exception for the NAC currently appears in 21 C.F.R. § 1307.31 (2014).

86. Peyote Way Church of God, Inc. v. Thornburgh, 922 F.2d 1210, 1216 (5th Cir. 1991). For a case involving the Native American Church of New York, which is not affiliated with the NAC and which has few Indian members, see Native American Church of New York v. United States, 468 F. Supp. 1247 (S.D.N.Y. 1979), aff'd, 633 F.2d 205 (2d Cir. 1980).

87. Smith v. Employment Division, 721 P.2d 445, 445–46 (Ore. 1986).

88. Id. at 446–49.

on religious activity is the "least restrictive" means of achieving a "compelling" state interest.[89] A companion case involved Galen Black, a non-Indian who belonged to the NAC. He was also denied unemployment benefits after being fired for ingesting peyote during a religious ceremony.

Under Oregon law, possession of peyote was a crime. Unemployment benefits could be denied when an employee was discharged for misconduct, in this case by ingesting peyote. Although the state defended the law as part of its general policy against drug use, the Oregon Supreme Court held that the state had not shown that the financial stability of the unemployment insurance fund would be "imperiled by claimants applying for religious exemptions if this claimant receives benefits."[90]

Dave Frohnmayer, Attorney General of Oregon, took the case to the U.S. Supreme Court. In 1988, the Court vacated the Oregon ruling and returned the case with the request that the Oregon Supreme Court decide whether the religious use of peyote was legal in that state. The U.S. Supreme Court pointed out that the results reached in *Sherbert* and other unemployment benefits cases "might well have been different if the employees had been discharged for engaging in criminal conduct."[91] The Oregon Supreme Court reaffirmed its earlier ruling by holding that the First Amendment entitled Smith and Black to their unemployment benefits.[92]

Frohnmayer urged the U.S. Supreme Court to review this latest decision of the Oregon Supreme Court. The case presented this question: Does the Free Exercise Clause of the First Amendment "protect a person's religiously motivated use of peyote from the reach of a state's general criminal law prohibition?" Frohnmayer objected strongly to the reliance by the state supreme court on congressional interpretations of the Constitution: "This process of canvassing congressional understanding to resolve an important first amendment question would be troubling under any circumstance."[93]

By the time the case returned to the U.S. Supreme Court, some of the original conditions had changed substantially to raise the question whether the dispute was still a live controversy. For example, as part of a federal consent decree, ADAPT agreed that religious use of peyote by NAC members would no longer be considered work-related misconduct. The conditions that led to

89. Id. at 449.
90. Id. at 451.
91. Employment Div. v. Smith, 485 U.S. 660, 671 (1988).
92. Smith v. Employment Division, 763 P.2d 146, 149 (Ore. 1988).
93. Petition for Writ of Certiorari to the Supreme Court of the State of Oregon, Employment Division v. Smith; 196 Landmark Briefs 425.

the denial of benefits to Smith and Black could not arise again in Oregon.[94] Smith and Black won back pay.[95]

In 1990, the U.S. Supreme Court attempted to settle the matter by holding that the Free Exercise Clause permits a state to prohibit sacramental peyote use and to deny unemployment benefits to persons discharged for such use. In *Employment Division v. Smith*, delivered by Justice Scalia, the Court ruled that state law may prohibit the possession and use of a drug even if it incidentally prohibits a religious practice, provided the state law is neutral and generally applicable to all individuals.[96]

Under this test, there was no need for the state to show a compelling interest or to use the least restrictive means. However, the issue of abandoning the compelling interest test was not before the Court. It was neither argued nor briefed. Remarkably, Scalia twice cited *Minersville School District v. Gobitis* (1940), the compulsory flag-salute decision that was bitterly attacked when it appeared and survived only three years before the Court overturned it.[97] Scalia acknowledged that his test would place religious minorities at the mercy of the political process, but discriminatory treatment was an "unavoidable consequence of democratic government."[98]

Scalia wrote for a 6–3 majority, with dissents from Blackmun, Brennan, and Marshall. O'Connor's concurrence read more like a dissent, accusing the Court of "dramatically" departing from "well-settled First Amendment jurisprudence" and finding the decision "incompatible with our Nation's fundamental commitment to individual religious liberty."[99] Her concurrence offered additional criticism of Scalia's decision.[100]

Immediately following the Court's decision, a broad coalition of religious groups expressed strong opposition to the ruling and sought a rehearing in the case. Among the organizations involved in this effort: American Friends Service Committee, American Jewish Committee, American Jewish Congress, Americans United for Separation of Church and State, Baptist Committee on Public Affairs, Christian Legal Society, Lutheran Church Missouri Synod, National Council of Churches, National Association of Evangelicals,

94. Brief in Opposition to Petition for Writ of Certiorari, Employment Division v. Smith; 196 Landmark Briefs 2.

95. Garrett Epps, "To an Unknown God: The Hidden History of *Employment Division v. Smith*," Ariz. St. L.J. 953, 989 (1998).

96. Employment Division v. Smith, 494 U.S. 872 (1990).

97. Id. at 879.

98. Id. at 890.

99. Id. at 891.

100. Id. at 892, 901, 902.

and the Presbyterian Church USA.[101] The Court denied the motion for a rehearing.[102]

With the judiciary offering no support for the individual rights involved in the case, interest groups turned to legislative remedies in Congress and Oregon. A bill introduced in Congress, the Religious Freedom Restoration Act (RFRA), was drafted to reinstate the *Sherbert* standard for protecting religious liberties. It was agreed that the objective should be to restore this constitutional standard and not focus on the sacramental use of peyote. Otherwise, the legislation would gain the reputation as "a drug bill."[103]

While Congress considered this proposal, the Oregon legislature repaired some of the damage of the U.S. Supreme Court's decision by enacting a bill to protect the sacramental use of peyote by the Native American Church. Al Smith testified in favor of the bill, advising the legislative committee that the "drug we have to worry about is alcohol."[104] As enacted in 1991, the bill states that in any prosecution for the manufacture, possession, or delivery of peyote, it is an affirmative defense that the peyote is being used or is intended for use (1) in connection with the good faith practice of a religious belief, (2) as directly associated with a religious practice, and (3) in a manner that is not dangerous to the health of the user or others who are in proximity to the user.[105]

Congressional hearings in 1992 explored the authority of Congress to enact legislation that would overturn the Supreme Court on constitutional issues. Representative Henry Hyde, a senior member of the House Judiciary Committee, argued that Congress had no authority to enact RFRA: "Congress is institutionally unable to restore a prior interpretation of the first amendment once the Supreme Court has rejected that interpretation. We are a legislature, not the Court."[106] He exaggerated the distinction between the legislative and judicial branches and offered no reason why Congress could not enact legislation that provided safeguards to individual rights that had been left unprotected by the Supreme Court.

At the hearing, Robert Dugan, Jr., of the National Association of Evangelicals testified that the Supreme Court, intended to be a guardian of constitutional freedoms, had "deprived us of our birthright as Americans" and

101. "High Court Urged to Reconsider," Wash. Post, May 12, 1990, at C11. See "Hail Mary Pass," Legal Times, May 14, 1990, at 11.

102. Employment Division v. Smith, 496 U.S. 913 (1990).

103. Long, Religious Freedom and Indian Rights, at 213.

104. "Panel Listens to Peyote Testimony," Salem, Oregon, Statesman Journal, April 6, 1991, at D1.

105. Oregon Laws, Chap. 329, § 1 (June 24, 1991), reprinted in 1995 Oregon Revised Statutes 475.992, § 5 (v. 9, p. 80).

106. "Religious Freedom Restoration Act of 1991," hearings before the House Committee on the Judiciary, 102d Cong., 2d Sess. 7 (1992).

emptied the Free Exercise Clause of its meaning. The system of checks and balances, he said, empowered Congress "to override the Court by restoring the compelling interest test."[107] Dallin Oaks from the Mormon Church and Nadine Strossen of the ACLU offered additional support for legislation designed to protect religious freedom.[108]

At Senate hearings, one witness called *Smith* "the Dred Scott of first amendment law."[109] In 1993 the House Judiciary Committee, voting 35 to 0, ordered RFRA reported.[110] For constitutional authority the committee pointed to Section 5 of the Fourteenth Amendment and the Necessary and Proper Clause embodied in Article I, Section 8. To the committee, Congress could provide "statutory protection for a constitutional value when the Supreme Court has been unwilling to assert its authority."[111] The House bill did not mandate that all states permit the ceremonial use of peyote; it merely subjected any prohibition to the compelling interest test.[112] The bill passed the House under suspension of the rules, which requires a two-thirds majority.[113]

The Senate Judiciary Committee, voting 15 to 1, reported RFRA for floor consideration.[114] By the time the bill headed for final passage, sixty-eight religious and civil liberties groups had lined up in support.[115] On final passage, the bill passed 97 to 3.[116] Under a motion of unanimous consent, the House passed the bill.[117] As enacted, RFRA provided that governments may substantially burden a person's religious exercise only if they demonstrate a compelling interest and use the least restrictive means of furthering that interest. The term "government" applied to any branch, department, agency, instrumentality, or official at the federal, state, and local levels.[118]

A year after enacting RFRA, Congress passed legislation to permit the use of peyote by Native Americans during religious ceremonies.[119] As Senator Paul Wellstone remarked, leaving the definition of standards for religious

107. Id. at 10, 14.
108. Id. at 25, 64–65.
109. Oliver S. Thomas, general counsel, Baptist Joint Committee on Public Affairs; "The Religious Freedom Restoration Act," hearing before the Senate Committee on the Judiciary, 102d Cong., 2d Sess. 42 (1992).
110. H. Rept. No. 103-88, 103d Cong., 1st Sess. 1–2 (1993).
111. Id. at 9.
112. Id. at 7.
113. 139 Cong. Rec. 9680–87 (1993).
114. S. Rept. No. 103-11, 103d Cong., 1st Sess. 2 (1993).
115. "Disparate Groups Unite behind Civil Rights Bill on Religious Freedom," Wash. Post, Oct. 16, 1993, at A7.
116. 139 Cong. Rec. 26416 (1993).
117. Id. at 27239–41 (1993).
118. 107 Stat. 1488 (1993).
119. 108 Stat. 3125 (1994).

freedom "up to the judiciary has not proven very effective for native American religions."[120] There had already been legislative and executive agency precedents to support a statutory exemption for peyote, including the American Indian Religious Freedom Act of 1978. Its legislative history explained that although previous congressional statutes "prohibit the use of peyote as a hallucinogen, it is established Federal law that peyote is constitutionally protected when used by a bona fide religion as a sacrament."[121] A rule issued by the Drug Enforcement Agency (DEA) in 1978 stated that the listing of peyote as "a controlled substance in Schedule I does not apply to the nondrug use of peyote in bona fide religious ceremonies of the Native American Church."[122]

Early in 1995, a district court in Texas held RFRA to be unconstitutional. Relying on dicta in *Baker v. Carr* (1962) and *United States v. Nixon* (1974), to the effect that the Court regards itself as the ultimate interpreter of the Constitution, the district court concluded that Congress cannot enact legislation that has the effect of overturning a Supreme Court decision.[123] That ruling was overturned a year later by the Fifth Circuit, which said the executive and legislative branches "also have both the right and duty to interpret the Constitution."[124] The Fifth Circuit found nothing unusual or illegitimate about Congress protecting constitutional right to a greater degree than the Supreme Court.[125]

Other courts also upheld the constitutionality of RFRA.[126] Whatever the Supreme Court decided to do with RFRA, it would acknowledge the role of nonjudicial bodies in protecting religious rights. If it upheld the statute, it would recognize that religious groups, acting in concert with Congress, could define religious freedom more generously than the Court. If it struck it down, it would merely reaffirm the 1990 *Smith* holding, which itself depended on the political process to protect religion. As the Court noted in *Smith*: "It may fairly be said that leaving accommodation to the political process will place at a relative disadvantage those religious practices that are not widely engaged in; but that unavoidable consequence of democratic government must be

120. 139 Cong. Rec. 10971 (1993).
121. S. Rept. No. 95-709, 95th Cong., 2d Sess. 3 (1978). The same sentence appears in H. Rept. No. 95-1308, 95th Cong., 2d Sess. 2 (1978).
122. 21 C.F.R. § 1307.31 (1978), referred to in 43 Fed. Reg. 56106 (1978).
123. Flores v. City of Boerne, 877 F. Supp. 355, 357 (W.D. Tex. 1995).
124. Flores v. City of Boerne, Tex., 73 F.3d 1352, 1356 (5th Cir. 1996).
125. Id. at 1363.
126. E.E.O.C. v. Catholic University of America, 83 F.3d 455, 470 (D.C. Cir. 1996); Abordo v. Hawaii, 902 F. Supp. 1220 (D. Hawaii 1995); Sasnett v. Department of Corrections, 891 F. Supp. 1305 (W.D. Wis. 1995), aff'd, Sasnett v. Sullivan, 91 F.3d 1018 (7th Cir. 1996); Belgard v. Hawaii, 883 F. Supp. 510 (D. Hawaii 1995). In 1996, a district court in Maryland held that RFRA usurped the Supreme Court's authority to determine the scope and meaning of the First Amendment and violated the separation of powers. Keeler v. Mayor & City Council of Cumberland, 928 F. Supp. 591 (D. Md. 1996).

preferred to a system in which each conscience is a law unto itself or in which judges weigh the social importance of all laws against the centrality of all religious beliefs."[127]

In *City of Boerne v. Flores* (1997), the Supreme Court ruled 6–3 that Congress exceeded the scope of its enforcement power under Section 5 of the Fourteenth Amendment in enacting parts of RFRA.[128] Writing for the Court, Justice Anthony Kennedy announced: "Under our Constitution, the Federal Government is one of enumerated powers."[129] Obviously that is not true. All three branches have implied powers drawn reasonably from express powers. Congress has the implied power to investigate, issue subpoenas, and hold individuals in contempt. The President has the implied power to remove certain executive officials. The Supreme Court has the implied power of judicial review.[130] In striking down parts of RFRA, the Court supplied this citation for support: *McCulloch v. Maryland* (1819).[131] However, in that decision the Supreme Court upheld the *implied* power of Congress to create a U.S. Bank.

Justice Kennedy warned that if Congress "could define its own powers by altering the Fourteenth Amendment's meaning, no longer would the Constitution be 'superior paramount law, unchangeable by ordinary means.'"[132] There is no intelligible distinction between what Congress does by statute and what Court does by case law in interpreting the meaning of the Fourteenth Amendment. Both actions are done outside the amendment process. Kennedy inserted some unintended humor with this grave admonition: "Shifting legislative majorities could change the Constitution and effectively circumvent the difficult and detailed amendment process contained in Article V."[133] The same risk flows from judicial decisions that reflect shifts in the composition or thinking of the Supreme Court. Two days before the Court invalidated RFRA, it overruled a decision from 1985 that had limited federal assistance to parochial schools.[134]

In various places, Justice Kennedy insisted on judicial supremacy: "When the Court has interpreted the Constitution, it has acted within the province of the Judicial Branch, which embraces the duty to say what the law is.

---

127. Employment Division v. Smith, 494 U.S. at 890.

128. City of Boerne v. Flores, 521 U.S. 507 (1997).

129. 521 U.S. at 516.

130. Louis Fisher, The Law of the Executive Branch: Presidential Power 58–62, 66–68 (2014).

131. 521 U.S. at 516.

132. Id. at 529.

133. Id.

134. Agostini v. Felton, 521 U.S. 203 (1997), reversing Aguilar v. Felton, 473 U.S. 402 (1985).

Marbury v. Madison, 1 Cranch, at 177."[135] The page cited has this famous sentence: "It is emphatically the province and duty of the judicial department to say what the law is." As explained in chapter 1, that merely says that courts *decide* cases, not that they are supreme over the other branches in interpreting the Constitution. Jerold Waltman, in his study of *Boerne*, regarded Kennedy's opinion as "one of the most extreme statements of unbridled judicial power." In effect, his words make Congress "a subordinate, not a coordinate, branch of government."[136]

A separate question concerned the constitutionality of RFRA as applied not to the states via the Fourteenth Amendment but to the federal government. In 1998, the Eighth Circuit held that RFRA was constitutional as applied to federal law. It did not violate the separation of powers doctrine or the Establishment Clause.[137] In 2001, the Tenth Circuit ruled that RFRA was a legitimate congressional action under Article I to govern the conduct of federal prison officials.[138]

Following *Boerne*, Congress in 1997 considered alternative legislation ("Son of RFRA") that relied not on the Fourteenth Amendment but on the Interstate Commerce Clause and the Spending Clause.[139] The following year, Senator Orrin Hatch introduced the Religious Liberty Protection Act to respond to *Boerne*, also relying primarily on the commerce and spending powers.[140] This legislation attracted broad support in Congress and among outside groups and became law in 2000.[141]

RFRA continues to provide a framework for religious liberty with regard to the federal government. In 2006, a unanimous Supreme Court ruled that the federal government failed under RFRA to demonstrate a compelling interest to justify a substantial burden on a religious group that used a hallucinogenic tea for communion services.[142] In 2014, the Supreme Court decided a case involving agency regulations regarding contraceptive methods available to employees. Those who owned and operated Hobby Lobby Stores objected that some of the contraceptives violated their Christian beliefs. The Court might have decided the case on First Amendment grounds but chose to interpret

135. City of Boerne v. Flores, 521 U.S. at 536.

136. Jerold Waltman, Congress, the Supreme Court, and Religious Liberty: The Case of *City of Boerne v. Flores* 162 (2013).

137. In re Young, 141 F.3d 854 (8th Cir. 1998), cert. denied, sub nom. Christians, Trustee v. Crystal Evangelical Free Church, 525 U.S. 811 (1998).

138. Kikumura v. Hurley, 242 F.3d 950 (10th Cir. 2001).

139. "Protecting Religious Freedom after Boerne v. Flores," hearing before the House Committee on the Judiciary, 105th Cong., 1st Sess. 2 (1997).

140. 144 Cong. Rec. 11386–89 (1998).

141. 114 Stat. 803 (2000).

142. Gonzales v. O Centro Espirita Beneficente Uniao do Vegetal, 546 U.S. 418 (2006).

the contraceptive mandate solely on the statutory policy established in RFRA.[143]

Edison Chiloquin and Klamath Indians

This book offers many examples of Congress protecting the rights of minorities. At times it protects a minority within a minority. Adult members of the Klamath Indians in Oregon were given the option of holding their land interests in common under state law or converting their interests to cash. In a 1958 election, approximately 77 percent of the tribal members voted to sell a portion of their property. Edison Chiloquin voted against this transfer.[144] The federal government used the land to create the Winema National Forest.

Legislation in 1973 directed the Secretary of Agriculture to acquire 135,000 acres of land to be added to the Winema National Forest. Purchase of the land resulted in the disbursement of $270,000 to each Indian beneficiary. Chiloquin refused to accept the money. Instead, he wanted land to establish a village founded on traditional values and the preservation of Indian culture, ways, and spiritual beliefs. To underscore his determination, he built a tipi in the forest, became a squatter, and kept a sacred fire lit. There was little reason for him to expect judicial relief. Could he count on Congress for protection?

The purpose of a private bill introduced in Congress in 1980 for Chiloquin was to avoid, as Senator Mark Hatfield said, "confrontation and all other kinds of unpleasantries of trying to expel this man from the lands that are his ancestral home."[145] The bill specified that the land set aside for Chiloquin "shall not be inconsistent with its cultural, historical, and archeological character." If Chiloquin or his heirs used the land for other than "traditional Indian purposes," it would revert to the United States to protect archaeological, cultural, and traditional values associated with the property. This private bill became law.[146]

The role of Congress and broad public involvement in basic constitutional questions of religious liberty underscore why it is impracticable and misleading, on both political and legal grounds, to look automatically (and

143. Burwell v. Hobby Lobby Stores, Inc., 573 U.S. ___ (2014).
144. Background on the Edison Chiloquin bill comes from H. Rept. No. 1406, 96th Cong., 2d Sess. (1980). See also Garrett Epps, To an Unknown God: Religious Freedom on Trial 49–52 (2001), and Theodore Stern, The Klamath Tribe: A People and Their Reservation 249–52 (1965).
145. 126 Cong. Rec. 30379 (1980).
146. 94 Stat. 3613 (1980).

optimistically) to the courts for the protection of individual and minority rights. Native Americans found victory not in courtrooms but in legislative chambers, both in Congress and at the state level. They prevailed because they were effective in working with many other interest groups that wanted to safeguard rights that were unattainable from the courts.

8

STRENGTHENING U.S. DEMOCRACY

This book has explored how individual rights are protected. The conventional answer—by the judiciary—is belied by U.S. history. Judicial safeguards are largely of the past six decades, and the pattern over those years has been quite uneven. Presidents can contribute important leadership at times, though their role has not been dominant. As with the other branches, Congress has violated individual rights, but the general legislative record has been steady and significant. Legislative contributions have also come the states.

Protection of individual rights often depends on pressures that build outside the three branches. In a speech in 1969, Justice Thurgood Marshall highlighted the importance of public participation: "No matter how solemn and profound the declarations of principle contained in our charter of government, no matter how dedicated and independent our judiciary, true justice can only be obtained through the actions of committed individuals, individuals acting both independently and through organized groups."[1] His own work as a private attorney in desegregation cases, leading to *Brown v. Board of Education* in 1954, underscores that point. Congress and state legislatures play a key role because public pressures are funneled through lawmakers and legislative committees.

How confident are we today that Congress can continue to protect individual rights? As witnessed by the Lilly Ledbetter legislation in 2009, Congress has the capacity to protect rights, but there are reasons to be concerned about its contemporary capacity. One factor is the manner in which constitutional law is taught in law schools and political science classes. The approach is case-driven, with students reading one judicial decision after another with little attention to contributions from the elected branches. As explained in chapter 1, the misleading assumption that the final word resides in the Supreme Court is widely accepted by reporters who cover the Court, while senior members of Congress who read the decisions are willing to offer some criticism but then defer to the Court's judgment. Those attitudes put Congress in a subordinate, not coequal, position.

---

1. Thurgood Marshall, "Group Action in the Pursuit of Justice," 44 N.Y.U. L. Rev. 661, 662 (1969).

159

This book has described the many accomplishments of Congress. What steps might be taken to restore and strengthen its institutional capacity? This chapter focuses on five areas: changing the way that Congress schedules its work, urging members of Congress to protect their prerogatives, providing better institutional resources, adopting congressional districts that are not gerrymandered, and addressing the problem of campaign expenditures that undermine congressional independence and effectiveness.

Making Time for Legislative Work

There has been concern in recent years that members of Congress are not in town a sufficient number of days to discharge their legislative duties and provide close oversight of the executive branch. Lawmakers typically arrive in Washington on Tuesday for votes scheduled that evening and leave after votes on Thursday afternoon. That leaves only one full day—Wednesday— for committee hearings, marking up bills, meetings, and floor action. Instead of holding formal hearings to hear executive officials and experts offer different views on public issues, committee staff are more likely to receive one-sided briefings from agency officials and rely on that information to provide advice to committee members.[2]

Representatives and Senators have extremely demanding jobs that require close attention to highly technical issues. Even after mastering substantive details, it takes time to draft compromise language that will permit passage and enactment. With a short workweek, lawmakers are less likely to spend time with members of the opposite party at social gatherings, meet their families, build mutual respect, and develop trust to reach across the aisle for bipartisan solutions. Because lawmakers have few such contacts, it is easier to demonize the other party and lose opportunities for constructive work.

The decline in the effectiveness of Congress prompted the creation of the Bipartisan Policy Center (BPC) in 2007, cochaired by these former members of Congress: Senator Tom Daschle, Representative Dan Glickman, Senator Dirk Kempthorne, Senator Trent Lott, and Senator Olympia Snowe. It seeks solutions in today's hyperpartisan climate where citizens and members of Congress are apt to get information from ideologically driven sources. The hope is to listen to each other and find common ground. In 2013, BPC launched the Commission on Political Reform to advocate specific reforms to improve the political process. It released a thoughtful report called

2. Michael L. Koempel, "Being a Member of Congress: Some Notable Changes during the Last Half Century," The Evolving Congress, S. Prt. 113–30, 113th Cong., 2d Sess. 66 (2014).

"Governing in a Polarized America: A Bipartisan Blueprint to Strengthen our Democracy."

One conclusion is that Congress is simply not performing the job it is required to do, including passing budgets and ensuring that the federal government will not close down. Bills often come to the floor without prior committee action. Lawmakers, particularly in the Senate, have difficulty in offering amendments. The commission's report recommends that the two chambers of Congress schedule three five-day workweeks in Washington, D.C., followed by one-week recesses to tend to issues in their home districts and states. The next requirement is to ensure that lawmakers carry out their constitutional duties while in session.

Protecting Congressional Prerogatives

Members of Congress take an oath to support and defend the Constitution, "without any mental reservations or purpose of evasion." Developments from World War II to the present time do little to support the Framers' expectation that each branch of government would protect itself by repulsing usurpations and transgressions by other branches. From 1789 to 1945, the Framers' constitutional design worked fairly well. The last six decades, however, witness members of Congress abdicating their institutional powers, including those over war and spending. Abdication means to relinquish a power that has been entrusted to you. In the case of Congress, it also means relinquishing a power that has been placed with the people. It marks a loss of self-government.

The contemporary shift of congressional authority to the President and at times to the Supreme Court belies a core belief by the Framers that each branch would protect its own prerogatives. This principle is basic to the system of checks and balances. James Madison argued in Federalist No. 51 that "the great security against a gradual concentration of the several powers in the same department, consists in giving to those who administer each department the necessary constitutional means and personal motives to resist encroachments of the others. . . . Ambition must be made to counter ambition. The interest of the man must be connected with the constitutional rights of the place."[3] In republican government, he said, "the legislative authority necessarily predominates."[4]

The Framers were particularly intent in vesting the power of the purse and the power of initiating war with Congress, as the people's representative.

3. The Federalist 356.
4. Id.

The U.S. Constitution places the power of the purse squarely in Congress. Under Article I, Section 9, "No Money shall be drawn from the Treasury, but in Consequence of Appropriations made by Law." In Federalist No. 48, Madison explained that "the legislative department alone has access to the pockets of the people."[5] The power of the purse, he said in Federalist No. 58, represents the "most complete and effectual weapon with which any constitution can arm the immediate representatives of the people, for obtaining a redress of every grievance, and for carrying into effect every just and salutary measure."[6]

From 1789 to 1945, all major military actions were either declared or authorized by Congress. Over that period, Presidents and executive officials uniformly acknowledged the need to come to Congress for authority to support anything other than purely defensive operations. Toward the end of World War II, however, the Joint Committee on the Organization of Congress, established in 1944, voiced its apprehension about the decline of Congress in relation to the executive branch. There was a growing tendency to shift policy making—domestic and foreign—to the Executive, "partly because of the comparative lack of effective instrumentalities and the less adequate facilities in the legislative branch." It was necessary for Congress to "modernize its machinery, coordinate its various parts, and establish the research facilities that can provide it with the knowledge that is power."[7] The Legislative Reorganization Act of 1946 restructured congressional committees and strengthened analytical resources within Congress.

In 1950, President Harry Truman ordered U.S. troops to engage in military operations against North Korea without ever seeking authority from Congress. This was the first time that a President used military force in a major war and Congress failed to protect its prerogatives. As a substitute for Congress, Truman obtained resolutions from the UN Security Council in flat violation of the UN Participation Act of 1945, which required the President to first seek approval from Congress for UN military operations.[8] This method of bypassing Congress was later used by President Clinton in Haiti and Bosnia and by President Obama in Libya. When Clinton could not receive support from the Security Council to use military force in Kosovo, he obtained "authority" from NATO allies.[9] The Constitution does not allow

---

5. Id. at 345.
6. Id. at 391.
7. S. Doc. No. 36, 79th Cong., 1st Sess. 2 (1945).
8. 59 Stat. 621, sec. 6 (1945); Louis Fisher, Presidential War Power 80–99 (3d ed., 2013); Louis Fisher, "The Korean War: On What Legal Basis Did Truman Act?," 89 Am. J. Int'l L. 21 (1995); http://www.loufisher.org/docs/wp/425.pdf.
9. Fisher, Presidential War Power, at 178–91, 197–200.

congressional prerogatives to be transferred to international and regional authorities.[10]

Through these presidential military initiatives and the appropriations they required, part of the power of the purse shifted to the executive branch. The next threat to the spending power came when President Richard Nixon claimed inherent authority not to spend funds appropriated by Congress. Both houses of Congress responded quickly and effectively by passing the Impoundment Control Act of 1974 to deny Nixon and his successors that kind of authority.[11] Having protected legislative prerogatives, Congress then proceeded to debate and finally pass the Line Item Veto Act of 1996, allowing the President to decide what he will and will not spend—precisely the power that Nixon had claimed unilaterally.[12] This loss of congressional spending power eventually led to a Supreme Court decision striking down the item veto legislation.[13]

When President Ronald Reagan took office in January 1981, the total national debt—covering the period from 1789 to his inauguration—stood at one trillion dollars. Because of his tax cuts and increased military spending, both of which Congress supported, the national debt tripled during his eight years in office. The national debt rose another trillion during the four years of President George H. W. Bush. Initiatives by President Bill Clinton brought the deficit under control and even projected surpluses. However, another round of tax cuts and military increases under George W. Bush led to sharp increases in the national debt, which now exceeds eighteen trillion dollars. The Congressional Budget Office projects even higher levels over the next decade. Throughout this period there has been little leadership from the President or members of Congress in controlling deficits.[14]

Members of Congress need to rededicate themselves to fulfilling institutional duties and protecting legislative prerogatives. They can help explain to their constituents the importance of maintaining constitutional checks on executive and judicial power. If citizens decide to continue bashing Congress, the result will be a continued shift of power to the President and the Supreme Court. The values of democracy and self-government will further decline. Constituents should recognize that their own interests coincide with the system of checks and balances and a Congress able and willing to discharge its constitutional powers.

10. Louis Fisher, "Sidestepping Congress: Presidents Acting under the U.N. and NATO," 47 Case W. Res. L. Rev. 1237 (1997); http://www.loufisher.org/docs/424.pdf.
11. Louis Fisher, Congressional Abdication on War and Spending 115–22 (2000).
12. Id. at 137–51.
13. Clinton v. City of New York, 524 U.S. 417 (1998).
14. Louis Fisher, "Presidential Fiscal Accountability following the Budget Act of 1974," 67 Maine L. Rev. 286 (2015).

Improving Institutional Resources

The Legislative Reorganization Act of 1946 sought to give Congress greater access to its own analytical experts rather than rely heavily on executive sources. The statute authorized the Librarian of Congress to appoint a corps of "Senior Specialists" to cover such broad fields as American government and public administration, American public law, full employment, housing, international affairs, money and banking, taxation, and fiscal policy. The grade for Senior Specialists was set at not less than the highest grade in the executive branch "to which research analysts and consultants without supervisory responsibility are currently assigned."[15]

The Legislative Reorganization Act of 1970 marked a second attempt to strengthen the research capacity of Congress. This statute was far more explicit, directing the Library of Congress to recruit high-level professionals capable of assisting Congress with its substantive duties. The statute changed the name of the Legislative Reference Service (which dated back to 1914) to Congressional Research Service (CRS), anticipating that it would triple in size from three hundred to about nine hundred and greatly deepen its analytical mission. Senior Specialists were to be paid at a level of GS-17. The clear intent was to create a congressional staff agency with the capacity and willingness to provide Congress with nonpartisan and expert analysis. Senior Specialists were required to do more than simply present two sides of a question. If one side was stronger, it was their duty to say so. The same obligation applied to newly created CRS research Specialists at the level of GS-16. Congress expected the work of CRS to involve "more creative effort than the mere acquisition, storage and retrieval of data and information produced elsewhere."[16]

When I became Senior Specialist in Separation of Powers in 1988, there were eighteen of us, housed in a separate office and supported by research assistants. To be selected, Senior Specialists had to compete against other "nationally recognized experts." CRS selected its last Senior Specialist through a competitive process in 1989. Since that time, CRS management allowed the number of Senior Specialists to drift down, by attrition and retirement. As of 2015, there are only three remaining Senior Specialists, all of them nearing retirement. The number will soon be zero.

Similarly, CRS management allowed the number of research Specialists at the GS-16 level to drop from about thirty-eight in the late 1980s to three by 2015, with that number heading to zero with pending retirements. Over a period of two decades, CRS management eliminated the two top levels of experts within the agency that Congress had established by law to assist it with substantive duties and constitutional analysis needed to protect legislative power. The violation of statutory policy increased because of another CRS decision.

From 1989 forward, CRS management began assigning the titles (and salaries) of "specialist" and "senior specialist" to administrative officials who did not compete for those positions, were not nationally recognized experts, and lacked the education, experience, and analytical skills to function in the substantive areas statutorily designated by Congress. They were unable to write reports, testify before committees, or meet with lawmakers and their staff to discuss policy issues. By law, Congress had announced: "We need substantive specialists with nationally recognized credentials to help us with our legislative and constitutional duties." By administrative action, CRS management responded: "No, you don't." House and Senate members who served on committees that provided oversight of the Library of Congress allowed this elimination of high-level professional assistance.[17]

This willingness to weaken the institutional capacity of Congress extends more broadly. On May 12, 2015, the House Appropriations Committee reported the legislative branch appropriations bill. It kept the Library of Congress at the previous year's budget level and denied CRS its requested increase of five million dollars. In 1980, CRS had 868 employees. Its current staffing level is just over six hundred. The committee report explained that its bill "reflects continued acknowledgment that the Legislative Branch must set itself as an example for fiscal restraint while continuing to serve the Nation."[18]

In fact, Congress cannot serve the Nation if it is inadequately staffed. Two members of House Appropriations objected: "this bill falls short in providing Congress with the resources needed to fulfill its constitutional duties."[19] "Vital Statistics on Congress," compiled by the American Enterprise Institute and the Brookings Institution, documents the loss of professional support in Congress. Although the personal staff for Representatives and Senators from 1979 to the present time has remained steady, there have been substantial reductions in committee staff. Congress lacks the capacity to adequately review and analyze executive branch claims.

An article by Harry Stein and Ethan Gurwitz in 2015 explains how Congress makes itself dysfunctional by reducing its own budget. The funding level for the legislative branch is now about 17 percent less than inflation-adjusted FY 2010 levels. Particularly hard-hit are cutbacks in professional

17. For further details on the decline of senior specialists and specialists within CRS, see Louis Fisher, Defending Congress and the Constitution 287–309 (2011).
18. H. Rept. No. 114-110, 114th Cong., 1st Sess. (2015).
19. Representatives Nita M. Lowey and Debbie Wasserman Schultz.

committee staff, which have fallen by about one-third.[20] One consequence is that Congress depends more heavily on outside organizations that have their own special interests to promote. Those groups are now positioned to exercise greater control over legislation that passes through Congress, enabling them to advance their policies and financial interests.[21]

Eliminating Gerrymandered Districts

Another institutional weakness is the manner in which House seats are drawn. In 1901 and 1911, statutory language required that congressional districts be "contiguous and compact territory."[22] That requirement was dropped in 1929.[23] In subsequent years, the Supreme Court decided a number of redistricting cases, for both Congress and the states, without providing clear guidelines on the constitutionality of "bizarre" districting designed to promote racial and political objectives.[24] As Justice Scalia acknowledged when writing for the Court in 2004: "no judicially discernable and manageable standards for adjudicating political gerrymandering claims have emerged."[25]

The boundaries of congressional districts are drawn by the states, either by their legislatures or by independent redistricting commissions.[26] However, Congress has the duty and authority to protect the effectiveness of its institution. Under Article I, Section 4, it is empowered to alter state regulations of elections "except as to the Places of chusing Senators." Congress does not have to leave this issue entirely to the courts or the states. Redistricting by states can produce oddly drawn House districts that are insular and ideologically based, often to protect incumbents. Those lawmakers are then less able and willing to participate in consensus legislation. Congress can act by statute, not

20. Harry Stein & Ethan Gurwitz, "Congress Makes Itself Dysfunctional with Legislative Branch Cuts," Center for American Progress, June 15, 2015; https://www.americanprogress .org/issues/economy/news/2015/06/15/114975/congress-makes-itself-dysfunctional-with -legislative-branch-cuts.

21. Austin Wright & Leigh Munsil, "In House Bill, Arms Makers Wrote Their Own Rules," Politico, May 12, 2015; see also Paul Glastris & Haley Sweetland Edwards, "The Big Lobotomy: How Republicans Made Congress Stupid," Washington Monthly, June/July/ August 2014.

22. 31 Stat. 734, sec. 3 (1901); 37 Stat. 14, sec. 3 (1911).

23. 46 Stat. 26, sec. 22 (1929).

24. E.g., Shaw v. Reno, 509 U.S. 630 (1993). See Louis Fisher & Katy J. Harriger, American Constitutional Law 1000–22 (10th ed., 2013).

25. Vieth v. Jubelirer, 541 U.S. 267, 281 (2004).

26. Royce Crocker, "Congressional Redistricting: An Overview," Congressional Research Service, Report R42831, Nov. 21, 2012.

to actually draw district lines but to establish requirements for contiguity and compactness, as it did in the past.

In an article in 2014, Norm Ornstein analyzed the harm done to Congress by gerrymandered districts that are fundamentally safe for one party, with many Republican districts containing "barely more than trace elements of minorities." Instead of heterogeneous districts, forcing lawmakers to confront and balance competing elements, the result is an "echo-chamber effect, where members' ideological predilections are reinforced, not challenged." The pattern is one of lawmakers "choosing their voters instead of voters choosing their lawmakers," creating "more disaffection and cynicism among the public."[27] No doubt the political hurdles here are substantial. Political gerrymandering can offer benefits to Democrats and Republicans. The question is whether it damages the institution of Congress and the aspiration for self-government. Those issues should be explored in committee hearings to consider remedial legislation.

On June 5, 2015, a panel of federal judges found that Virginia lawmakers had illegally concentrated black voters into one congressional district to reduce their influence elsewhere. The court ordered the Virginia House of Delegates to redraw the state's eleven-district congressional map by September 1. By diluting the number of blacks in the black-majority district, adjacent districts would be less Republican and more vulnerable to Democratic challenges. An appeal is likely.[28]

In its report "Governing in a Polarized America," the Commission on Political Reform points out that the number of competitive House districts has declined by more than one-third since the 1970s. With so many seats firmly in the control of a single party, the essential vote is not in the general election but in the primaries, where a candidate can appeal to a small section of the party's base and win the seat. That individual is poorly equipped by ideology and experience to work jointly and effectively with other members of Congress. Voting in favor of moderate legislation could jeopardize chances in the next primary fight. The Commission on Political Reform recommends that states adopt redistricting commissions that have the bipartisan support of the legislature and the electorate. That process should be guided by congressional legislation requiring that House districts be contiguous and compact.

During oral argument on March 2, 2015, the Supreme Court heard from contending sides on Arizona's method of drawing lines for congressional districts. In 2000, a voter initiative in Arizona placed that responsibility with a five-member independent commission. Opponents argued that it was

27. Norm Ornstein, "Gerrymandering's Fallout," National Journal Daily, Dec. 4, 2014, at 7.
28. Jenna Portnoy & Laura Vozzella, "Virginia Inches toward New Congressional Map," Wash. Post, June 6, 2015, B1.

unconstitutional to vest that duty in an unelected commission instead of the state legislature. Divided 5–4, the Supreme Court upheld the Arizona voter initiative.[29] Other states have experimented with transferring to commissions the task of deciding the contours of congressional districts.[30]

Limiting Campaign Expenditures

In response to the impact of money on federal and state elections, E. J. Dionne has written: "The fact that so many Americans see politics as dominated by wealthy interests that make large campaign contributions remains one of the central reasons why Americans continue to mistrust politics—and sometimes come to hate it."[31] To what extent does the amount of money in political campaigns weaken the ability of Congress to perform its constitutional duties and protect individual rights?

The time needed to perform legislative and oversight responsibilities is consumed when lawmakers must seek money for their individual races and their party. In Congress, about 20–25 percent of a member's week is spent raising money. Precious time to fulfill constitutional functions is lost. If members fall short in meeting the party's quota assigned to them, they can be removed from committees and denied the right to ever chair a committee or subcommittee, no matter how long they have served or the level of their expertise. The pursuit of money affects not only individual lawmakers but how the entire institution operates.

Congressional efforts to control campaign expenditures have been blocked by Supreme Court decisions in *Buckley v. Valeo* (1976) and *Citizens United* (2010), concluding that corporations are "persons," money is "speech," and corporations' political contributions are therefore protected by the First Amendment.[32] It is important to closely evaluate the quality and reasoning of those decisions to determine how Congress should respond. This book has provided many examples of congressional legislation being invalidated by the Court, with Congress later able to prevail: legislation regarding public accommodations for blacks, the right of women to practice law, child-labor regulations, and the Lilly Ledbetter case for equal pay. Do the rulings in *Buckley* and

29. Arizona State Legislature v. Arizona Independent Redistricting Comm'n, 576 U.S. ___ (2015).

30. Adam Liptak, "Court Skeptical of Arizona Plan for Less-Partisan Congressional Redistricting," N.Y. Times, March 3, 2015, A18; Robert Barnes, "Supreme Court Looks at Arizona's Redistricting Commission," Wash. Post, March 3, 2015, A3.

31. E. J. Dionne, Jr., Why Americans Hate Politics 10 (2004 ed.).

32. Buckley v. Valeo, 424 U.S. 1 (1976); Citizens United v. Federal Election Comm'n, 558 U.S. 310 (2010).

Citizens United merit a congressional challenge? To answer that question, it is necessary to review judicial decisions to form a judgment about them.

First, we need to understand the difference between natural persons and corporations. In the *Dartmouth College* case in 1819, Chief Justice John Marshall used plain talk to describe a corporation as "an artificial being, invisible, intangible, and existing only in contemplation of law." As the "mere creature of law," it possesses "only those properties" conferred upon it.[33] Natural persons are not creatures of law. They do not possess only those properties recognized in law. One property conferred by law on corporations, Marshall said, is immortality. No such property extends to natural persons.

The idea that corporations are persons under the Constitution surfaced in the 1886 *Santa Clara* case, even though the issue was never *briefed, argued, reasoned, analyzed, or even decided*. Does such a judicial process sound possible or even conceivable? Before oral argument began, Chief Justice Morrison Remick Waite told the parties: "The court does not wish to hear argument on the question whether the provision in the Fourteenth Amendment to the Constitution, which forbids a State to deny to any person within its jurisdiction the equal protection of the laws, applies to these corporations. We are all of opinion that it does."[34] His remarks appear not in the Court's decision but in the headnote prepared by the clerk to summarize the holding.

Nowhere in the unanimous decision in *Santa Clara* did Justice John Marshall Harlan refer to corporations as "persons" under the Fourteenth Amendment. Yet the headnote begins: "The defendant Corporations are persons within the intent of the clause in section 1 of the Fourteenth Amendment to the Constitution of the United States, which forbids a State to deny to any person within its jurisdiction the equal protection of the laws."[35] Apparently the clerk did not bother to read the Fourteenth Amendment. Section 1 opens with: "All persons born or naturalized in the United States." Obviously that refers to natural persons, not artificial creations. Corporations are not born or naturalized. Calling a corporation a person is a metaphor, a legal fiction.[36]

Over the years, the Supreme Court has made many false and misleading claims about *Santa Clara*. In 1896, Justice Harlan said it was "now settled that corporations are persons under the Fourteenth Amendment," citing *Santa Clara*.[37] In fact, his ruling in *Santa Clara* said nothing about that.

33. Trustees of Dartmouth College v. Woodward, 17 (4 Wheat.) 518, 636 (1819).
34. Santa Clara Co. v. South. Pac. Railroad, 118 U.S. 394 (1886).
35. Id. at 394–95. For background on this headnote, see Jack Beatty, Age of Betrayal: The Triumph of Money in America, 1865–1900, at 110–11, 171–78 (2008 ed.).
36. Jess M. Krannich, "The Corporate 'Person': A New Analytical Approach to a Flawed Method of Constitutional Interpretation," 37 Loy. U. Chic. L.J. 61 (2005).
37. Covington &c. Turnpike Co. v. Sandford, 164 U.S. 578, 592 (1896).

A decade later he corrected his error. Writing for a unanimous Court, he said the liberty guaranteed by the Fourteenth Amendment "is the liberty of natural, not artificial persons."[38] A year later, in another unanimous Harlan decision, the Court said the Fourteenth Amendment applies to "natural, not artificial, persons."[39]

Those decisions attempted to correct the erroneous headnote in *Santa Clara*. However, the record of the Supreme Court demonstrates that once an error appears in a decision—or rather in this case a headnote—it will continue to be cited as authority and create confusion. A dissent by Justice Hugo Black in 1938 wrote falsely that the Court in *Santa Clara* "decided for the first time that the word 'person' in the Fourteenth Amendment did in some instances include corporations."[40] There was no such decision. A dissent by Justices William O. Douglas and Black in 1949 stated it was "so held" in *Santa Clara* that a corporation is a "person" under the Equal Protection Clause of the Fourteenth Amendment.[41] There was no such holding.

A dissent by Justice William Rehnquist in 1978 presented a better understanding. He pointed to Justice Harlan's opinion for a unanimous Court in 1906 that the liberty under the Fourteenth Amendment is "the liberty of natural, not artificial persons."[42] Rehnquist added: "it cannot be disputed that the mere creation of a corporation does not invest it with all the liberties enjoyed by natural persons," pointing out that corporations do not enjoy the privilege against self-incrimination.[43]

With this checkered judicial history, why should we accept that (1) corporations are persons under the Fourteenth Amendment, (2) they are entitled under the First Amendment to spend money as "speech" in political elections, and (3) Congress and state legislatures may not limit those expenditures? In 1976, the Court in *Buckley v. Valeo* reviewed legislation passed by Congress two years earlier to reform the funding of federal elections. The statute responded to political abuses that "culminated in the 1972 presidential campaign and its aftermath, commonly called Watergate. Congress found that those excesses were fueled by money collected for political purposes."[44]

The Court in *Buckley* accepted the judgment of Congress that contributions give rise to concern about quid pro quos and may invite political corruption.

38. Northwestern Life Ins. Co. v. Riggs, 203 U.S. 243, 255 (1906).
39. Western Turf Association v. Greenberg, 204 U.S. 359, 363 (1907).
40. Conn. General Co. v. Johnson, 303 U.S. 77, 87 (1938) (Black, J., dissenting).
41. Wheeling Steel Corp. v. Glander, 337 U.S. 562, 576 (1949).
42. First National Bank of Boston v. Bellotti, 435 U.S. 765, 822 (1978) (Rehnquist, J., dissenting).
43. Id. at 824.
44. J. Skelly Wright, "Politics and the Constitution: Is Money Speech?," 85 Yale L.J. 1001, 1003 (1976).

Although *expenditures* are not immune from corruption, the Court reasoned that limits "on the amount of money a person or group can spend on political communications during a campaign necessarily reduces the quantity of expression by restricting the number of issues discussed, the depth of their exploration, and the size of the audience reached."[45] No doubt that is true, but on what constitutional grounds were corporations entitled to spend unlimited money for political campaigns, and wouldn't such expenditures raise concerns about corruption, which is what Congress found in passing the law?

In one of the dissents in *Buckley*, Justice Byron White said the majority had accepted the maxim that "money talks."[46] Anthony Lewis of the *New York Times* remarked: "We know that money talks; but that is the problem, not the answer."[47] To Judge Harold Leventhal, who served on the D.C. Circuit that upheld the 1974 legislation, the central question is not whether money is speech or not, but "the need to maintain confidence in self-government, and to prevent the erosion of democracy which comes from a popular view of government as responsive only or mainly to special interests."[48]

As explained by Judge Leventhal, Theodore Roosevelt in the early 1900s was "sensitive to the accusation that the Republican Party was the party of the monied interests," a charge later supported by investigations in 1905 about life insurance financial contributions to campaigns in New York.[49] In 1907, Congress passed the Tillman Act to prohibit any national bank or federal corporation from making "a money contribution in connection with any election to any political office." Nor could corporations make a financial contribution to any election "at which Presidential and Vice-Presidential electors or a Representative in Congress is to be voted for or any election by any State legislature of a United States Senator." Corporations in violation of this statute were subject to fines and imprisonment.[50] In 1934, while upholding a provision of the Federal Corrupt Practices Act of 1925, the Supreme Court underscored the authority of Congress to protect federal elections from corruption: "To say that Congress is without power to pass appropriate legislation to safeguard such an election from the improper use of money to influence the result is to deny to the nation in a vital particular the power of self protection."[51]

For nearly seven decades, it was understood that Congress possessed constitutional authority to keep federal elections free from the corrupting

45. 424 U.S. 1, 19 (1976).
46. Id. at 262.
47. Harold Leventhal, "Courts and Political Thickets," 77 Colum. L. Rev. 345, 359 (1977).
48. Id. at 362.
49. Id. at 363.
50. 34 Stat. 864 (1907).
51. Burroughs and Cannon v. U.S., 290 U.S. 534, 545 (1934).

influence of corporate spending. There was no claim that corporations were natural persons at liberty to spend unlimited amounts in elections to exercise their First Amendment right of speech. Why did things change with *Buckley v. Valeo* and *Citizens United*?

Part of the answer lies in Justices who misread Supreme Court decisions. In 1978, the Court divided 5–4 in striking down a Massachusetts statute that prohibited corporations from making contributions or expenditures to referenda and elections.[52] Speaking for the Court, Justice Powell said: "If the speakers here were not corporations, no one would suggest that the State could silence their proposed speech. It is the type of speech indispensable to decisionmaking in a democracy."[53] He added this footnote: "It has been settled for almost a century that corporations are persons within the meaning of the Fourteenth Amendment," citing *Santa Clara*.[54] But the Court in *Santa Clara* did not *decide* that question, much less "settle" it. Powell seemed unaware that Justice Harlan later corrected the misconception caused by the clerk's headnote.

The difficulty of following judicial reasoning on campaign finance cases is evident by reading Court decisions from 1982 forward.[55] Of special interest is a decision in 2000 that produced dissents from Justices Kennedy, Thomas, and Scalia.[56] Kennedy, who would write for the Court in *Citizens United*, stated: "The plain fact is that the compromise the Court invented in *Buckley* set the stage for a new kind of speech to enter the political system."[57] That statement is extraordinary. It meant that *Buckley* did not reflect careful and reliable constitutional analysis. Instead, it represented a compromise "invented" by the Court to yield a type of speech that did not previously exist.

Kennedy found sufficient grounds "to reject *Buckley*'s wooden formula."[58] He warned that the "melancholy history of campaign finance in *Buckley*'s wake shows what can happen when we intervene in the dynamics of speech and expression by inventing an artificial scheme of our own."[59] His advice was to "overrule *Buckley* and then free Congress or state legislatures to attempt some new reform, if, based upon their own considered view of the First Amendment,

52. First National Bank of Boston v. Bellotti, 435 U.S. 765 (1978).
53. Id. at 777.
54. Id. at 780, n.15.
55. Common Cause v. Schmitt, 455 U.S. 129 (1982); FEC v. National Right to Work Committee, 459 U.S. 197 (1982); FEC v. National Conservative PAC, 470 U.S. 480 (1985); FEC v. Massachusetts Citizens for Life, Inc., 479 U.S. 243 (1986); Austin v. Michigan Chamber of Commerce, 494 U.S. 652 (1990); Colorado Republican Federal Campaign Comm. v. Federal Election Comm'n, 518 U.S. 604 (1996).
56. Nixon v. Shrink Missouri PAC, 528 U.S. 377 (2000).
57. Id. at 406.
58. Id. at 407.
59. Id.

it is possible to do so."[60] In other words, take the issue away from the Supreme Court and let it be handled by the elected branches. Nevertheless, in deciding *Citizen United* ten years later, Kennedy relied repeatedly on *Buckley*.[61]

A campaign finance decision in 2003 consumed 272 pages, with seven Justices dissenting in part: Scalia, Thomas, Kennedy, Rehnquist, Stevens, Ginsburg, and Breyer.[62] Despite chronic problems with *Buckley*, a plurality of the Court in 2006 relied on it to prevent Vermont from imposing limits on campaign expenditures.[63] Thomas and Scalia rejected the plurality's approach, pointing to "the continuing inability of the Court (and the plurality here) to apply *Buckley* in a coherent and principled fashion."[64] A 2007 case found the Court once again divided 5–4 in holding unconstitutional a federal statute that made it a crime for any corporation to broadcast shortly before an election day any communication that names a federal candidate for elected office and that is targeted for the electorate.[65]

The Supreme Court often invalidates legislation when it decides that Congress has provided inadequate justification.[66] What about inadequate justification by the Court? In writing for the Court in *Citizens United*, Justice Kennedy offered several assertions about corporate spending in elections unsupported by any evidence. One claim: "we now conclude that independent expenditures, including those made by corporations, do not give rise to corruption or the appearance of corruption."[67] Based on actual data, experience, and findings, Congress and a number of states have determined that corporate spending in political campaigns not only provides the appearance of corruption but results in actual corruption. The Court gave no deference to those elected branch judgments and analysis.

Here is a second assertion by Kennedy unaccompanied by any corroborating evidence: "The appearance of [corporate] influence or access, furthermore, will not cause the electorate to lose faith in our democracy."[68] Courts need to anchor their decisions on reliable information and convincing reasoning. Mere assertions are hollow, especially when they fly in the face of contrary findings by Congress and state legislatures.

60. Id. at 409–10.
61. Citizens United v. Federal Election Comm'n, 558 U.S. 310, 339, 340, 345–46, 349–50, 356–60, 363, 365, 365–67, 369 (2010).
62. McConnell v. Federal Election Comm'n, 540 U.S. 93 (2003).
63. Randall v. Sorrell, 548 U.S. 230 (2006).
64. Id. at 266.
65. Federal Election Comm'n v. Wisconsin Right to Life, 551 U.S 449 (2007).
66. E.g., Shelby County v. Holder, 570 U.S. ___ (2013), striking down reauthorization of a section of the Voting Rights Act.
67. Citizens United v. Federal Election Comm'n, 558 U.S. at 357.
68. Id. at 360.

In 2012, the Supreme Court had an opportunity to actually learn something about the link between corporate expenditures and campaign corruption. Montana had experienced a century of "copper kings" and other mining interests largely able to control the state's politics through financial power.[69] It enacted legislation to prohibit a corporation from making "an expenditure in connection with a candidate or a political party."[70] The Supreme Court could have taken the case, ordered briefs and oral argument, and had some of its beliefs and assertions tested by actual evidence and experience. Instead of opening its door to learning something, it issued a short per curiam reversing the Supreme Court of Montana.[71] A dissent signed by four Justices (Breyer, Ginsburg, Sotomayor, and Kagan) stated that *Citizens United* "should not bar the Montana Supreme Court's finding, made on the record before it, that independent expenditures by corporations did in fact lead to corruption or the appearance of corruption in Montana."[72]

Public attitudes do not alone decide constitutional questions, but it is apparent throughout U.S. history that public support can eventually convince the Supreme Court that a prior position was untenable and needs to be changed. That is evident in such decisions as the child-labor cases, the 1940 compulsory flag-salute case, and contemporary issues of sodomy and same-sex marriage. As to the judicial doctrine that supports unchecked corporate expenditures in elections, Americans from both parties broadly reject the Court's ruling in *Citizens United*. They support legislative limits on money spent by "super PACs" and other wealthy donors. More than four in five Americans say that money exerts too large a role in political campaigns.[73]

Critics of *Citizens United* offer two remedies: the Court could confess error and reverse itself, or Congress and the states could pass and ratify a constitutional amendment to empower legislative action to regulate campaign expenditures. There is a third remedy. In the field of campaign finance, the Court stands on shaky ground by relying on strained and artificial judicial creations: corporations are persons, money is speech, and the First Amendment protects unlimited corporate expenditures in political campaigns. Congress should hold hearings, invite expert testimony on the influence of money in

69. Robert Barnes & Dan Eggen, "Justices Reject States Law, Uphold Citizens United Ruling," Wash. Post, June 26, 2012, at A7.

70. Mont. Code Ann. § 13-35-227(1) (2011).

71. American Tradition Partnership, Inc. v. Bullock, 567 U.S. ___ (2012).

72. Id. at ___.

73. Nicholas Confessore and & Megan Thee-Brenan, "Poll Shows Americans Favor an Overhaul of Campaign Financing," N.Y. Times, June 3, 2015, A16.

elections, and produce legislation that is coherent, principled, and evidence-based to protect popular control and self-government.[74]

Such a bill, if enacted, would be litigated, and the Supreme Court could declare the statute contrary to its rulings. It would be institutionally risky to strike down the statute merely because it conflicts with evidence-free Court decisions. Instead, the Court could announce: "Congress has assembled evidence that was not available to us when we decided *Buckley* and *Citizens United*. We now, after due consideration, defer to the legislative judgment and override our decisions." If that were to happen, the Court would be under appropriate pressure to adopt a more deferential attitude toward state efforts to control campaign expenditures.

Would it be difficult for the Supreme Court to confess error? A dissenting opinion by Justice Brandeis in 1932 observed: "The Court bows to the lessons of experience and the force of better reasoning, recognizing that the process of trial and error, so fruitful in the physical sciences, is appropriate also in the judicial function."[75] The Court is judged on the basis on the quality of its decisions, its respect for the elected branches, and the principle of self-government, not on some abstract, illusory, and groundless theory of judicial finality. An essential test of credibility for all three branches is the capacity to admit error and correct it.

This book has offered many examples of the Supreme Court deciding against individual rights, followed by Congress passing protective legislation. What we have seen in recent years is a Congress less willing and able to provide that independent check. For example, after the Supreme Court in *Shelby County* in 2013 struck down the Justice Department preclearance procedure for voting rights, Congress could have held hearings to gather evidence to pass legislation to reinstate preclearance. It has not done so. Nor has it passed legislation to challenge *Citizens United*.

In an interview on February 13, 2015, Justice Ruth Bader Ginsburg expressed concern about congressional inaction. She said: "The current Congress is not equipped to do anything. The kind of result that we got in the Ledbetter case is not easily achieved today. Someday, we will go back to having the kind of legislature that we should, where members, whatever party they belong to, want to make the thing work and cooperate with each other to see that will happen."[76] It is in the interest of constitutional government to have that day come quickly.

74. Louis Fisher, "Saying What the Law Is: On Campaign Finance, It's Not Just for the Court; Congress Has an Equal Say," Nat'l L.J., Feb. 22, 2010, at 38.

75. Burnet v. Coronado Oil & Gas Co., 285 U.S. 393, 407–8 (1932).

76. "Ruth Bader Ginsburg on Abortion, Race and the Broken Congress," MSNBC, Feb. 15, 2015; http://www.msnbc.com/msnbc/ruth-bader-ginsburg-abortion-race-and-the-broken-congress.

ABOUT THE AUTHOR

Louis Fisher is Scholar in Residence at the Constitution Project. Previously he worked for four decades at the Library of Congress as Senior Specialist in Separation of Powers (Congressional Research Service, from 1970 to 2006) and Specialist in Constitutional Law (the Law Library, from 2006 to 2010). During his service with CRS he was research director of the House Iran-Contra Committee in 1987, writing major sections of the final report. Fisher's specialties include constitutional law, war powers, budget policy, executive-legislative relations, and judicial-congressional relations.

After completing his doctoral work in political science at the New School for Social Research in 1967, he taught full-time at Queens College for three years. Later he taught part-time at Georgetown University, American University, Catholic University law school, Indiana University, Catholic University, the College of William and Mary law school, and Johns Hopkins University. Currently he is a Visiting Scholar at the William and Mary law school.

This book marks Fisher's twenty-fourth. The others are listed in the front of this book. He is the author of more than five hundred articles for law reviews, political science journals, encyclopedias, books, magazines, and newspapers. He has twice won the Louis Brownlow Book Award (for *Presidential Spending Power* and *Constitutional Dialogues*). The encyclopedia he coedited with Leonard W. Levy was awarded the Dartmouth Medal. In 1995, Fisher received the Aaron B. Wildavsky Award "For Lifetime Scholarly Achievement in Public Budgeting" from the Association for Budgeting and Financial Management. In 2006 he received the Neustadt Book Award for *Military Tribunals and Presidential Power*. In 2011 he received the Walter Beach Pi Sigma Alpha Award from the National Capital Area Political Science Association for strengthening the relationship between political science and public service. In 2012 he received the Hubert H. Humphrey Award from the American Political Science Association in recognition of notable public service by a political scientist. The July 2013 issue of *PS: Political Science and Politics* includes a symposium on his work, "Law and (Disciplinary) Order: A Dialogue about Louis Fisher, Constitutionalism, and Political Science."

Fisher has been invited to testify before Congress more than fifty times on such issues as war powers, state secrets privilege, NSA surveillance, executive spending discretion, presidential reorganization authority, Congress and the Constitution, the legislative veto, the item veto, the Gramm-Rudman deficit control act, executive privilege, committee subpoenas, executive lobbying, CIA whistleblowing, covert spending, the pocket veto, recess appointments, the budget process, the balanced budget amendment, biennial budgeting, and presidential impoundment powers.

He has been active with CEELI (Central and East European Law Initiative) of the American Bar Association, traveling to Bulgaria, Albania, and Hungary to assist constitution writers; participating in CEELI conferences in Washington, D.C., with delegations from Bosnia-Herzegovina, Lithuania, Romania, and Russia; serving on CEELI "working groups" on Armenia and Belarus; and assisting in drafting constitutional amendments for the Kyrgyz Republic. As part of CRS delegations he traveled to Russia and Ukraine to assist on constitutional questions. For the International Bar Association he helped analyze the draft constitutions for Swaziland and Zimbabwe.

Fisher has been invited to speak in Albania, Australia, Belgium, Bulgaria, Canada, China, the Czech Republic, Denmark, England, France, Germany, Greece, Israel, Japan, Macedonia, Malaysia, Mexico, the Netherlands, Oman, the Philippines, Poland, Romania, Russia, Slovenia, South Korea, Sweden, Taiwan, Ukraine, and the United Arab Emirates. The topics include a range of constitutional, political, and institutional issues.

INDEX OF CASES

Abelman v. Booth, 21 How. 506 (1859), 49

Abingdon School Dist. v. Schempp, 374 U.S. 203 (1963), 18

Abordo v. Hawaii, 902 F. Supp. 1220 (D. Hawaii 1995), 154

Adkins v. Children's Hospital, 261 U.S. 525 (1923), 76, 101

Agostini v. Felton, 521 U.S. 203 (1997), 155

Aguilar v. Felton, 473 U.S. 402 (1985), 155

Akron v. Akron Center for Reproductive Health, 462 U.S. 416 (1983), 82

American Tradition Partnership, Inc. v. Bullock, 567 U.S. ___ (2012), 174

Arizona v. Attakai, Criminal No. 4098, Coconino County (1960), 148

Austin v. Michigan Chamber of Commerce, 494 U.S. 652 (1990), 172

Bailey v. Drexel Furniture Co., 259 U.S. 20 (1922), 98–99, 113

Baker v. Carr, 369 U.S. 186 (1962), 17, 154

Barnette v. West Virginia State Board of Ed., 47 F. Supp. 251 (D.W.Va. 1942), 111

Belgard v. Hawaii, 883 F. Supp. 510 (D. Hawaii 1995), 154

Bitterman v. Secretary of Defense, 553 F. Supp. 719 (D.D.C. 1982), 131

Boumediene v. Bush, 553 U.S. 723 (2008), 27

Boynton v. Virginia, 364 U.S. 454 (1960), 61

Bradwell v. State, 83 U.S. (16 Wall.) 130 (1873), 16–17, 71–72

Browder v. Gayle, 142 F. Supp 707 (M.D. Ala. 1956), 61

Brown v. Allen, 344 U.S. 443 (1953), 14

Brown v. Board of Education, 347 U.S. 483 (1954), 13, 17, 61–63, 159

Brown v. Board of Education, 349 U.S. 294 (1955), 17, 63–64

Buckley v. Valeo, 424 U.S. 1 (1976), 168–69, 170–71, 172–73, 175

Burnet v. Coronado Oil & Gas Co., 285 U.S. 393 (1932), 175

Burroughs and Cannon v. U.S., 290 U.S. 534 (1934), 171

Burton v. Wilmington Pkg. Auth., 365 U.S. 715 (1961), 65

Burwell v. Hobby Lobby Stores, Inc., 573 U.S. ___ (2014), 157

Busey v. District of Columbia, 129 F.2d 24 (D.C. Cir. 1942), 111

Carpenter v. Dane, 9 Wis. 248 (1859), 17

Champion v. Ames, 188 U.S. 321 (1903), 94

Cherokee Nation v. Georgia, 30 U.S. 1 (1832), 140

Child Labor Tax Case (Bailey v. Drexel Furniture Co.), 259 U.S. 20 (1922), 98–99, 113

Christians, Trustee v. Crystal Evangelical Free Church, 525 U.S. 811 (1998), 156

Citizens United v. Federal Election Comm'n, 558 U.S. 310 (2010), 168–69, 172, 173, 174, 175

City of Boerne v. Flores, 521 U.S. 507 (1997), 14, 155–56

Civil Rights Cases, 109 U.S. 8 (1883), 56–58, 59, 61, 65, 66, 113

Clark Distilling Co. v. West'n Md. Ry. Co., 242 U.S. 311 (1917), 129

Clinton v. City of New York, 524 U.S. 417 (1998), 163

Colorado Republican Federal Campaign Comm. v. Federal Election Comm'n, 518 U.S. 604 (1996), 172

Committee to Defend Reprod. Rights v. Myers, 625 P.2d 779 (Cal. 1981), 84

Common Cause v. Schmitt, 455 U.S. 129 (1982), 172

Conn. General Co. v. Johnson, 303 U.S. 77 (1938), 170

Cooper v. Aaron, 358 U.S. 1 (1958), 64

Covington &c. Turnpike Co. v. Sandford, 164 U.S. 578 (1896), 169

Dawson v. Mayor, 220 F.2d 386 (4th Cir. 1955), 61

Doe v. Bolton, 410 U.S. 179 (1973), 82

Doe v. Maher, 515 A.2d 134 (Conn. Super. 1986), 84

Dred Scott v. Sandford, 60 U.S. (19 How.) 393 (1857), 23, 51–52, 98, 113, 153

E.E.O.C. v. Catholic University of America, 83 F.3d 455 (D.C. Cir. 1996), 154

Employment Division v. Smith, 485 U.S. 660 (1988), 150

Employment Division v. Smith, 494 U.S. 872 (1990), 149, 151, 152, 154–55

Engel v. Vitale, 370 U.S. 421 (1962), 18

Ex parte Virginia, 100 U.S. 339 (1880), 56, 58

FEC v. Massachusetts Citizens for Life, Inc., 479 U.S. 243 (1986), 172

FEC v. National Conservative PAC, 470 U.S. 480 (1985), 172

FEC v. National Right to Work Committee, 459 U.S. 197 (1982), 172

Federal Election Comm'n v. Wisconsin Right to Life, 551 U.S. 449 (2007), 173

First National Bank of Boston v. Bellotti, 435 U.S. 765 (1978), 170, 172

Fisher v. Hurst, 333 U.S. 147 (1948), 62

Flores v. City of Boerne, 877 F. Supp. 355 (W.D. Tex. 1995), 154

Flores v. City of Boerne, Tex., 73 F.3d 1352 (5th Cir. 1996), 154

Fraina v. United States, 255 F. 28 (2d Cir. 1918), 122

Geduldig v. Aiello, 417 U.S. 484 (1974), 85

General Electric Co. v. Gilbert, 429 U.S. 125 (1976), 86

Gibbons v. Odgen, 22 U.S. (9 Wheat.) 1 (1824), 103

Gideon v. Wainwright, 372 U.S. 335 (1963), 17

Gillette v. United States, 401 U.S. 437 (1971), 124

Girouard v. United States, 328 U.S. 61 (1946), 123

Gobitis v. Minersville School Dist., 21 F. Supp. 581, 583 (E.D. Pa. 1937), 104

Gobitis v. Minersville School Dist., 24 F. Supp. 271 (E.D. Pa. 1938), 105

Goeseart v. Cleary, 335 U.S. 464 (1948), 76

Goldman v. Secretary of Defense, 530 F. Supp. 12 (D.D.C. 1981), 131

Goldman v. Secretary of Defense, 734 F.2d 1531 (D.C. Cir. 1984), 132

Goldman v. Secretary of Defense, 739 F.2d 657 (D.C. Cir. 1984), 132

Goldman v. Weinberger, 475 U.S. 503 (1986), 16, 131, 134–35

Gonzales v. Carhart, 550 U.S. 124 (2007), 85

Gonzales v. O Centro Espirita Beneficente Uniao do Vegetal, 546 U.S. 418 (2006), 156

Gray v. Sanders, 372 U.S. 368 (1963), 17

Griffin v. School Bd., 377 U.S. 218 (1964), 64

Griswold v. Connecticut, 381 U.S. 479 (1965), 17

Haley v. Ohio, 332 U.S. 596 (1948), 19

Halter v. Nebraska, 205 U.S. 34 (1907), 107

Hammer v. Dagenhart, 247 U.S. 251 (1918), 96–97, 103, 113

Hannah v. Larche, 363 U.S. 420 (1960), 65

Harper v. Virginia Board of Elections, 383 U.S. 663 (1966), 17

Harris v. McRae, 448 U.S. 297 (1980), 84

Heart of Atlanta Motel v. United States, 379 U.S. 241 (1964), 66

Henfield's Case, 11 F. Cas. 1099 (C.C. Pa. 1793) (No. 6, 360), 42

Herrera v. Collins, 506 U.S. 390 (1993), 14

Hirabayashi v. United States, 320 U.S. 81 (1943), 22

Holmes v. City of Atlanta, 223 F.2d 93 (5th Cir. 1955), 61

Hoyt v. Florida, 368 U.S. 57 (1961), 77

In re Bradwell, 55 Ill. 535 (1869), 70
In re Goodell, 39 Wis. 232 (1875), 72
In re Grady, 394 P.2d 728 (Cal. 1964), 148
In re Latrecchia, 26 A.2d 881 (N.J. 1942), 110
In re Rahrer, 140 U.S. 545 (1891), 26
In re Summers, 325 U.S. 561 (1945), 122
In re Young, 141 F.3d 854 (8th Cir. 1998), 156

Jones v. Opelika, 316 U.S. 584 (1942), 111

Katzenbach v. McClung, 379 U.S. 294
    (1964), 66
Katzenbach v. Morgan, 384 U.S. 641
    (1966), 67
Keeler v. Mayor & City Council of
    Cumberland, 928 F. Supp. 591 (D. Md.
    1996), 154
Kikumura v. Hurley, 242 F.3d 950 (10th Cir.
    2001), 156
Korematsu v. United States, 323 U.S. 214
    (1944), 22

Ledbetter v. Goodyear Tire & Rubber Co.,
    550 U.S. 618 (2007), 28, 87–88
Leisy v. Hardin, 155 U.S. 100 (1890), 25
Lochner v. New York, 198 U.S. 45 (1905),
    113
Lorance v. AT&T Technologies, Inc., 490
    U.S. 900 (1989), 86

Marbury v. Madison, 5 U.S. (1 Cr.) 137
    (1803), 14–15, 16, 155–56
McConnell v. Federal Election Comm'n, 540
    U.S. 93 (2003), 173
McCulloch v. Maryland, 17 U.S. (4 Wheat.)
    316 (1819), 24, 155
McLaurin v. Oklahoma State Regents, 339
    U.S. 637 (1950), 62
McNabb v. United States, 318 U.S. 332
    (1943), 19
Minersville School District v. Gobitis, 310
    U.S. 586 (1940), 106–09, 113–14, 151
Minersville School Dist. v. Gobitis, 108 F.2d
    683 (3d Cir. 1939), 105
Minor v. Happensett, 88 U.S. (21 Wall.) 162
    (1875), 75
Miranda v. Arizona, 384 U.S. 436 (1966), 19

Missouri ex rel. Gaines v. Canada, 305 U.S.
    337 (1938), 62
Moe v. Secretary of Administration, 417
    N.Ed.2d 387 (Mass. 1981), 84
Morehead v. N.Y. ex rel. Tipaldo, 298 U.S.
    587 (1936), 76, 101
Mormon Church v. United States, 136 U.S. 1
    (1890), 127
Muller v. Oregon, 208 U.S. 412 (1908), 76
Murphy v. Ramsey, 114 U.S. 14 (1885), 126

Native American Church of New York
    v. United States, 468 F. Supp. 1247
    (S.D.N.Y. 1979), 149
Native American Church v. Navajo Tribal
    Council, 272 F.2d 131 (10th Cir. 1959),
    145, 148
Nebbia v. New York, 291 U.S. 502
    (1934), 101
New York Times Co. v. Sullivan, 376 U.S.
    254 (1964), 20
Nixon v. Shrink Missouri PAC, 528 U.S. 377
    (2000), 172
Northwestern Life Ins. Co. v. Riggs, 203 U.S.
    243 (1906), 170

Obergefell v. Hodges, 576 U.S. ___
    (2015), 16

Pace v. Alabama, 106 U.S. 583 (1883), 58
Paterson v. McLean Credit Union, 491 U.S.
    164 (1989), 86
Pearson v. Murray, 182 A. 593 (Md. 1936), 62
Pennsylvania v. Wheeling and Belmont
    Bridge Co., 18 How. 421 (1856), 29
Pennsylvania v. Wheeling and Belmont
    Bridge Co., 54 U.S. (13 How.) 518
    (1852), 25
People v. Woody, 394 P.2d 813 (Cal. 1964),
    148
Peyote Way Church of God, Inc. v.
    Thornburgh, 922 F.2d 1210 (5th Cir.
    1991), 149
Planned Parenthood Ass'n v. Dept. of Human
    Res., 663 P.2d 1247 (Or. App. 1983), 84
Planned Parenthood of Southeastern Pa. v.
    Casey, 505 U.S. 833 (1992), 83

Plessy v. Ferguson, 163 U.S. 537 (1896), 17, 58–61, 63, 113

Prigg v. Pennsylvania, 16 Pet. 539 (1842), 49

Quick Bear v. Leupp, 210 U.S. 50 (1908), 143

Radice v. New York, 264 U.S. 292 (1924), 76

Randall v. Sorrell, 548 U.S. 230 (2006), 173

Reed v. Reed, 404 U.S. 71 (1971), 77

Reynolds v. United States, 98 U.S. 145 (1879), 126

Right to Choose v. Byrne, 450 A.2d 925 (N.J. 1982), 84

Roe v. Wade, 410 U.S. 113 (1973), 80–83, 113

Santa Clara Co. v. South. Pac. Railroad, 118 U.S. 394 (1886), 169–70, 172

Sasnett v. Department of Corrections, 891 F. Supp. 1305 (W.D. Wis. 1995), 154

Sasnett v. Sullivan, 91 F.3d 1018 (7th Cir. 1996), 154

Selective Draft Law Cases, 245 U.S. 366 (1918), 121

Shaw v. Reno, 509 U.S. 630 (1993), 166

Shelby County v. Holder, 570 U.S. ___ (2013), 67–68, 173, 175

Sherbert v. Verner, 374 U.S. 398 (1963), 149, 150, 152

Sipuel v. Board of Regents, 332 U.S. 631 (1948), 62

Slaughter-House Cases, 83 U.S. (16 Wall.) 36 (1873), 56, 60

Smith v. Employment Div., 721 P.2d 445 (Ore. 1986), 149

Smith v. Employment Division, 763 P.2d 146 (Ore. 1988), 150

South Carolina v. Katzenbach, 383 U.S. 301 (1966), 67

State v. Big Sheep, 242 P. 1067 (Mont. 1926), 146

State v. Lefebvre, 20 A.2d 185 (N.H. 1941), 110

State v. Smith, 127 P.2d 518 (Kans. 1942), 110

State v. Whittingham, 504 P.2d 950 (Ariz. 1972), 148

Stenberg v. Carhart, 530 U.S. 914 (2000), 84

Swann v. Charlotte-Mecklenburg Bd. of Ed., 402 U.S. 1 (1971), 67

Sweatt v. Painter, 339 U.S. 629 (1950), 62

Torcaso v. Watkins, 367 U.S. 488 (1961), 18, 123

Trustees of Dartmouth College v. Woodward, 17 (4 Wheat.) 518 (1819), 169

United States v. Bland, 283 U.S. 636 (1931), 123

United States v. Carolene Products Co., 304 U.S. 144 (1938), 13

United States v. Cruikshank, 92 U.S. 542 (1876), 54, 56

United States v. Curtiss-Wright Export Corp., 299 U.S. 304 (1936), 7

United States v. Darby, 312 U.S. 100 (1941), 103

United States v. F. W. Darby Lumber Co., 32 F. Supp. 734 (S.D. Ga. 1940), 103

United States v. Jefferson County Board of Education, 372 F.2d 836 (5th Cir. 1966), 64

United States v. Lovett, 328 U.S. 303 (1946), 22

United States v. Macintosh, 283 U.S. 605 (1931), 122, 123

United States v. Morrison, 529 U.S. 598 (2000), 90

United States v. Nixon, 418 U.S. 683 (1974), 154

United States v. Reese, 92 U.S. 214 (1876), 54

United States v. Seeger, 380 U.S. 163, 165 (1965), 123–24

United States v. Top Sky, 547 F.2d 486 (9th Cir. 1976), 145

United States v. Virginia, 518 U.S. 515 (1996), 90

United States v. Yazell, 382 U.S. 341 (1966), 77

Vieth v. Jubelirer, 541 U.S. 267 (2004), 166

Wards Cove Packing Co. v. Atonio, 490 U.S. 642 (1989), 86

Watson v. Memphis, 373 U.S. 526 (1963), 61

Webb v. Baird, 6 Ind. 13 (1854), 17

Webster v. Reproductive Health Services, 492 U.S. 490 (1989), 83

Welch v. United States, 398 U.S. 333 (1970), 124

West Coast Hotel Co. v. Parrish, 300 U.S. 379 (1937), 76, 101

West Virginia State Board of Education v. Barnette, 319 U.S. 624 (1943), 14, 111–14

Wheeling Steel Corp. v. Glander, 337 U.S. 562 (1949), 170

Whitehorn v. State, 561 P.2d 539 (Okla. 1977), 148

Whitney v. California, 274 U.S. 357 (1927), 30

Williams v. Zbaraz, 448 U.S. 358 (1980), 84

Worchester v. Georgia, 32 U.S. 515 (1832), 140

Youngstown Co. v. Sawyer, 343 U.S. 579 (1952), 8

Zivotofsky v. Kerry, 576 U.S. ___ (2015), 7

INDEX OF SUBJECTS

abdication, congressional, 161–63
abolitionist movement, 47–50
abortion rights, 80–85
Adams, Brock, 136
Adams, John, 7, 19, 20, 41
Adams, John Quincy, 50, 139, 140
Alien and Sedition Acts, 19–20, 41
Alien Friends Act, 19–20
Alito, Samuel, 87–88
Allen, James B., 78
Allen, Michael, 125
amendments, constitutional, 18, 99–100,
   115–16, 128, 129, 130, 174
American Anti-Slavery Society, 50
American Bar Association, 106
American Civil Liberties Union, 21, 106, 153
American Enterprise Institute, 165
American Friends Service Committee, 151
American Indian Religious Freedom Act of
   1978, 145–46, 154
American Jewish Committee, 151
American Jewish Congress, 151
American Legion, 136
American Temperance Society, 127
Andrews, George, 18
Anti-Saloon League, 128
Articles of Confederation, 32, 35

Baker, Howard, 79
Baptist Committee on Public Affairs, 151
Baptists, 46
Barnes, Robert, 16
Bates, Edward, 52
Bay of Pigs, 10, 12
Beck, James M., 98
Benson, Egbert, 118
Beveridge, Albert, 93
bill of attainder, 22, 40, 145
Bill of Rights, American, 19, 40–41, 112

Bill of Rights, British, 31
Bill of Rights, Virginia, 40
Bipartisan Policy Center, 160
Black, Galen, 150, 151
Black, Hugo, 18, 63, 101, 109, 110, 111,
   112, 113, 170
blacks, rights of, 47–68
Blackstone, William, 31–32, 69, 70, 71, 73, 76
Bolling, Richard, 4
Born-Alive Infants Protection Act, 84
Boschwitz, Rudy, 136
Bosnia, 162
Boy Scouts, 21
Bradley, Joseph P., 71
Bradwell, Myra, 70–72
Brandeis, Louis, 21, 30, 101, 175
Breaux, John, 136
Brennan, William, 134, 151
Brewer, David J., 75–76
Breyer, Stephen, 68, 84, 90, 173, 174
Bright, John, 6
British model, 30–32, 35–37, 38, 70, 73, 74
Britt, James J., 94–95
Brookings Institution, 165
Brown, Henry Billings, 59–61
Bruff, Harold, 10
Buchanan, James, 51
Burdick, Quentin, 136
Burger, Warren, 81, 82
Burke, John, 10
Burns, James McGregor, 5
Burton, Harold, 63
Bush, George H. W., 10, 86, 163
Bush, George W., 10, 11, 163
Butler, Benjamin, 55, 73, 101
Butler, Pierce, 36, 37
Butler, Pierce (Justice), 101
Byrd, Robert, 136
Byrnes, James, 101, 111

184

Calhoun, John C., 139
Camp Fire Girls, 21
Cardozo, Benjamin, 101
Carpenter, Matthew H., 71
Catholic Association for International
    Peace, 21
Catholics, 21, 124, 127, 128, 143
Celler, Manny, 130
chaplains, 124–26
Charles I, King, 31
Chase, Samuel, 15
Cherokees, 139–42
Chickasaws, 142
child-labor legislation, 17, 92–103, 168, 174
children, rights of, 92–114
Chiloquin, Edison, 157
Choctaws, 142
Christian Legal Society, 151
Christians, 71, 107–08, 112, 124, 125, 126,
    128, 129, 130, 137–39, 148, 151, 156
Civil Rights Act of 1866, 53, 57
Civil Rights Act of 1875, 55, 56
Civil Rights Act of 1957, 64
Civil Rights Act of 1960, 65
Civil Rights Act of 1964, 58, 65–66, 85,
    88, 89
Civil Rights Act of 1991, 86, 88
Civil War (American), 49, 51–53, 57, 69, 92,
    98, 107–08, 118–19, 124, 126
Clark, Joseph S., 4
Clark, Tom, 63
Clarke, John, 99
Clinton, Bill, 2, 10, 84, 132, 162, 163
Collier, John, 143
commerce power, 24–25, 66, 85, 90, 93,
    94–97, 101, 103, 129, 156
Commission on Political Reform, 160–61, 167
Communism, 21, 23, 62
Compromise of 1850, 49
confiscation acts (Civil War), 52
Congressional Research Service, 164
conscience, 29, 104–05, 106, 115–16, 117,
    118, 121, 123, 126
conscientious objectors, 116–19, 120–24
Continental Congress, 32–34, 35, 117, 124,
    137, 144
Conyers, John, 28, 89

corporations as "persons," 168, 169–72, 174
Corwin, Edward S., 7
Court of Appeals in Cases of Capture, 34
court-packing plan (FDR), 100
Courts of Admiralty, 34
coverture, 69, 71, 76–77
Creeks, 142
Cronin, Thomas, 9–10
Curtis, Charles, 78

Dagenhart, Roland H., 96
Danforth, John, 136
Daschle, Tom, 136, 160
Declaration of Independence, 29, 32, 47, 50,
    55, 69, 70, 117
Declaration of Rights, Virginia, 32
Declaration of Sentiments, Seneca Falls, 70
"Democratic Societies," 44–46
Denison, Edward E., 99
Denvir, John, 61
Dickens, Charles, 69
Dickinson, William, 132
Dies, Martin, 21
Dionne, E. J., 168
Dodd, William E., Jr., 22
Domenici, Pete, 136
Douglas, William O., 17, 18, 63, 81, 101,
    109, 110, 111, 112, 113, 170
Duché, Jacob, 124
Dugan, Robert, Jr., 152
Dunham, Allison, 109
Dunkards, 121
Dworkin, Ronald, 13

Eagles, religious use of, 144–45
Eighteenth Amendment, 129, 147
Eisenhower, Dwight D., 8, 9, 10
Ely, John Hart, 82
Emancipation Proclamation, 52–53
eminent domain, 57
Enforcement Act of 1870, 54
Enlightenment, 29
Equal Pay Act of 1963, 85, 87
equal pay legislation, 14, 85–90
Equal Protection Clause, 62, 76, 170
Equal Rights Amendment (ERA), 77–80
Ervin, Sam, 79

Establishment Clause, 145, 156
ex post facto law, 40, 145

Fair Labor Standards Act of 1938, 102
Faubus, Orval, 64
Federal Corrupt Practices Act of 1925, 171
Feldman, Noah, 13, 17
Fenno, Richard, 4–5
Fifteenth Amendment, 53, 54, 67, 75
First Amendment, 50, 111, 115–16, 121,
    131, 132, 145, 148, 149, 150, 151, 152,
    156, 168, 172–73
Fischel, Arnold, 125
flag-salute, compulsory, 13, 14, 99,
    103–14, 174
force acts, 53
Ford, Gerald, 10
Fourteenth Amendment, 53, 54, 55, 56–57,
    58, 59, 60, 61, 65, 66, 71, 75, 76, 81, 82,
    90, 111, 145, 153, 155, 169–70, 172, 174
Frankfurter, Felix, 63, 76–77, 101, 106–08,
    109–10, 111, 112, 113–14
Free Exercise Clause, 41, 116, 131, 132,
    149–50, 151, 153
Fried, Charles, 133
Frohnmayer, Dave, 150
fugitive slave statutes, 49

Genet, Edmond, 44
George III, King, 47
Gerry, Elbridge, 37, 117–18
gerrymandered districts, 166–68
Giles, William, 46, 118
Ginsburg, Ruth Bader, 68, 83, 84, 88, 90,
    132, 173, 174, 175
Glickman, Dan, 160
"Glorious Revolution," 31
Gobitas, Lillian, 104
Gobitas, William, 104
Goldman, Simcha, 16, 130–35
Goldstein, Leslie Friedman, 80
Goldstein, Tom, 16
Goodell, Lavinia, 72
Gore, Al, 136
Graham, Bob, 136
Grant, Ulysses S., 54, 56, 142
Greeley, Horace, 141

Greenhouse, Linda, 81
Greenstein, Fred, 10
Grier, Robert, 25
Griffiths, Martha, 77, 78
groupthink, 2
Guantánamo, 27
Gurwitz, Ethan, 165

habeas corpus, writ of, 40, 54
Haiti, 162
Hamilton, Alexander, 36, 40, 43
Hardwick, Thomas W., 95
Harkin, Tom, 136
Harlan, John Marshall, 57–58, 61, 65, 169–70
Harris, Ira, 118
Hart, John, 9
Hatch, Orrin, 27–28, 156
Hatfield, Mark, 157
Healy, Gene, 10
Hitler, Adolf, 62, 104, 109
Hoar, George, 74–76
Hobby Lobby Stores, 156
Holmes, Oliver Wendell, Jr., 63, 96–97, 129
Horst, Amos, 122
House Committee on Un-American Activities
    (HUAC), 21
Hughes, Charles Evans, 51, 101, 111
Hussein, Saddam, 12
Hutterites, 121
Hyde, Henry J., 83, 152
Hyde Amendment, 83–84

Impoundment, 163
Impoundment Control Act of 1974, 163
Inaugural addresses, 18, 23, 51, 52
Indian Civil Rights Act of 1968, 145
Indian removal, 139–42
Indian Reorganization Act of 1934, 143–44
Innocent III, Pope, 31
institutional resources, improving, 164–66
intoxicating liquors, 25–26
Iran-Contra, 9, 10, 12
Iraq War, 2, 10, 11–12
Iredell, James, 37

Jackson, Andrew, 6, 24, 140, 141
Jackson, James, 118

Jackson, Robert H., 14, 63, 111–13
James II, King, 31
Japanese Americans, 17, 22
Jay Treaty, 7
Jefferson, Thomas, 20, 32, 47, 138
Jehovah's Witnesses, 13, 104, 105, 106, 109, 110, 111
Jews, 62, 107–08, 113, 124, 125, 127, 130
Jews, Orthodox, 16, 130–36
John, King, at Runnymede, 31
Johnson, Andrew, 53
Johnson, Lyndon B., 9, 10, 67
Johnston, J. Bennett, 136
Joint Committee on the Organization of Congress (1944), 162
judicial finality. *See* last-word doctrine
jurors, independent, 42

Kagan, Elena, 68, 174
Kansas-Nebraska Act of 1854, 49, 51
Karnes, David, 136
Katzmann, Robert, 27
Kempthorne, Dirk, 160
Kennedy, Anthony M., 27, 82, 83, 84, 86, 90, 155–56, 172, 173
Kennedy, John F., 10, 66, 85
Kennedy, Robert F., 66
Kennedy, Ted, 88
Kenyon, William S., 95
King, Martin Luther, Jr., 65
Klamath Indians, 149, 157–58
Klarman, Michael, 64
Knox, Henry, 138
Korean War, 2, 8, 12, 162
Kosovo, 162
Ku Klux Klan Act, 54

last-word doctrine, 1, 14–16, 23–26, 92, 97, 98, 103, 109, 113, 152, 159, 175
Leahy, Patrick, 26–27
Ledbetter, Lilly, 14, 17, 28, 86–89, 159, 175
Legislative Reference Service, 164
Legislative Reorganization Act of 1946, 162, 164
Legislative Reorganization Act of 1970, 164
Legislative work, making time for, 160–61
Leventhal, Harold, 171

Lewin, Nathan, 133
Lewis, Anthony, 171
Lewis, David J., 94
Library of Congress, xii–xiii, 164–65
Libya, 2, 162
Lilly Ledbetter Fair Pay Act of 2009, 28, 86–89, 159, 168, 175
Lincoln, Abraham, 5, 23, 52–53, 107, 111, 112, 119, 125
line item, presidential, 163
Line Item Veto Act of 1996, 163
Liptak, Adam, 16
Livermore, Samuel, 116
Lockwell, Belva, 73–75
Lott, Trent, 160
Louisiana Purchase, 49, 138
Lovett, Robert Morss, 22
Loyalty investigations, 23
Lutheran Church Missouri Synod, 151

MacArthur, Douglas, 8
Madison, James, 29–30, 37, 39, 40, 41, 44, 46, 48, 115–16, 117, 118, 161, 162
Magna Carta, 31
Mansbridge, Jane, 80
Marshall, John, 7, 15, 24, 140–41, 169
Marshall, Thurgood, 47, 134, 135, 151, 159
Mary II, Queen, 32
Mason, George, 32, 37, 40
Mayaguez, 10
Mayhew, David, 1–2
McCarthy, Joseph, 23
McGovern, Jim, 88–89
McReynolds, James, 101, 108
Mennonites, 116, 119, 121, 122
Methodist Conference, 50
Methodists, 46
Mexican War, 49
Mikulski, Barbara, 136
Military Coalition, 136
militia, 41–42, 43, 116–18
Militia Act, 41–42, 43
Minor, Virginia, 75
Minton, Sherman, 63
Miranda warnings, 19
Missouri Compromise Act of 1820, 49
Moe, Ronald, 7

money as "speech," 168–71, 174
Monroe, James, 139, 140
Moravians, 116, 118
Mormons, 126–27, 153
Morris, Gouverneur, 38
Morris, Robert, 39
Muhammed, Abdul-Rasheed, 125–26
Murphy, Frank, 101, 109, 110, 111, 112, 113
Murray, William Vans, 41
Muslims, 125–26

Nadler, Jerrold, 89
National Association of Evangelicals, 151–52
National Child Labor Committee, 92–93
National Council of Churches, 151
National Prohibition Act of 1919, 130
National Temperance Society, 128
Native American Church (NAC), 146, 148–50, 152, 154
Native Americans, 128, 137–58
NATO allies, 162
Navajos, 148
Nazi Germany, 104, 105
Necessary and Proper Clause, 24, 153
Nelson, Samuel, 25
Neustadt, Richard, 5, 7–9
Neutrality Act, 42
Neutrality Proclamation, 42
Nicholas, John, 45
Nickles, Don, 136
Nineteenth Amendment, 75, 76
Ninth Amendment, 81
Nixon, Richard M., 9, 163
Northwest Ordinance, 47
Nullification Ordinance, 141

Oaks, Dallin, 153
oath of office, 18, 123
Obama, Barack, 10, 89, 91, 162
Oberly, Kathryn, 134
O'Connor, Sandra Day, 82, 83, 84, 90, 135, 151
Ornstein, Norm, 167
Owen, Robert L., 97

pacifism, 116–19, 120–24
Parker, Ely S., 142

Parker, Josiah, 45–46
Parks, Rosa, 64
Paterson, William, 48
Pennsylvania Abolition Society, 50
Peters, Richard, 43
petition, right of, 44, 50
Petition of Right, 31
peyote, religious use of, 146–49, 149–53, 153–54
Pfiffner, James, 10
Pinckney, Charles, 35, 36, 37
Pious, Richard, 10
Pledge of Allegiance, 30
Plessy, Homer, 59
poll taxes, 17–18
polygamy, 126–27
Posner, Eric, 11–12
Powe, Lucas, 63
Powell, Lewis, 82, 86, 133, 172
prayer, official, 18
Pregnancy Discrimination Act of 1978, 86
prerogative, royal, 32, 35, 36
prerogatives, congressional, 161–63
Presbyterian Church, 50, 152
press, freedom of, 20, 41, 115, 116, 145
privileges and immunities, 40, 71, 75
Prohibition Movement, 127–30, 147
property, 29, 48
Protestants, 127, 128, 143
public accommodations, 55–58, 60, 65–66, 168
public participation, 41–46

Quakers (also Society of Friends), 46, 50, 116, 117, 118, 119, 122, 142, 143

Randolph, Edmund, 45
Raphall, Morris J., 124
Rawle, William, 43
Reagan, Ronald, 9, 10, 136, 163
reapportionment, 17
"Red Scare," 21
Reed, Stanley, 63, 101, 113
"Regents' Prayer," 18
Rehnquist, William H., 14, 15, 81, 82, 83, 84, 90, 133, 170, 173
Reid, Harry, 136

Religious Freedom Restoration Act (RFRA) of 1993, 149–57
religious liberty, 40, 41, 115–36, 137–39, 143–46, 146–59
Religious Liberty Protection Act, 156
Removal Act of 1830, 140
Rhodes, John J., 4
right to counsel, 17
Robert, John G., Jr., 16
Roberts, Owen, 101, 111, 113
Rockefeller, John, 136
Rogers, Will, 4
Roosevelt, Franklin D., 7, 8, 9, 10, 22, 100–01
Roosevelt, Theodore, 6–7, 171
Rossiter, Clinton, 5–6
Russell, Howard, 128
Russell, John, 128
Rutledge, John, 35
Rutledge, Wiley, 111
Ryan, Chief Justice, 72

same-sex marriage, 16, 174
Sargent, Aaron, 73–74
Scalia, Antonin, 82, 83, 84, 90, 132, 151, 166, 172, 173
Schlesinger, Arthur M., Jr., 5, 6–7
Schneider, George J., 102
school busing, 66–67
school desegregation, 17, 61–64
Scott, Dred, 51
Second Amendment, 117, 118
Sedgwick, Theodore, 138
sedition, 20–21, 44
Sedition Act of 1798, 20, 41
self-created societies, 43–46
Seminoles, 142
Senior Specialists (CRS), 164–65
"separate but equal" doctrine, 58–61, 62
Seventh Day Adventist, 122
Shakers, 117, 118
Shane, Peter, 10
Sherman, Roger, 35, 37
Shortridge, Samuel M., 100
Simon, Paul, 136
slavery, 23, 47–50, 52–53, 55, 59, 98, 119
slaves, fugitive, 47–49

Smith, Alfred, 149, 151, 152
Smith, Howard, 65
Smith, William, 45
Smith Act, 21
Snowe, Olympia, 160
Society of United Brethren, 138
Solarz, Stephen, 132
sole-organ doctrine, 7
Sotomayor, Sonia, 68, 174
Souter, David, 83, 90
Specialists (CRS), 164–65
speech, freedom of, 20–21, 31, 116, 145, 168, 170, 171, 172
spending power, 139, 142, 143, 156, 161–62, 163
Starr, Kenneth, 132
Stein, Harry, 165
Stevens, John Paul, 84, 90, 134, 173
Stewart, Potter, 18, 81
Stone, Harlan Fiske, 13, 101, 103, 108–09, 121
Strossen, Nadine, 153
Sutherland, George, 7, 101

Taft, William Howard, 93, 98, 127
Take Care Clause, 43
Taney, Roger, 51, 52
taxing power, 97–99
Thirteenth Amendment, 53, 55, 56, 59
Thomas, Clarence, 83, 84, 90, 172, 173
Tillman Act of 1907, 171
titles, presidential, 38–39
Tocqueville, Alexis de, 1
Tonkin Gulf Resolution, 2
Toobin, Jeffrey, 15–16
Treaty of Hopewell, in 1785, 139
Treaty power, 7, 32, 36, 139, 140, 142, 143
Tribe, Lawrence, 12
Truman, Harry, 8–9, 23, 162
Tucker, Thomas, 39
Twain, Mark, 1
Twenty-First Amendment, 130

U-2 flights, 10
UN Participation Act of 1945, 162
UN Security Council, 162–63
U.S. Bank, 24, 155

U.S. democracy, strengthening, 159–75

Van Devanter, Willis, 101, 129
Venable, Abraham Bedford, 46
Vermeule, Adriane, 11–12
Vietnam War, 2, 9, 10, 12, 124
Vinson, Fred, 63
Violence against Women Act (VAWA) of
    1994, 90–91
Virginia Military Institute (VMI), 90
Volstead Act of 1919, 130
voting, for women, 70, 71, 75–76
voting rights, 53, 54, 67–68, 71, 75, 76, 175
Voting Rights Act of 1965, 18, 67–68

Waite, Morrison Remick, 169
Waltman, Jerold, 156
war power, 10, 11–12, 32, 33, 35, 36–37,
    40, 161–63
Warren, Earl, 17–19, 22, 63
Washington, George, 5, 39, 41, 42,
    43–46, 138
Watergate, 9, 170
Watson, Goodwin B., 22
Webb, Edwin Y., 94

Webb-Kenyon Act of 1913, 129
Weinberger, Caspar, 136
Wellstone, Paul, 153–54
Wharton, Francis, 34
Whiskey Rebellion, 42–44, 45
White, Byron, 81, 82, 83, 133, 134, 171
White, Edward Douglass, 121
white-slave act, 95
Wilkinson, J. Harvie, 67
William III, King, 31
Wilson, James, 35, 37, 43
Wilson, Raymond, 122
Wilson, Woodrow, 7, 93, 120–21
Wirt, William, 140, 141
Wirth, Tim, 136
Wolfensberger, Donald, 3
Woman's Christian Temperance Union, 128
women, rights of, 69–91
women practicing law, 70–75, 168
Worchester, Samuel A., 140
World War I, 20–21, 104, 120–22, 129, 143
World War II, 1, 4, 5, 13–14, 22, 122–23,
    161, 162

yarmulke case, 16, 17, 130–36